PART ONE
PREPARE IT

Mrs Fixit Everyday DIY

Paula Lamb

Mrs Fixit Everyday DIY

Paula Lamb

Collins

For my sister Isobel, without whom none of this would have happened.

First published in 2005 by Collins
an imprint of HarperCollins Publishers
77-85 Fulham Palace Road
London W6 8JB

www.collins.co.uk

A catalogue record for this book is available from the British Library

Designed and produced by Airedale Publishing
Art Director: Ruth Prentice
PA to Art Director: Amanda Jensen
Designer: Hannah Attwell
Project Editor: Emma Callery
Colour: Max Newton
DTP: Lucy Jensen
Index: Hilary Bird
Paula Lamb photographs by David Murphy
All project photography by Sarah Cuttle
and David Murphy

For HarperCollins
Publishing Director: Denise Bates
Senior Managing Editor: Angela Newton
Editor: Alastair Laing

Additional non-technical text: Clare George

Back cover photographs: David Murphy

ISBN 0 00 720531 7

Pre-Press by F. E. Burman, London
Printed and bound in Thailand by Imago

Contents

Why DIY is important to women

Just as men used to miss out by not learning to cook, many women still miss out by not learning about DIY for themselves. Yet more and more women are choosing to live alone, whether it's because they've lost their husband, like me, or because they're just setting out in life, or because they have a career and 15 godchildren and have quite full enough a life already. And those who do have a partner to help around the house can't always rely on them being as handy as their fathers or grandfathers were, because the men sometimes know even less than the women these days.

While it's often better to call out a professional for the big jobs, women who haven't learnt about DIY are vulnerable every time the tap drips or a fuse blows. When I first grew up, even I found myself getting angry with things that went wrong in my house, and though my dad had taught me so much here and there, he'd always done the more complicated things himself. The only way for me to learn was to ask him not to do things for me any more, and to teach me how to do them instead.

These days, many women's fathers live miles up the motorway, and brothers are on the other side of the world. So how can we learn? This book is designed to help you find your way through the maze, but a bit of help and support is a real advantage. Many jobs can only be done safely by two people, so find a friend who also needs work done, and help one another. You can have so much fun doing DIY (or DIP, as I like to call it – Doing It Properly) – there's such a satisfying sense of achievement when you've changed your first fuse or redecorated your first room. As well as saving money, doing it yourself can save you from waiting weeks or months for a tradesman to become available.

Of course, some people find that DIY just isn't their thing, and there's no reason why it should be when you've got a taxing job or so many commitments that your time at home is for spending with family or friends. But the extra confidence you'll get from a bit of know-how will also help when you need to call in a tradesman. It's all too easy to panic and think that a problem is going to mean a bill for thousands of pounds that you don't have, and sometimes lack of confidence can make it easier for a rogue to charge you for things that don't need to be done. If you learn a little bit of the language used by builders, plumbers and electricians, and understand a bit about what they're doing so that you can use your own common sense, you'll have a head start in making sure that you're in control of what's in your house, whether you do it yourself or not. So go ahead, and take control! It's easy when you know how.

CHAPTER ONE

Know your house

Compiling a House Bible

The House Bible is a book containing as much information about the guts of your house as possible. Ideally, you should start compiling it when you move in and keep adding to it as you go along. In that way, you will always have a record of the essential pieces of information.

Get your info together

> Start out by gathering all the instruction books, guarantees and receipts for everything from the boiler to the damp course, and put them in a file. Then, in a notebook, draw a rough floorplan for each storey of the house. Mark in the following details:
> The width, length and height of each room.
> The positions and measurements of all the doors and windows.
> The positions of radiators, sockets, switches, the TV aerial socket and the telephone sockets.
> The boiler and any central heating tanks, such as a supply tank, a top-up tank and a feed-and-expansion tank (how many and which types you have will depend on your central heating system – for more information, see page 16).
> Then add perhaps the most important information of all, which is the details of where all the main utilities come into the house, and how to turn them off. This is essential for maintenance and especially for emergencies. Here is a checklist of the information you need to find out for each utility.

Water

Stop cocks

> If you live in a house or a ground floor flat, the mains water will usually enter through the cellar or kitchen. Usually this will also be where you'll find the stop cock or isolator valve, which allows you to turn off the water. Good places to look include the cupboard under the stairs, under the kitchen sink or even in the depths of the cellar.
> If you live in a flat, there may be a separate stop cock for your property, or there may be one for the whole building, in which case you should always remember to give your neighbours an hour's notice before turning off the water so that they can fill the kettle for drinks and the bath for flushing the toilet.
> Mark the stop cock on your house plan, and also the place where the water comes into the house – the supply pipe will follow a straight line from the hatch marked 'water' in the pavement outside your house. Knowing where it is will help you to avoid accidents if any work needs to be done near the pipe.

Sewers and inspection hatches

You can get information about the layout of the sewers from you local authority – find out where the inspection hatches are and which way the sewer runs. This will be invaluable if you need to get your drains unblocked – it's very difficult to rod or jet drains in the wrong direction.

TOP TIP: ASK A PLUMBER

If you can't find a stop cock inside your property, get a plumber to find it – or if there isn't one there, ask him to fit one for you. Probably the most accessible place to have it installed is under the kitchen sink. Make a detailed diagram of its location for your House Bible.

Gas

If you have a gas supply, there will be a valve for turning it off. It will be close to the gas meter, perhaps under the stairs or in a cupboard in the front hall. If the valve is in a place that isn't easily accessible, you may prefer to get another one installed nearer to your equipment by a Corgi registered professional, because if something goes wrong you won't want to spend time foraging in a dark, dirty cellar while the gas builds up. Mark the position of the valve on your plan of the house, and draw a line showing where the supply comes in from the street. As with the water, it will come in deep under the ground in a straight line from the hatch marked 'Gas' in the pavement outside your house.

Electrics

Mains electricity comes into your house from under the ground and goes straight into your electricity meter where the supplier measures all the electricity you use. After that, it goes on to the master switch, which allows you to turn off all the electricity in your property, and then to your fuse box (see page 76).

You'll find the fuse box inside your front door, under the stairs or in the garage. Inside it, the current is split to feed the different circuits in your house, with a miniature circuit breaker (MCB) or, in older-style boxes, a fuse guarding each one. The purpose of the MCBs/fuses is to react to strong surges in electricity and automatically shut off the current to that circuit without disrupting the rest. (For more information, see pages 77–9). Mark the fuse box on your plan, and also show where the supply comes into the house. Keep a torch close by, but don't ever keep matches there as electricity can arc and you can imagine what would happen then.

A living document

Add details to the House Bible as you get to know your house better, including the colour codes for all the paints and the construction of each of the walls – see overleaf . You can use the book as an equivalent of the MOT book in your car – each year your car is thoroughly tested, and your home is worth so much more. So make a list of all the jobs that need to be done on an annual basis to keep your property ticking over, and every year go through them before awarding yourself a HAT certificate after the Household Annual Test. To the right is a checklist to get you started. If you go through this checklist every year, you'll save a fortune in repairs – a stitch in time saves nine.

ANNUAL CHECKLISTS

Clean and repair gutters and downpipes, and check roof tiles and the mortar around the chimney.

Clean the drains and check for blockages (see pages 104–7).

Oil all external latches and hinges, and apply a coat of Vaseline to all window locks.

Go round all the plugs and sockets and check for burn marks and cracks (see pages 80–3).

Check for damp and mould inside airing cupboards, underneath tanks and in the loft (see pages 200–1).

Take off the bath panel and check the waste unit for leaks. Make the same check on all the sinks. If you're feeling really scrupulous, turn the water off, take out the waste traps and clean them out (see page 104).

Check the windows for cracked and broken panes (see page 196), and make sure all sash cords are working properly.

Nail down any creaking floorboards and stick or nail down any loose floor tiles or boards (see pages 168–9).

Check the smoke alarms (see pages 56–7).

Wash down the 'white work' (skirting boards, door and window frames, etc.) (see pages 192–3).

House construction

Get to know how your home is built and you will have an even greater understanding of how to tackle problems as diverse as fixing loose floorboards (you won't accidentally puncture a pipe) and mending a hole in plasterboard (you won't accidentally electrocute yourself).

Wall types

It pays to be aware of what each of your walls is made of, as it will affect what tools you will use when working on them and what loads they can support.

> **Supporting walls:** If you live in a property with more than one storey, it will have at least five supporting walls, and sometimes more, depending on its size. These are the four at each side of the property, and one or more internal wall carrying the floor joists for the storey above. Supporting walls are usually made of brick, and you can tell whether a wall is made of brick by tapping it. If there is only a small, dull noise, it is likely to be a brick wall, whereas if it sounds hollow it's probably made of lath and plaster or plasterboard, depending on the age of the wall.

> **Lath and plaster:** Lath and plaster walls were used for internal walls before the invention of plasterboard. Narrow strips of wood, known as laths, are nailed to the studs to provide a supporting framework for the plaster. A mixture of horse hair and cow hair can often be found coating the laths in older houses, and sometimes even human hair mixed with the plaster.

> **Plasterboard:** Plasterboard is very easy both to put up and knock down. It has the great advantage that it doesn't need plastering. A plasterboard wall will normally consist of two pieces of plasterboard on each side of a wooden stud frame (see page 131).

Floors and ceilings

> **Foundations:** Unless you have a cellar, the ground floor will rest on the foundations of your house. They carry the whole weight of the building and spread it as evenly as possible across the area. The type, size and depth will depend on the house and the characteristics of the soil. Any extensions to the house should have foundations of the same weight and depth as those used for the rest of the house, otherwise there will be uneven movement between the two structures and cracks will appear where they meet – never a good thing.

> **Ground floor:** Ground floors are usually built from either solid concrete or suspended timber. Concrete floors usually incorporate a damp-proof membrane to prevent rising damp. Suspended timber floors are made up of floorboards resting on joists. The floorboards run at right angles to the joists, and the ends of the joists are supported by brickwork or metal wall plates. (See page 164 for more details.)

> **Upper floors:** As with suspended timber floors on the ground floor, these are supported by joists, this time bedded in all the supporting walls.

> **Ceilings:** Ceilings are also supported by joists. Where there is another floor above the ceiling, the same joists may support both ceiling and floor and will be 20–38cm (8–15in) deep and 10–15cm (4–6in) wide, depending on the size of the room. Where joists support only a ceiling, they will be smaller and are unlikely to be adequate to support a floor. If you want to put a floor down in the loft, you'll usually need to get proper floor joists installed.

> **Roof:** Where the house has a sloping roof (also called a pitched roof), the ceiling joists on the top storey connect with angled rafters, which are supported by wall plates on the top of the walls and are attached to a ridge board at the top of the roof. This triangular structure is held together by a number of other planks of wood and metal fittings, including ties, purlins and struts. There will usually be a felt

membrane laid over the rafters to keep out the rain and, on top of this, horizontal tile battens run at right angles to the rafters and support the roof tiles.

> **Utilities:** The walls carry all the electricity cables, and the pipes that feed your radiators are more likely to be under the floorboards or running around the skirtingboards. You can buy pipe and cable detectors that will locate these for you (see page 38), and these should always be used before you drill or hammer into a wall or floor. Make sure you mark the pipes and cables on your house plan when you do.

> **Fireplaces and chimneys:** If your fireplaces have properly built chimneys that are open and clean, they will take the smoke and fumes from the rooms. They'll also help to circulate the air and get rid of dust – houses without chimneys are 50% dustier than those that have them.

Period houses

If you live in a period building, it can be very useful to know exactly what period it comes from. This will help you to understand how it was built and the materials used, and also what features and decoration will work well. However, there might be building restrictions, too – check with your building control officer at the local council offices. Look at the other properties on your street to see what original features they've kept, and if you don't have the original drawings and architect's plans, a library or your local authority website may help you to track down the history of your home.

A client of mine had her house for more than 50 years, and never had the drawings. When the floorboards rotted, she got a carpenter in to replace them, and as soon as he'd pulled up a few boards he discovered the most beautiful cellar, full of interesting stuff. I've heard stories of people checking out the drawings of their homes and realising they didn't tally with the floor space – when they've poked a hole in the wall they've found real treasure troves from the past.

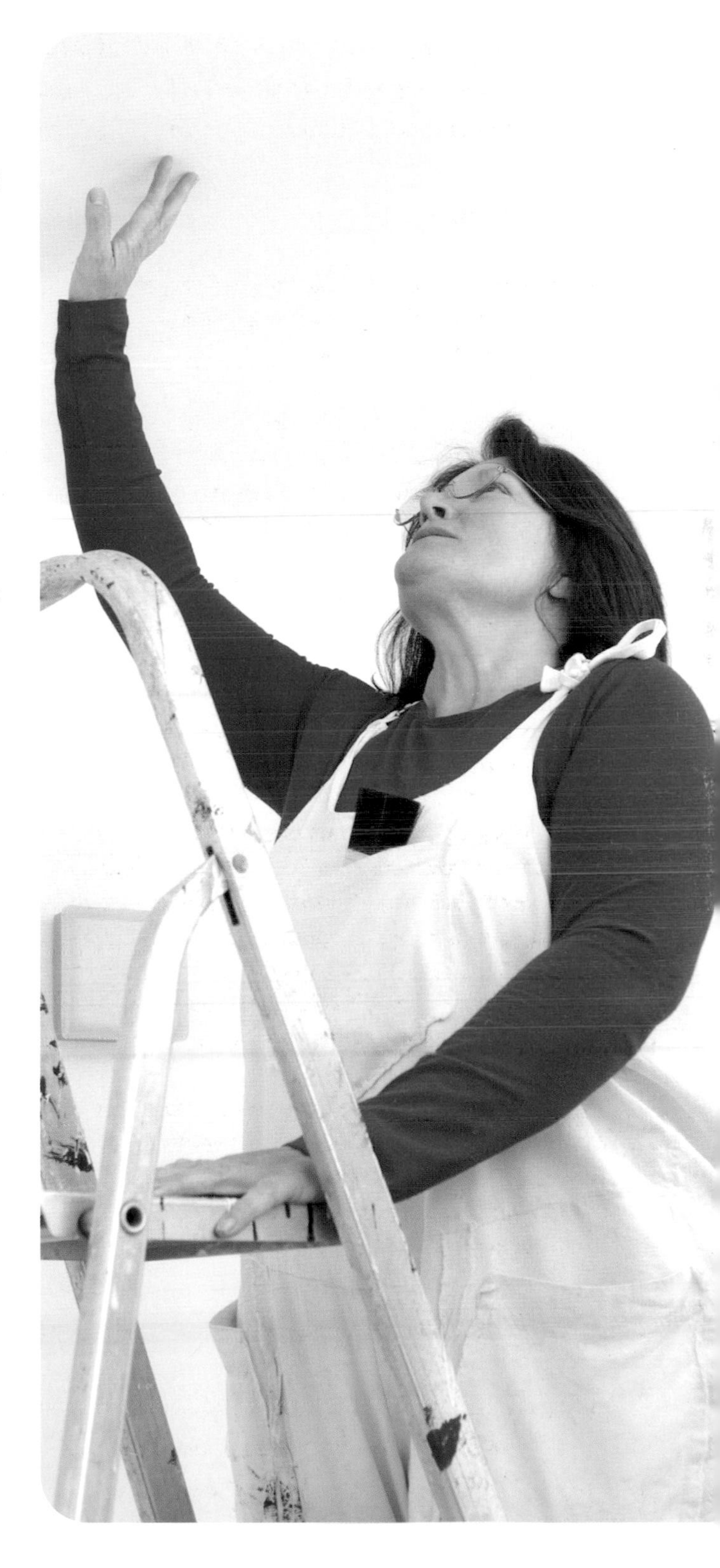

open-vented system

1 boiler
2 pump
3 radiators
4 feed-and-expansion tank
5 storage tank
6 hot water cylinder
7 mains water supply
8 overflow

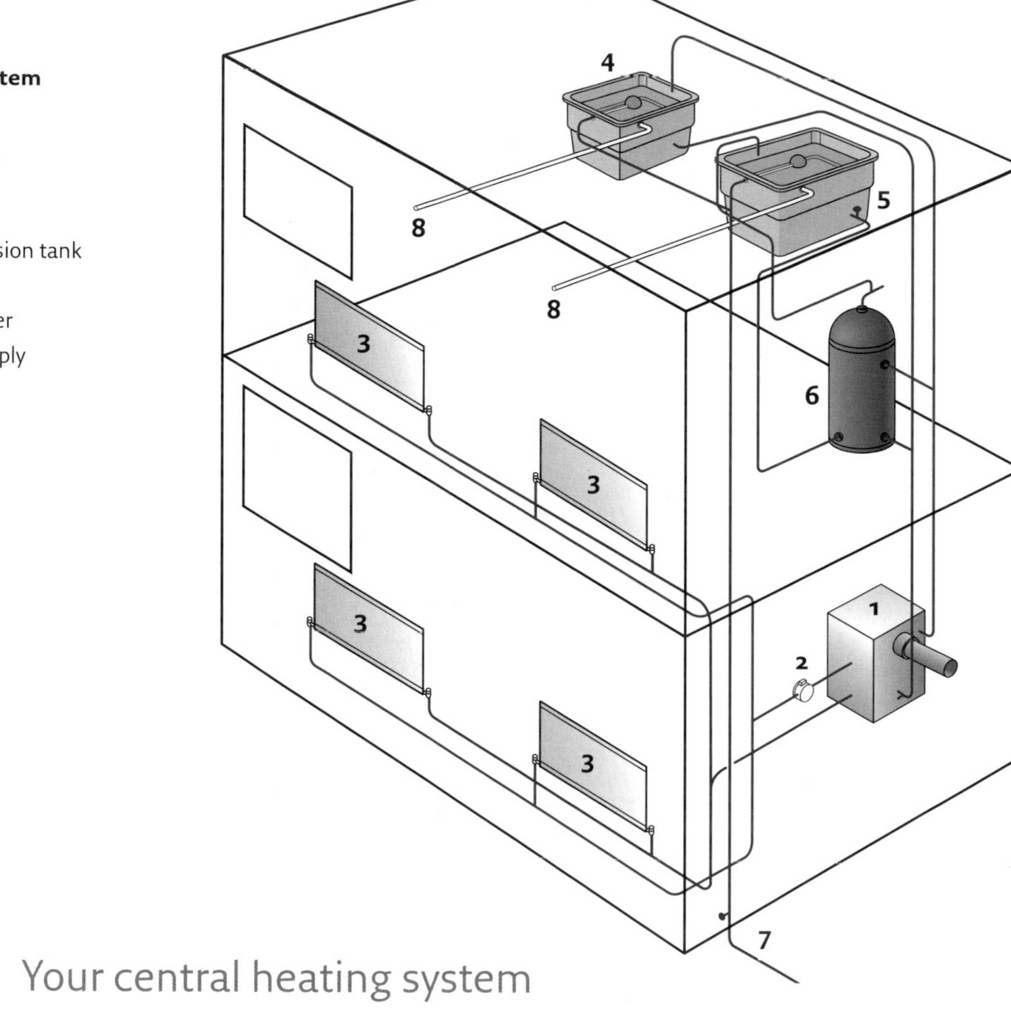

Your central heating system

All central heating systems consist of a boiler, a pump, a network of pipes and enough radiators to heat each room. They work by heating up water at the boiler, then pumping it around the pipes to each radiator in turn and finally bringing it back to the boiler to be heated again. The water loses heat when the radiators are heating up the room, so you can usually find out which way it flows around your system by feeling the pipes going into and out of the radiator – the warmer one is the inbound pipe, and the slightly cooler one is the return pipe.

When you move into a new house or flat, it's useful to find out a bit about your central heating system. There are many different kinds, but the most important distinction here is between open-vented systems and sealed systems.

> **Open-vented systems** are more commonly found in houses rather than flats. The boiler is separate from any hot water tank supplying the taps, and the system usually includes a storage tank and a feed-and-expansion tank. The storage tank is between the mains supply and the boiler, and the feed-and-expansion tank is found close to the boiler on the outbound pipe, giving space in the system for the water to expand when heated and also for the displaced air to then escape. The open-vented system gives a lot of flexibility.

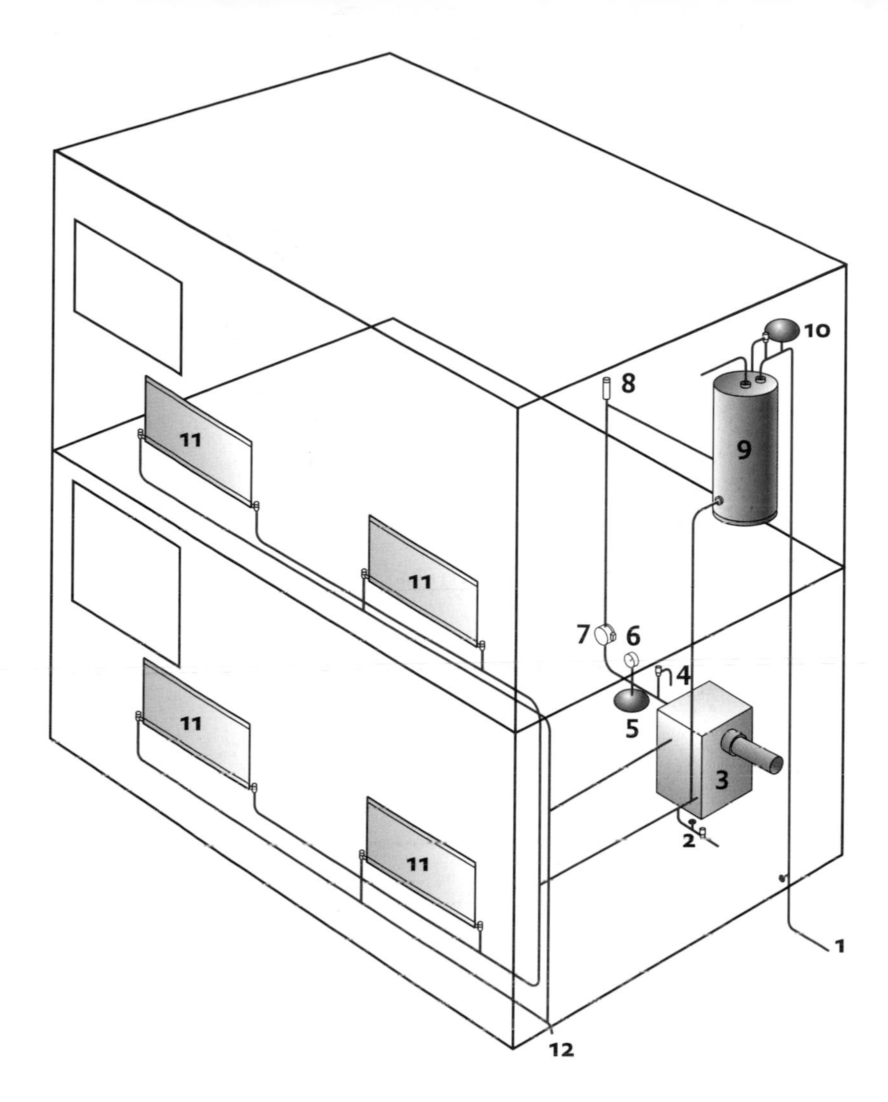

sealed system

1 cold mains supply
2 filling loop with non-return valve
3 boiler
4 safety valve
5 expansion vessel
6 pressure gauge
7 pump
8 air-release point
9 unvented hot-water cylinder
10 hot-water expansion vessel
11 radiators
12 draincock

> **Sealed systems** are often found in flats or smaller houses in conjunction with a combination boiler, or 'combi boiler' as they are often called. Combination boilers supply hot water both to a sealed central heating system and to the taps. They can be very handy because the boiler turns on to heat the water whenever you run a hot tap. However, because it supplies the tap water as it is heated, the supply is notoriously slow, and you may find that there is no supply to one hot tap if there is another on at the same time.

IMPORTANT FEATURES OF YOUR CENTRAL HEATING SYSTEM

The drain cock is used for emptying all the water from your central heating system for certain types of repair. It resembles a tap, and will usually be close to the boiler on the pipe that brings the water from the last radiator in the system back to the boiler. Failing this, try the pipes near to the back or front door.

The feed-and-expansion tank allows the system to be topped up when water is low, and gives room for the water to expand as it heats up.

Health and safety girl

Here are some essential common sense tips for avoiding a trip to A&E. But before moving on to them, remember that the most important DIY tool is your brain. It's all too easy to rush into a job, eager to get it done, but if you just stop and think before you do anything, taking time to work out what the risks are and how to avoid them, you can ensure that you won't finish your session laid up in hospital.

Take care!

These pages highlight the most important safety tips and others are brought to your attention throughout the book in the special Safety First boxes. But don't use these as an excuse not to think the consequences through for yourself. Always try to think ahead and try to see the risk of an accident before it happens. Even after all these years I still have accidents – just recently I over-reached while standing on a flight of stairs to attach a BT cable to the wall, and slipped because I had no shoes on. The only bit that does not hurt is the tip of my nose.

> Always wear shoes, and make sure they are rubber-soled for any jobs involving electricity. For other jobs, shoes with hard toecaps save years of pain. I have trainers with hard toecaps and solve both problems in one.

> Wear **goggles, a mask and protective clothing for any jobs that involve fumes or mess.** Masks must be the correct one for the job you're doing, and avoid breathing anything in other than the aroma of your coffee at break time.

> Don't run when carrying tools or go up and down stairs with tools in your hands. Always use a tool tray or tool box for carrying them.

> Be very careful with Stanley knives and scalpels – always retract the blades when you've finished with them, and NEVER keep one in a pocket.

> Keep dust sheets flattened while you're working, and if they get mucky, shake them out and lay them again.

Electricity and protection

> When using power tools, always plug a circuit breaker into the socket and plug the tool into the circuit breaker. This can be bought from any DIY store and will protect you if you cut through the cord, if your tools come into contact with water or in any other life-threatening circumstance.

> Do use a cordless drill if you can. Instead of working off mains electricity, they run off a battery, which can be recharged.

> If you're using a steamer, use your fuse box to turn off the sockets in the room where you're working (see pages 76–7). Then use an extension lead and a circuit breaker, and plug the steamer into a socket on a different socket circuit.

LADDER LORE

Ladders should never be bent, broken or without their rubber feet. Replace them if you are concerned – they're so cheap, and it's a small price to pay to prevent it from collapsing with you holding a drill at the top.

Make sure that the ladder's legs are on a firm and level base.

Keep the steps on the ladder clean and dry – wallpaper paste is particularly dangerous.

Make sure that your ladder is high enough for the job and don't over-reach

Make sure that the ladder faces the wall rather than being side on.

If you are leaning a long ladder against an outside wall, ensure the base is at least your body height away from the wall.

Never work on big extension ladders on your own – always have someone holding the bottom.

Don't get up a ladder with loads of tools in your arms, or put them loose on the ladder – instead, attach a tool tray to the top, placing the tools on the tray before you get up the ladder.

Don't climb a ladder holding a power tool with the cord trailing – strap the drill to the tool tray before getting up the ladder, and pick it up when you're at the top.

If you think you're going to fall and you're holding a tool, throw the tool away from yourself and anyone else in the room.

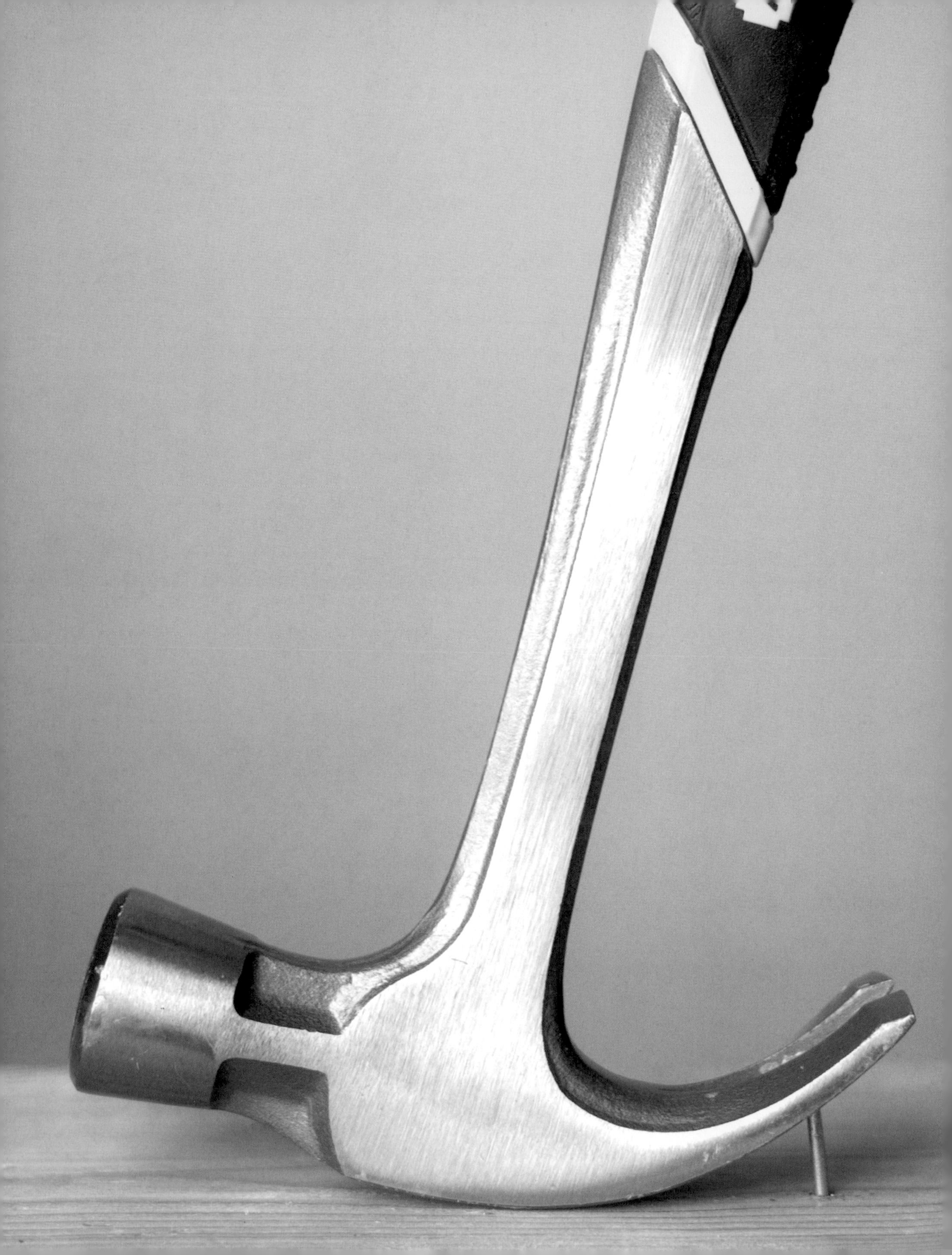

CHAPTER TWO

The ultimate tool box

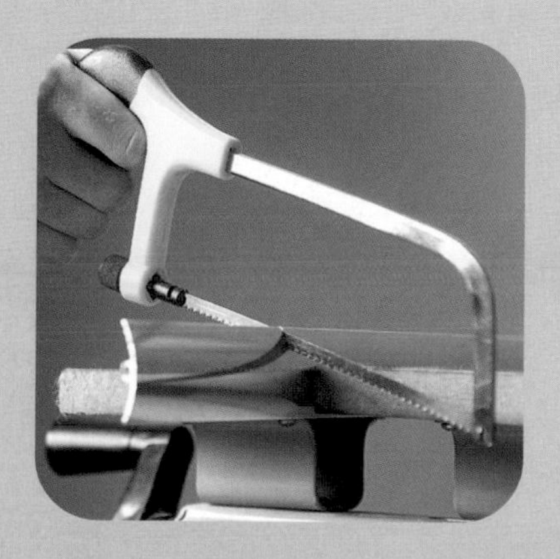

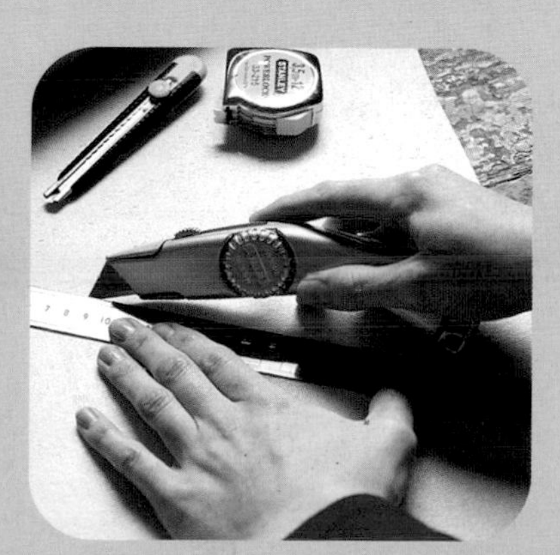

Building the ultimate tool box

Every home should have an essential DIY toolbox – it will come to the rescue, with even the smallest job, so often that you'll wonder how you ever survived without it. The time and energy it saves you in the long run makes it worth every penny.

The importance of good tools

Investing in the right tools makes a fantastic difference to the way you work (and to the way you feel about your work), which always reflects in the quality of the finished job.

> Always select the best quality tools you can afford – but remember that these don't have to be the most expensive tools on the market. These won't always be the best ones for you.
> The right tool comes down to the individual and the weight and balance of each item – it has to feel good in your hand, with a good weight for you to be able to hold it properly.
> Trips to superstores are great because you can see what they have, all easily displayed along miles of racks. Furthermore their own brand goods can be extremely good value.
> There are also more specialist stores to visit, such as that little tool shop around the corner – or look in the yellow pages. Many women I speak to either don't realise these small stores exist or think they are the exclusive domain of men or trade (or both). In fact, they are an invaluable source for information and advice. Not all their tools will necessarily be on display so talk to an assistant about what you need to do; be quite clear about the kinds of jobs you will be carrying out and ask lots of questions. Once they know you, they're more than helpful and will supply all the wonderful tools that craftsmen use.
> For specialist or one-off jobs, however, consider hiring a particular tool, such as a floor sander.
> Power tools are ever evolving so if what you want is currently too expensive, wait a little and the price will come down (just like it does with cars when new models are unveiled). Or perhaps try the own brand ranges from the superstores.

TOP TIP: BE INVENTIVE

Remember that the tool specified for the job doesn't always do the job best. My relatively blunt chisel covers a multitude of tasks, from removing old silicone from the side of the sink to raking out cracks in walls and ceilings so that filler will work properly.

ESSENTIAL TOOL KIT

> **Allen keys**
> **Bolster or cold chisel**
> **Bradawl**
> **Chisels**
> **Continental filling knifes**
> **Craft knife**
> **Electric drill and drill bits**
> **Electric sander**
> **Extension lead**
> **Hammers**
> **Joist and pipe detectors**
> **Metal ruler**
> **Mitre block**
> **Nail punches**
> **Paintbrushes**
> **Paint rollers**
> **Pincers**
> **Plane**
> **Pliers**
> **Sandpaper**
> **Saws**
> **Screwdrivers and screws**
> **Spanners**
> **Spirit levels**
> **Tape measure**
> **Tiling tools**
> **Toggle bolts**
> **Wallpapering tools**
> **Wall plugs**
> **Washers**
> **Wire cutters**
> **Wrenches**

STANLEY

Choosing your tools

Here I look at each of the key elements that your tool box should contain. The basic tool box will include important tools like hammers and screwdrivers, and support materials like wall plugs, screws and spirit levels, which will sort out most everyday DIY tasks. If you are doing tasks such as wallpapering or tiling, specific tools are also needed, which are included on these pages too. On pages 40–3, I then go on to highlight other helpful things to have on hand, like glues, epoxy resins and a notebook.

Buying a tool box is a matter of personal preference. There are so many on the market that it's best to just go and see what's available. However, I would suggest one that comes on wheels, which you can pull around. Usually they come apart into sections so you can carry the individual bits up stairs if you need to. Try to always carry tools from room to room in a tool box, even if all you need is the screwdriver. If you fall downstairs with a screwdriver in your hand, it is more likely to be fatal than if you fall with a box of tools, everyone in the house and street will know and it will just be messy.

TOOLS FOR WOMEN

If you have small hands, seek out smaller tools, such as hammers, screwdrivers, pliers, craft knives, tape measures and spirit levels, as shown here. There are also smaller drills on the market together with tiny saws. Tool shops will be only too happy to help you find the right size and weight of tool for your purposes and there are some tools available that have been designed specifically with women in mind – they are lighter weight but not necessarily lighter duty.

STORING TOOLS

CLEANED, OILED AND COVERED: that is the mantra for tools.

A little oil is invaluable on any bladed tool, except a craft knife.

Always put your saws away in their cardboard jackets. If the jackets get tatty, tape them back up with heavy duty tape.

Keep the blades on a craft knife retracted.

Treat tools like your friends: don't ignore them or mistreat them or they, in turn, will let you down badly.

Spirit levels (below)

Purchase two spirit levels: a very short one and another about 90cm (3ft) long.

> **Short spirit level:** Always carry this in your tool box so you can carry it from room to room while you are working.

> **The longer spirit level:** Essential for ensuring your work, whether wallpapering or a shelf, is completely level. It is also vital that all electrical goods, such as a stereo and the washing machine, fridge and cooker, are level so they perform at their best and have as long a life as possible.

> **To use a spirit level effectively,** ensure the little bubble in the glass phial is facing you. Then raise or lower the level so that the bubble is exactly between the two black lines.

TOP TIP: PREVENT SLIPPAGE

To stop a spirit level or metal ruler from slipping all over the wall, run a strip of masking tape along the back of it.

Tape measure (1)

Essential for measuring the spaces you're working within. Have two metal ones that whiz in and out, one tape measure is never enough as it always gets hidden underneath something. Ensure they have metric and imperial measurements on them and don't let them get dirty. Electronic measuring tapes are great for measuring big distances.

Metal ruler (2)

A metal ruler (30–45cm/12–18in long) can be used as a marker when needing to draw or score a straight line, or for cutting along.

Craft knife (3)

Perfect for cutting everything from cords and wires to insulation bats (wire connectors that come in a strip). Buy a curved blade, too – it's useful for cutting the likes of vinyl.

Saws

There are quite a few saws that you can and should use as a beginner. Only ever purchase a saw that has a cardboard cover: without one, you cannot be sure that the blade has not been damaged if it has banged or rubbed against other saws.

> **Medium-sized wood saw (bottom):** Choose one with 8.5 teeth/cm (22 teeth/in) if you are cutting laminate. They will ruin very quickly, with an average floor using up three or four saws. Sharpening saws is a lengthy procedure as modern metals do not lend themselves to sharpening easily. So either throw them away or give to a charity that recyles them.

> **Box saw:** Use this for a really fine, absolutely straight cut. It is nearly but not quite like a tenon saw, which is used for making dove-tailed joints cut on special pieces of wood that will be on show and for which you need a really good finish. This is also a good saw for cutting mitres.

> **Junior hacksaw (below):** For cutting that plastic curtain rail or for that screw that got lost in the wood and the head got ripped off. Change the blades regularly and throw the old ones away carefully.

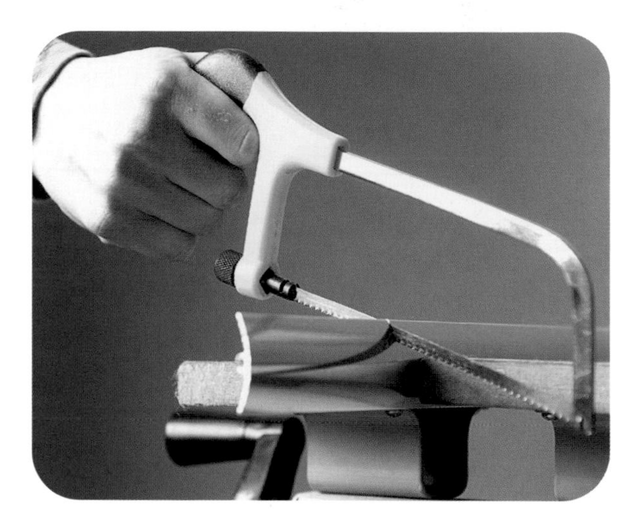

TOP TIPS: USING A SAW

If you hold a brand new saw with the handle towards you and look down its blade, you'll see that it's absolutely straight. The teeth are razor sharp and it's ready for action.

Using a steel rule, draw a line on the wood where you will cut it, and put it in a vice on a workbench.

Hold the saw and make an indentation at the edge where you will start the cut. Rest the saw in this mark at a right angle to the wood. Slowly draw the saw upwards so the teeth bite into the wood, and using no pressure, let the saw slide back down the groove you have made.

Continue up and down, letting the weight of your arm do the work and keeping your strokes light and even. Slow but sure is the key to cutting.

Don't rush and, as a novice, don't try holding the wood down with your hand alone – use a vice.

> **Jig saw (left):** The jig saw is a bonus if you have a lot of cutting to do. Make sure you have the right blades and that you follow the instructions for changing the blade to the letter. When it comes to choosing your jig saw get one that has a pendulum action, which is great for every kind of cutting. Resist the temptation to buy a cheap jig saw as the blades are more likely to bend under pressure.

Mitre block (above)

A mitre block is made of wood or plastic and provides a 45-degree cutting line. It is usually made of wood but can also be made of hard plastic. The wooden one is kinder to your saw. You should buy one with a straight cutting facility, you can use the block to help you make frames for pictures, to cut the Scotia to edge your new laminate floor, and to hold pieces of wood straight so you can measure and make a really good 45-degree cut. Sometimes known as a combi (or combination) block, there are a few different types of mitre block on the market – you must choose the right one for your needs.

TOP TIP: RECYCLE TOOLS

When any of your tools become blunt, consider taking them to a charity that specialises in recycling old tools, because you then don't have to bin them.

Electric drills and drill bits

There are many drills, cordless or otherwise, on the market, and some of them have a lot of features. Talking to the experts will tell you what drill is going to be best for you. A quick explanation of what work you intend to do will point you in the right direction. You should check things out on the internet before you go in order to give yourself a head start.

The slot drive system drill is the best, although for beginners it might be too big, too heavy and too fast. It purrs through concrete like butter, but if you're not careful, with a long enough drill bit you could drill right through the wall it's that tough. I would therefore suggest that you buy a re-charge drill, sometimes called a cordless drill; a cord can be dangerous so it is best avoided if possible.

> The most important thing when purchasing a drill is to hold the drill PLUS the battery in your hand and feel the weight. They can be very heavy.
> Go for one with as powerful a motor as you can afford.
> Having a variable speed allows you to choose an appropriate speed for the material you are drilling into.
> A hammer drill setting – at the flick of a switch – is valuable for drilling into brick or stone and slowly getting through tiles.

See pages 48–53 for practical advice on using a drill.

TOP TIP: GET A DRILL BIT COLLECTION

If you can afford it, buy one of those big drill bit boxes – an all-singing, all-dancing one makes the perfect Christmas or birthday present. Some of the contents you will never use and some things will be a bit suspect, but you will have everything you will ever need in the way of sizes and bits for nearly every material.

KNOW YOUR DRILL BITS

Each material in the home requires a different drill 'bit' depending on the surface. Here's a list of the main types of drill bit that a beginner might need to use.

Material	Drill bits
Brick/plaster	Masonry bit **1** (a silver bit with a flat head)
Plasterboard	Masonry bit
Lathe and plaster	Masonry bit (plus you'll need a wood bit)
Wood	Wood bit **2** (a blackish blue bit with a sharp point) and countersink bit **3** (small and stubby like the end of a candle)
Tiles	Starter bit **4** (with a spade-shaped tip), plus a masonry bit
Metal	Metal bit **5** (blackish blue bit with a fairly flat end but very sharp)
Concrete	Tungsten carbide masonry bit **6**
Plastic one),	Either a wood bit or a metal bit (always use a brand new but try it on a scrap piece first, and a countersink bit
Glass	Diamond drill (always use a brand new one)

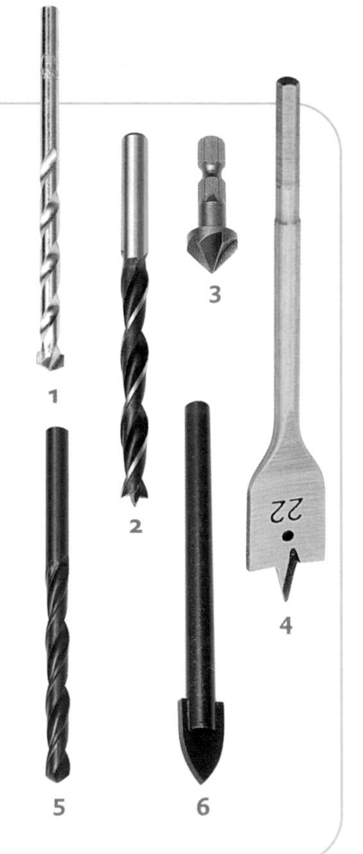

Extension lead

Never use an extension lead coiled up in its stand. The coil will create heat and if left on, may start to burn. Use short leads for short distances and don't have wires dragging all over the room. Instead, keep wires round the edges of the room for safety and do watch wires with ladders. If you have to work up high, use a recharge drill or recharge sander.

CIRCUIT BREAKER

A circuit breaker is either installed as part of your fuse box or is a box that you would plug into your socket and then plug your equipment into the box. If there is any deviation in the current at all, the circuit breaker will cut out – 'break the circuit' – saving you and your equipment from becoming brown and crispy. Always use a circuit breaker no matter what power tools you are using.

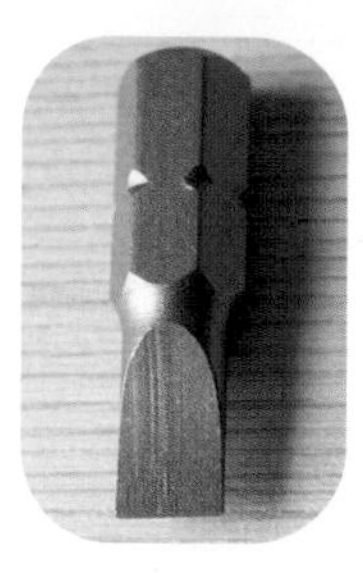

Screwdrivers

> **Craft screwdriver with multiple bits (right):** Buy a driver with a pack of bits or one where the bits are stored in the handle – this is an incredibly useful tool. The three main types are illustrated left (from top to bottom: flat-headed, Phillips and posidrive).

> **Flat-headed screwdriver:** If you choose not to buy a screwdriver with multiple bit attachments, you should have two flat-end screwdrivers in different sizes – one reasonably small and one with a bigger blade.

> **Phillips screwdriver:** These are the screwdrivers with a star-shaped fitting and are invaluable in a tool box. Buy one with a small head and a large one that is as long as you can get.

> **Posidrive screwdriver:** Posidrive screwdrivers and Phillips screwdrivers can be purchased in a very handy set from most superstores. In a set like this you will have all the most used types of screwdriver, saving you a big search for the right one.

> **Neon electrical screwdriver (see below):** This screwdriver lights up when in contact with electrical wiring that has a current running through it. Test yours on a wire that you know is working and it will glow brightly. The screwdriver has a plastic sheath up the length of the driver to protect you if there is faulty wiring and you touch something that is still live.

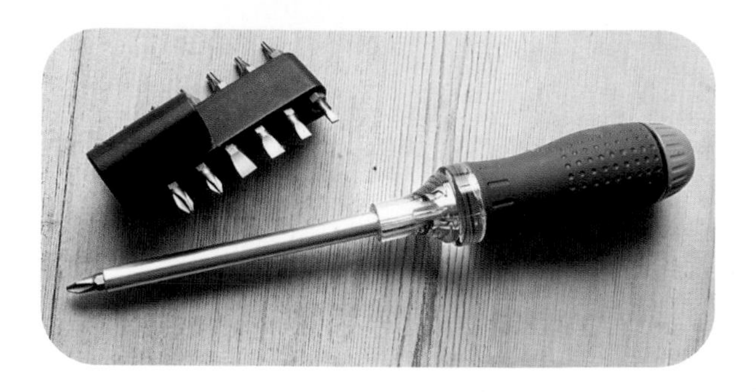

> **Electric screwdriver (below):** There are lots of small rechargeable electric screwdrivers on the market, ranging from the tiniest battery operated to the more useful recharge with a lot more power, to the big drivers with big recharge batteries that could, at a push, be used for drilling. So once again it's down to research, seeing how adaptable it is and feeling the weight of the tool in your hand. An electric screwdriver is comparatively cheap, so if you do need to change or upgrade it, it won't cost a fortune. In some stores, combination packs of screws and wall plugs are available, which are incredibly useful. They usually come in size 6, 8 and 10.

TOP TIP: USING A SCREWDRIVER

Always check your screwdrivers are clean and try not to use them for anything other than screwing. A screw will easily be ruined if the wrong sized screwdriver is used. So ensure the bit fits perfectly into the depth and width of the slot of the screw. Hold the screwdriver firmly, and if it has a slippery surface or you can't get a tight grip, wear rubber gloves. If you're unscrewing something and the screw won't budge, hold the screwdriver in the screw head slot and give it a few light whacks with a hammer – this will dislodge paint or dirt that's stopping it from turning.

Allen keys (1)
Purchase two sets of Allen keys – one imperial and the other metric – (or a combination set) as there are still many products that contain Allen screws to be turned with imperial-size keys. Keep all keys in their own small box (food containers work well), and keep them dry as they will rust if they come in contact with water.

Wall plugs (2)
Used to plug a drilled hole to fix screws in place. Buy a pre-selected set of wall plugs still attached to their strip of plastic. All the sizes you need will be here.

Washers (3)
Have a selection of sizes of galvanised and rubber washers in your tool kit. Essential for repairing leaking taps, the galvanised versions are also sometimes used with toggle bolts and large screws.

Toggle bolts (4)
These are specifically designed for plasterboard or lath and plaster and distribute the load over a larger area than an ordinary wall plug. They come in various sizes and it's always wise to have two or three different sizes in your tool box as you may find that one size just does not work, but the next one up will.

The toggle bolt is a long thin bolt with two wings attached on the end. Drill an appropriate size of hole in the wall so the wings can be popped through to the inside. As you tighten the bolt, so the wings open up to create a bar, making a secure flat fixing on the back of the plasterboard or lath and plaster wall. On a lath and plaster wall, try to ensure the bar runs vertically against the horizontal lathes. You may also have to add a steel washer to give extra strength to the screw end – the wings of the bolt may be larger than the screw end so a larger hole than usual will have been drilled. By using a steel washer, you will spread the load over the hole.

Screws (5)
When you buy your screwdriver(s), purchase a small box of assorted screws. Nearly all the screws you will need are in these boxes and you can buy larger ones, too. The bigger box has more screws for the price.

TOP TIPS: USING SCREWS

Most of the screws that you get in packs with products and instructions are pretty useless as they are very cheap or just not long enough to hold the weight of the product. Furthermore, with an electric driver, the heads usually get ripped off.

So please look at what you are putting on the wall and ask at a store or your tool shop for what they think is best.

If no screws are in with your purchase, it is probably because the manufacturer is giving you the decision as to what to use and not that they have been left out.

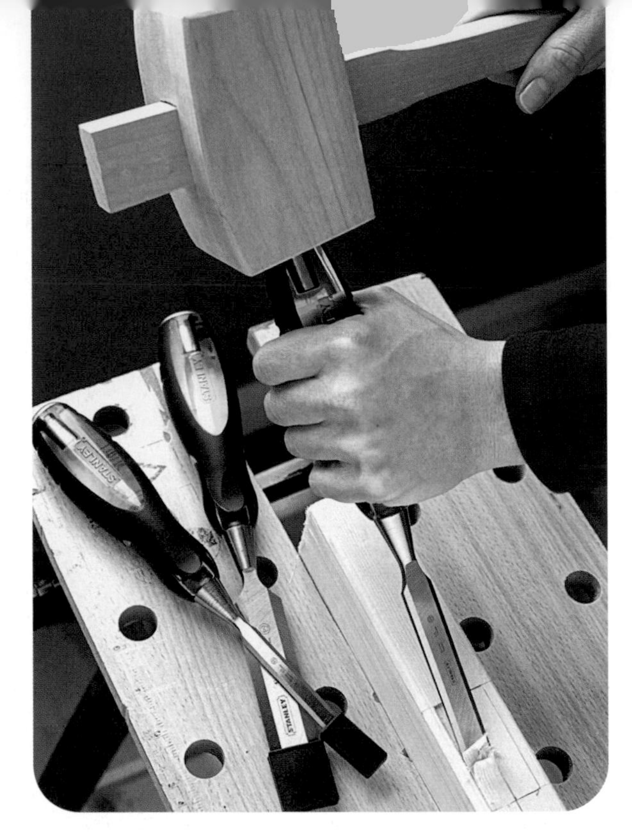

Chisels (left)

Buy a set of three chisels – they usually come in a box – and a sharpening stone. Also keep an oily rag in the chisel box to protect the chisels from damp. (See page 178–9 for practical advice on using a chisel, including using a stone.)

Bolster or cold chisel (bottom left)

It is always good to have a small bolster in your tool box as it has multitude of uses from chipping tiles off walls or floors to cutting out bricks and cutting bricks. A bolster looks like a very wide chisel and should always have a plastic hand guard.

Plane (below)

The small hand plane is a boon for all sorts of woodwork, especially the bottom or the sides of doors that may be sticking. Always oil the blade before you put it back in its box after use.

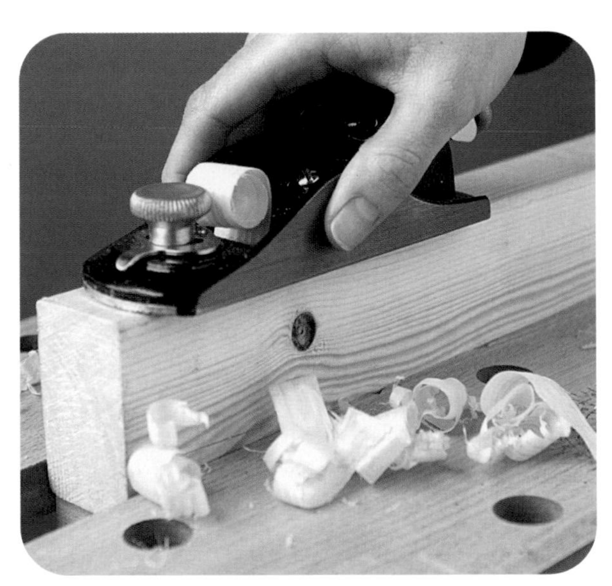

TOP TIP: BE SAFE

Always place the tools you are using in a shoe box or on a high-sided tray and NOT on the floor; it's amazing what you can end up standing on or losing just when you need it.

Hammers (right)

Hammers range from the dinkiest little jeweller's hammers to the well-known sledge hammer that only King Kong could lift. If it's too heavy or badly balanced, it's wrong – it is good technique not brute force that gets the nail in.

> **Claw hammer (1):** You only need one small and one large one. The weight for a large hammer should feel comfortable and will weigh between 400 and 560g (15 and 20 oz).

> **Pin hammer (2):** A lightweight hammer for pins and tacks. It has the normal striking head of a hammer and a wedge-shaped blunt end for tapping in pins.

> **Wooden mallet (see page 178):** This is used for tapping chisels and for that famous flat pack.

> **Rubber hammer (3):** Essential for flat packs and for coaxing anything in place where you don't want to mark the surface.

> **Double-headed hammer (4):** This is a great new innovation – it has a rubber head at one end and a yellow plastic head at the other, which doesn't mark.

Nail punches

Nail punches are invaluable and come in packs of three, with different indents in the heads to take most nails. Tap the nail until the head just reaches the surface of the wood and then place the nail punch over the head of the nail. Give a few taps and the head will start to disappear under the surface. You can then fill the hole with filler and paint or use a coloured wood filler prior to varnish. Use a drip of oil to maintain the punches.

TOP TIP: USING A HAMMER

When you strike a nail, leave a second before the next strike as this will allow the wood to accept the nail and ease. If you hit too quickly and repeatedly, you'll risk splitting the wood. Make sure that the top of the hammer head is kept clean and regularly rubbed with wet and dry paper to keep the head matt. A shiny head leads to bent nails.

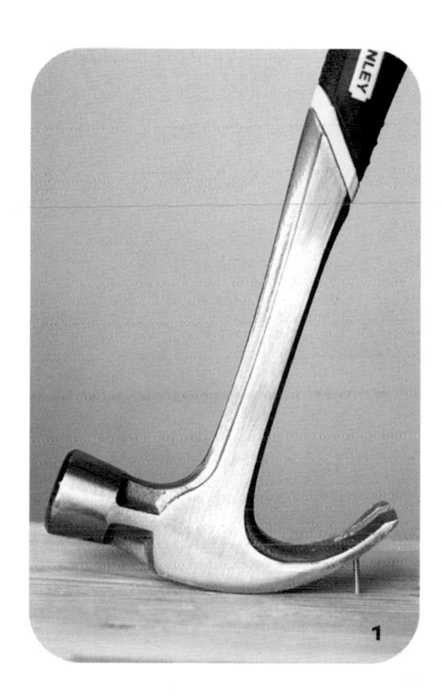

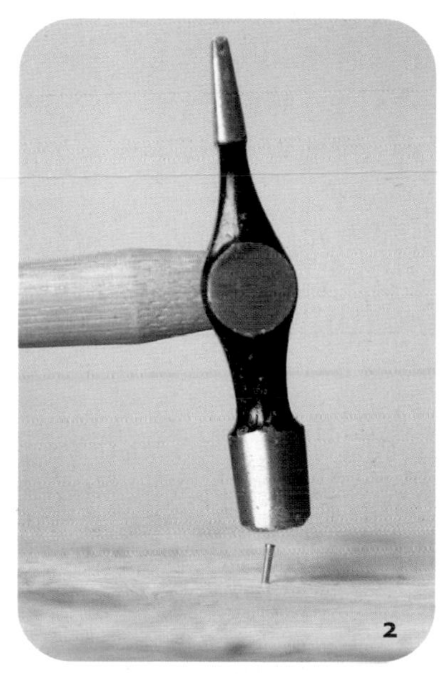

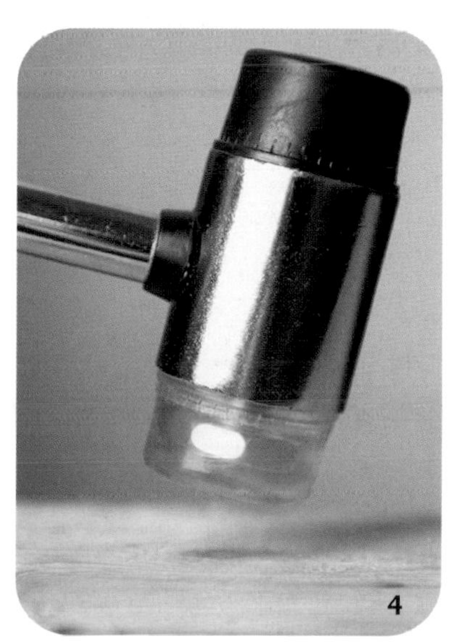

Paintbrushes (above)
Buy a set of five brushes in a plastic pack ranging from a width of 5mm (¼in) to 10cm (4in). The new ones with manmade fibre bristles are fantastic as they give such a good finish and they have little to no fallout. The rubber-handled ones do not do well in the white spirit that you use for cleaning the brushes.

Be disciplined with cleaning brushes properly in the appropriate solvent as soon as you have finished painting. Never leave brushes sitting in water or white spirits as the bristles will bend and the handles start to disintegrate. Instead, let them dry out by wrapping the bristles tightly in kitchen paper secured with masking tape so that the bristles dry straight and together.

> **Fitches:** Get two or three of these specialist brushes. These are a bit more expensive but if you keep them clean after every job they will last a lifetime. They are a boon for cutting in (painting along the edge of walls or against a window or door frame), and consist of a long wooden handle with a flat bristle tip. They come in various sizes, and you'll need to try them all to find out which size works for you, on the basis of its weight and how it feels in your hand. A lot of my decorating time is spent cutting in with a 7.5cm (3in) white-tipped brush made of manmade fibres – it paints like a dream.

Paint rollers (above)
Rollers come in various sizes and lengths. They also range from heavy-duty fluffy ones for painting over Artex, to the finest tiny 15cm (6in) roller with such an incredibly fine nap that I can paint my van with it. Different companies make differently sized handles and different colour codes to indicate the type of roller. Pick yours in the same way as you would a brush – it's the weight and the feel in your hand that's important.

> **Radiator rollers:** This is my favourite roller. With its extra long handle, this little beauty has so many uses, not just painting behind radiators but also for brushing wallpaper down the back of the radiator.

Continental filling knives (above)

Having a set of these in your tool kit is invaluable (they come in sets of different sizes) as they can be used for a whole variety of tasks. Choose a really flexible knife with a narrow blade and, if you have to fill awkward corners and niches, find a knife with a narrow blade. Remember these are very sharp, so be careful.

Sandpaper (below)

Buy a very large pack of assorted grades, a large roll of medium grade and a large pack of wet and dry paper.

All the grades are an invaluable asset in your tool box, plus you should always have a sanding block. This is a small block of wood or cork that will nestle nicely in your hand and around which you wrap sandpaper, checking that you are keeping the sanding area absolutely flat.

Start sanding with a coarser grade of paper and move to finer grades as the surface you are working on becomes smoother. Wet and dry paper is used for rubbing down fine surfaces such as painted wood or for polishing plastic.

Electric sander (below right)

The best electric sander for the beginner is a small hand-held sander that fits comfortably into the palm of your hand and has a strap that goes over the back of your hand. It is comfortable, neat and very effective.

TOP TIP: SAND WITH EASE

For finishing small pieces of wood, find a 30 x 30cm (12 x 12in) square of MDF and choose a different grade of sandpaper to glue to each side. You will then be able to deal with small pieces considerably more easily.

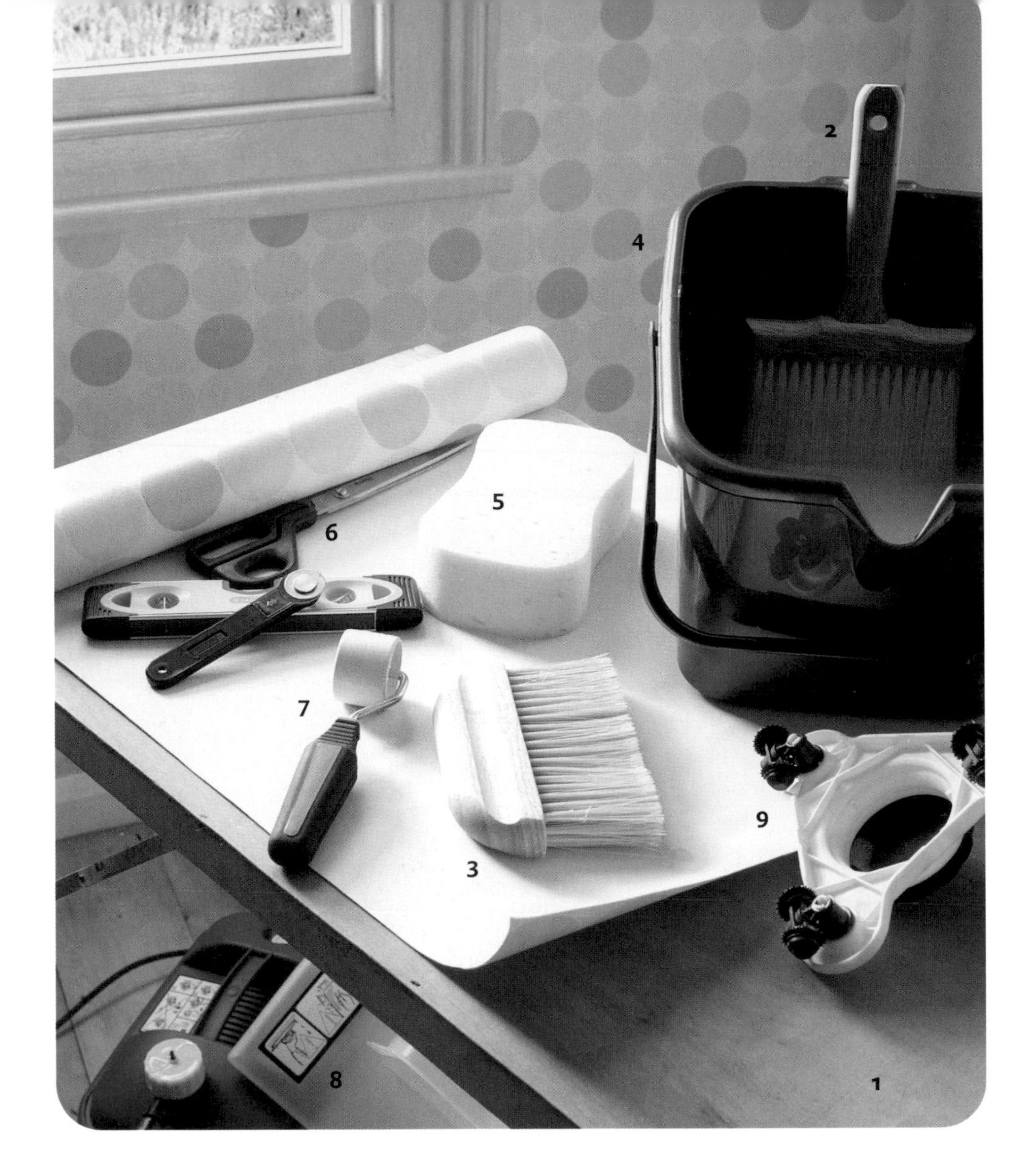

Wallpapering tools (above)

> **Pasting table (1):** A lightweight foldable table that is a good length for pasting wallpaper on. It also tends to be narrower than a conventional table. You don't have to have one of these for hanging wallpaper – but it helps, especially if you are working in a room a long way away from the nearest table.

> **Pasting and paper-hanging brushes (2 & 3):** A pasting brush is a wide, synthetic-bristled brush with a handle, used for applying paste to the back of the paper. A paper-hanging brush has shorter bristles, no handle and is used for smoothing paper onto the wall.

> **Bucket and sponge (4 & 5):** For holding the wallpaper paste and smoothing paper.

> **Wallpaper scissors (6):** With their ultra-long blades, wallpaper scissors make cutting strips of wallpaper and trimming excess a far more straightforward job than using ordinary kitchen scissors. Cutters with roller blades are also available for trimming edges of wallpaper once it is on the wall.

> **Seam roller (7):** A seam roller is a very narrow roller made of plastic, used for pressing seams in place. One of these will give you the best of finishes.

> **Wallpaper steamer (8)** If you are planning on stripping a lot of wallpaper, you might want to buy one of these gadgets. However, you can also hire one for a day or two. The steamer has a reservoir of water, which is heated to boiling point and forces steam through the plate that is pressed against the wallpaper. It makes you very warm, but it is also a very efficient way of removing paper.

> **Wallpaper perforator (9):** What a fine gadget – by rolling the little wheels across the wall, hundreds of tiny perforations are made in the paper. These allow water to soak through more readily, and the wallpaper just falls off.

Tiling tools (below)

> **Electric tile cutter (1):** This is a simple but effective tool and is used for cutting straight lines on thinner tiles. Also used for cutting tiles at an angle.

> **Tile spacers (2):** Made of plastic, by using these you will ensure your tiles are equally spaced. Special corner ones are also available.You can use matchsticks, if you prefer.

> **Tile nibblers (3):** For removing just a part of a tile, for example, to fit around a socket. Draw a line on the tile and then 'nibble' away. Continue to remove small pieces of tile until you have reached the marked line.

> **Grout float (4):** A grout float has a large handle on it, which allows the user to apply plenty of pressure when smoothing grout between tiles.

> **Notched spreader (above):** This is an essential tool for spreading tile adhesive. The notches on one side make the adhesive ridged, so providing better purchase for the tiles to adhere to.

> **Score-and-snap pliers (below):** Looking a little like a can opener, this tool is used for cutting straight lines on tiles that aren't too thick. Use the wheel on one side of the pliers to mark the scoring line first. Then snap apart with the pincers.

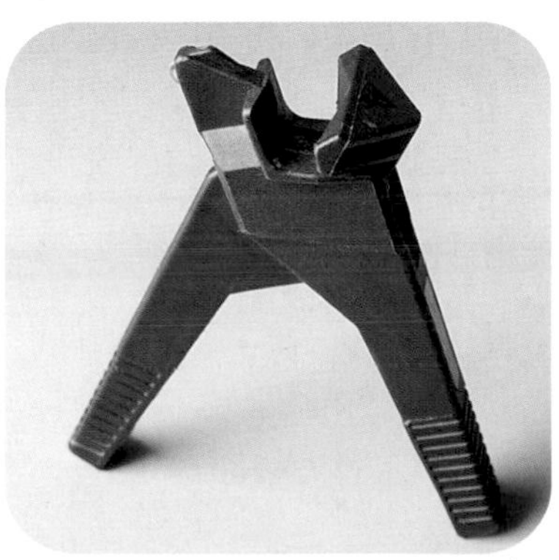

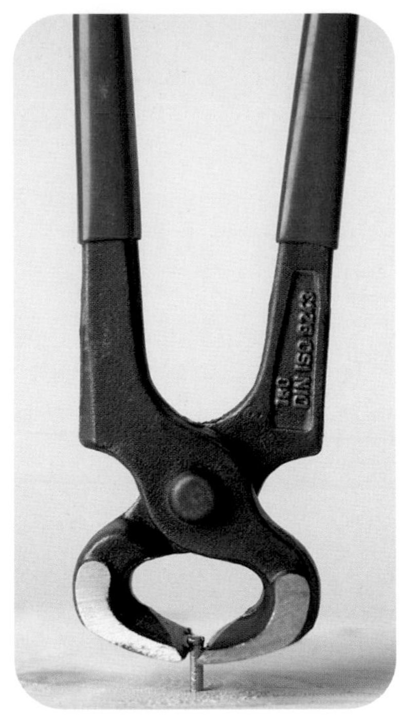

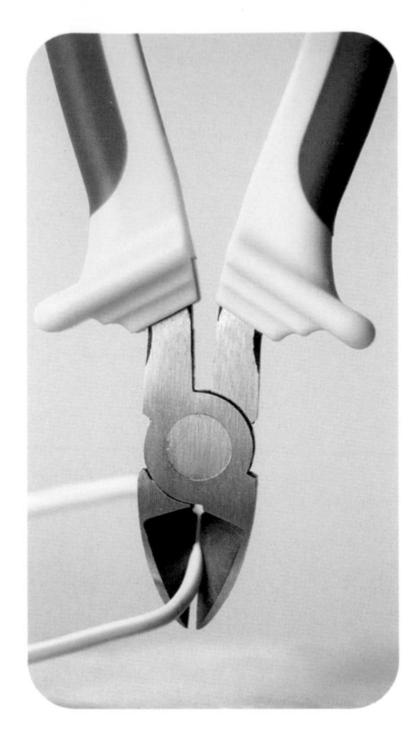

Pliers and long-nosed pliers (left and bottom left)
Pliers are long and very pointed and have ridges inside to help grip, pull and twist in the most awkward places. A drip of oil every now and again helps maintain a perfect plier that will last a lifetime. A small pair of long-nosed pliers with rubber handles are useful for such things as guiding wires through plugs, for getting things out of small spaces and for holding things while you screw, cut or bang.

Pincers (above, centre)
Pincers are seldom bought by beginners but I would always recommend getting a pair early on as they are the best tool for extracting nails – they usually have a little fork on the end of one part of the handle, which is a magic tool for pulling out such items. Use a rocking action when using them to pull out a nail so that you do not damage your wood. As with other metal tools, pincers respond well to a clean with an oily cloth.

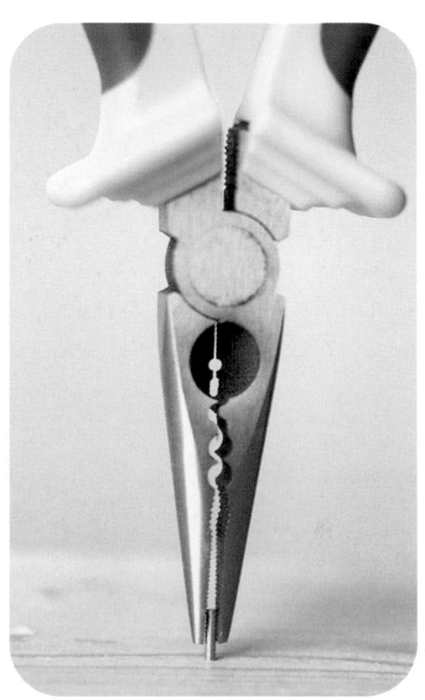

Wire cutters (above right)
Also called side cutters, this looks like a pair of pliers but has a curved top that can cut wire and wire nails. Choose a pair that fits snugly in your hand and is lightweight. It must also have rubber handles for a good grip.

Joist and pipe detectors (see page 165)
The joist detector is an electrical gadget that, when it is switched on, gives out a high-pitched tone when it detects a joist under your floorboards or behind your plaster wall. The same applies to the pipe detector: it gives off a high-pitched note when it finds a wire or a pipe.

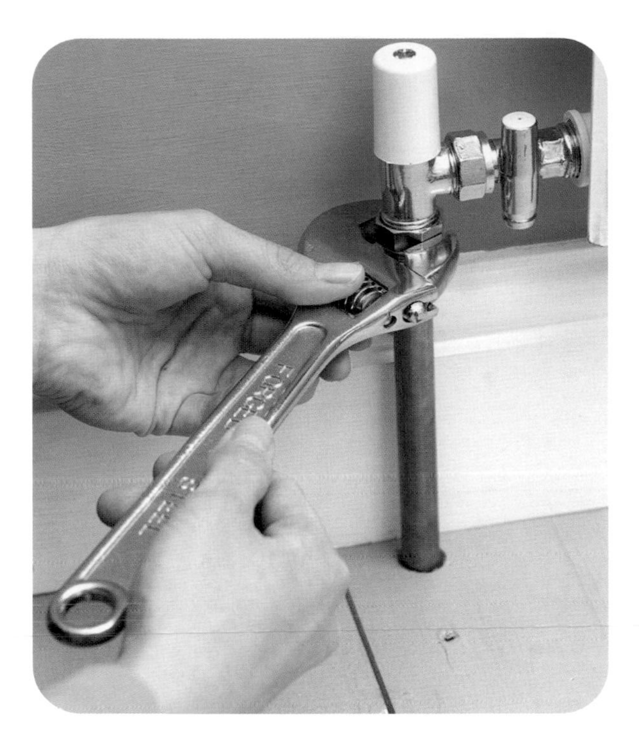

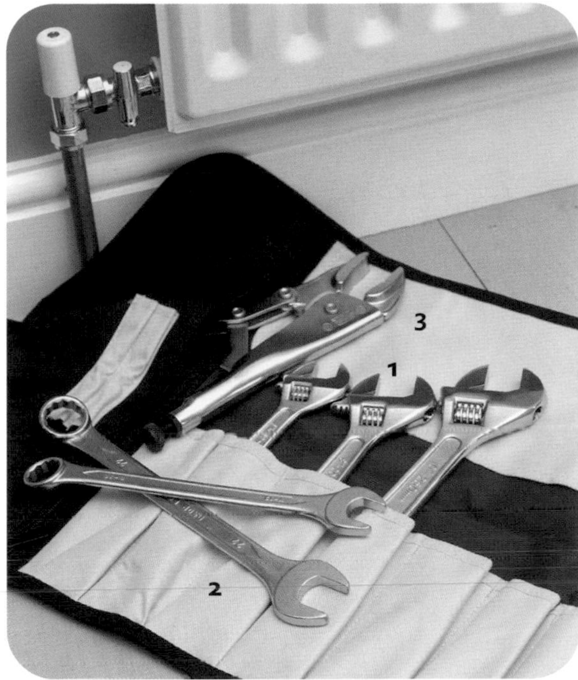

Spanners

- **Adjustable spanner (above left and right, 1):** This has two moving parts, allowing the head of the spanner to widen to whatever size you need. This spanner will tackle a number of jobs and two sizes are helpful (the smallest and the largest you can get).
- **Open spanner:** These are inserted from the side of the nut, which is ideal when you have no head clearance and no clearance from behind. If you look carefully at the open spanner you will see that the head of the spanner is at a helpful angle for when movement is restricted. You can also turn the spanner over and gain more leverage.
- **Ring spanner:** A ring spanner encircles the nut completely, ensuring that it won't slip off. They should be used when you can make a full rotation of the spanner and when you can get the spanner over the head of the nut (the ring fitting ensures the spanner won't slip from the nut).

Buy a small, cheap set of six to eight open spanners or **look for a set of combination spanners, each of which is an ordinary spanner on one end and a ring spanner at the other end (above right, 2).** A combination spanner is particularly ideal when you are working in a tight space because it is much easier having both the ring end and the open end together in the one tool – perfect for getting a good grip on a tight nut (if one end cannot get on to the nut, the other one will). If a spanner gets wet, add a few drips of oil and then dry it before putting away.

Spanners are designed to fit nuts tightly so they do not rub the edges of the nut or jeopardise the thread. Keep trying different spanners until you find the perfect fit or use an adjustable one.

Wrenches (above, 3)

Having two wrenches in your tool box makes tackling work on pipes or taps quite straightforward. Hold the bottom of a nut with one wrench while turning the top of the nut with the other one. Rubber handles are good for grip. The wrench works by the two parts of the head opening along a long slot, which gives you different settings for the head to clamp on to whatever you are working on.

TOP TIP: BE KIND TO TOOLS

When you buy suitcases or handbags you will find small packets of silica gel in the bottom to stop moisture from rotting the bag. Save them and throw into the tool box.

OTHER ESSENTIAL ITEMS

- Adhesives
- Blu-Tack
- Carpenter's pencil
- Chinagraph or wax pencil
- Cling film
- Earth wire cover
- Electrical tape
- Fuses
- Masking tape
- Notebook and pencil
- Plastic bags
- PTFE tape
- Rubber, large white
- Scissors
- Velcro
- Workbench

Adhesives

> **PVA (1):** PVA is a liquid membrane or a glue. It stabilises surfaces by rendering particles unable to move and it forms a barrier by penetrating many surfaces and creating a fine film. This acts as a key for many types of paint and wallpaper and PVA also prepares surfaces for decorating.

> **Contact (2):** Contact adhesive is a spirit-based adhesive used where you need a very tight and hard bond between two substances. It is applied on both parts to be joined together and is left to dry for a short period of time before the two pieces are joined together (usually under pressure, such as in a vice or beneath a couple of bricks).

> **Super glue (3):** Super glue is a substance that will melt the surface of plastic. So by using it to join together two pieces of plastic, super glue acts as a weld. You will find that if the join then breaks, it is the plastic on either side of the weld that will give under stress. Super glue has many uses – even in forensic science.

> **Epoxy putty (4):** This is a very good repairer. It either comes as two strips of what looks like Plasticine – usually beige and yellow, but you can get white too. To use it, cut pieces of the same length and mould them together. Sometimes the two strips are moulded into one piece, cut a slice off and mould it to soften it. There is then a chemical reaction which means the putty eventually sets as hard as a rock. The best application for epoxy putty is when you have drilled a deep hole in the wall and you need maximum strength for the screws: put a tiny bit of the mixed resin in the hole, insert the wall plug and then the screw.

But be warned – the only way you will get the screw out again is to drill it out with a metal drill bit.

> **Epoxy resin (5):** This is an adhesive that has two parts: the glue itself and a hardener, known as a catalyst. Epoxy resin can stick most things, especially metal.

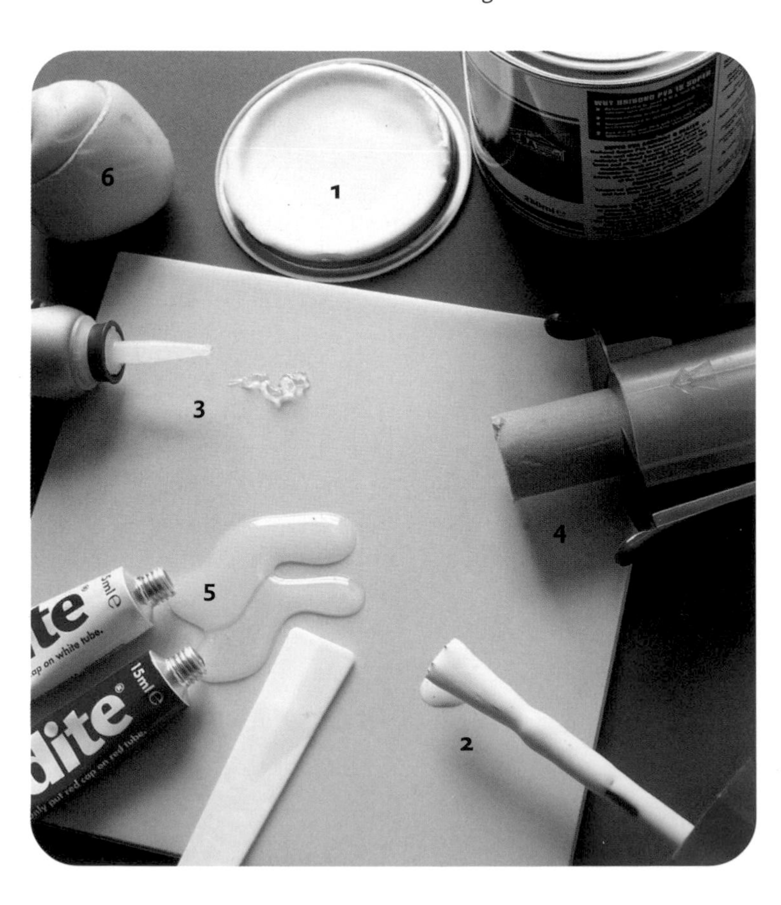

Blu-Tack (6)

Before you use Blu-Tack on a wall, do a test spot to ensure it doesn't leave a mark behind or tear delicate wallpaper. When removing the Blu-Tack, resist the temptation to pull it off; rolling it off is much better.

Notebook and pencil (1 & 2)

Choose a notebook that will last and fit in your tool box; spiral bound is good because it stays flat when open. Always have two pencils – they seem to go missing just when you need to put your hands on them.

Carpenter's pencil (3)

This is a flat pencil that gives you more control of the lead if, say, you are making a long mark down the length of a piece of wood freehand. If you are using a ruler, you can get the lead right into the edge. The other wonderful thing about a carpenter's pencil is that the lead doesn't keep breaking as it is so thick. And if you have ever seen a carpenter wield one, you will understand how many uses it has and how clever it is to be flat.

Chinagraph pencil or wax crayon (4)

This is a wax pencil that is invaluable for marking tiles and glass and for any material that will not take a pencil or for surfaces where you need to use water or oil in the cutting process. You can use a child's crayon instead.

Rubber (5)

No, this is not a red herring – a white rubber is really useful for just rubbing dirty marks from a wall and pencil marks and mistakes in your notebook.

Scissors (6)

Have a variety of sizes to hand; you can buy them in sets from any good superstore.

TOP TIP: KEEP NOTES

Make a note of EVERYTHING you do in your notebook: it's a vital tool for remembering what went right and wrong with each job. It also saves you from re-measuring everything in the future and you'll always have notes on tools and paints so that if they are discontinued, the store can help you find the best equivalent.

TOP TIP: PROTECT LENSES

If you are going to paint a ceiling and you need to wear glasses and/or goggles, stretch cling film over the lenses. Then when you can't see any more, just peel it of and replace with a fresh piece. I also use cling film for wrapping up my hair and if I want to keep my boots clean.

Cling film

There are so many uses for this when decorating. Cover the doors with dust sheets or plastic, but someone will always touch the handles with paint on their hands, so wrap them up in cling film. Or when you loosen a light switch or plug socket to paint and wallpaper, tape the screws to the front of the socket
or switch and wrap the face in cling film to ensure safe-keeping and to keep the paint off.

Plastic bags

Keep a roll of small bags that you tear off as you need them. All the bits you take out of light fittings, plugs, etc., can be put in a bag and taped to the switch or light fitting. Then when you come to re-install these items, there everything is to hand and saves you losing any small vital part.

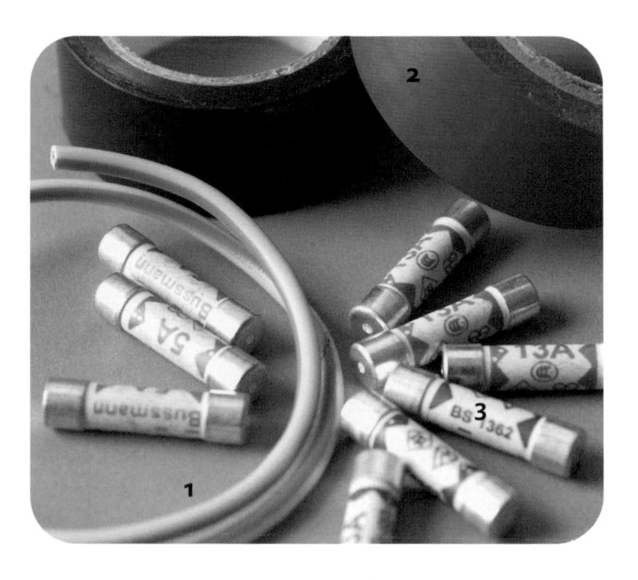

Earth wire cover (1)

Some builders use a cable that has a neutral and a live wire properly encased in plastic and tucked tightly into its plastic sheath. But down the middle of this there is a bare wire, which is the earth and should have been covered by the builder. If not, you should cover it to prevent any possibility of an earth fault occurring. You can purchase a green and yellow plastic cover from your superstore and just slide it on should you have any bare wires in your appliances (see page 83).

Electrical tape (2)

It is useful to have two rolls of electrical tape in different colours, e.g. red and black, as they can be used for flagging up certain things. For example, you may need to use tape on both your neutral and live wires. Your superstore will sell a pack very cheaply with all the colours that you may come across.

Fuses (3)

It is always good to have a collection of fuses in a variety of amperages in your tool box so that you can change a plug's fuse at a moment's notice.

Masking tape (4)

You can buy rolls of masking tape in different widths – 2.5cm (1in) wide is the optimum, anything wider can be difficult to use. Its uses are myriad, from marking a spot for drilling to masking edges of areas of painting.

PTFE tape (5)

PTFE tape is wound around the thread of nuts on water or gas pipes. When the nut is tightened, the tape ensures a water- or gastight connection. It is widely used by professional plumbers.

Velcro (6)

If you have this in the tool box you will find a million ways to use it. Get a pack of the black heavy-duty Velcro and also a roll of the white 5cm x 5m (2in x 5yd) for quick insulation without nails and screws – it's perfect.

Workbench (above)

For drilling pieces of wood and similar materials, invest in a workbench, preferably one with locking devices for your material or a vice. Most DIY stores carry simple workbenches – look for one that is light and easy to carry as well as being simple to store.

PART TWO
THE BASICS

wolfcraft®

CHAPTER ONE

Drill it and Screw it

Learning to drill

When you are choosing a power drill there are various features that you should bear in mind. Go for one with as powerful a motor as you can afford and also consider a cordless drill, which is good for safety. Having a variable speed allows you to choose an appropriate speed for the material you are drilling into, and a hammer drill setting – at the flick of a switch – is valuable for drilling into brick or stone.

Remember to breathe!

Holding a drill

> Don't grip the drill as if your life depends on it. **Hold it firmly with both hands, tuck your arms into your sides** (squeezing your body with your elbows) and lean into the drill. As you do this, slightly extend your arms, but stay tucked in and use the weight of your body to drive the force of the drill.

> Don't force the drill – control it by pressing lightly on the spot where you need the hole. Then, when the drill bit has gone in about 1cm (½in), relax. With a final gentle push, let the tool do the work.

> If you don't feel comfortable, stop and reposition yourself. Keep doing this until you find a position that feels naturally comfortable. Waving the drill around in one hand while trying to hold a piece of wood is a recipe for disaster.

> It helps to have a non-slip mat under your feet when you're drilling.

TOP TIP: DRILL FIRST HOLE ONLY

This is the best top tip that I know of for drilling. When attaching an object with two holes, NEVER drill the second hole until you have the first screw in place. Lightly fasten the first screw and then mark the second hole. Rotate the fitting away from the hole and drill again. Then, and only then, insert the second screw for a perfect fixing.

General drilling technique

> Before drilling, measure twice and mark once. Mark out where you need to drill your holes with a pencil, creating two neat fine lines that cross.

> Drill only as deep as the length of your screw. Measure your screw against the drill bit and **mark this depth with a piece of red electrical tape** wrapped around the drill bit.

> Make sure the drill bits are the right size to take the fixing you are using, whether it's a plastic wall plug or a metal toggle bolt.

> With the drill on ordinary drill setting (not hammer setting), start drilling your hole slowly. Let the drill go through the top layer of material you are drilling. Stop, leaving the drill in the hole, and switch the drill to hammer setting and continue to drill to the correct depth (marked by the red tape).

> **Tap in wall plugs with a rubber hammer** – ensure the masonry drill bit matches the size of the wall plug and the plug should go in fairly easily. Don't hit it too hard or you will damage the wall.

For wood

> Drilling into wood can be tricky. Always use a sharp wood drill bit and, if possible, **hold the piece of wood flat on a work bench or table with another piece of wood or MDF underneath it.** This will help to prevent the back of the wood you are drilling from shattering. **If the wood does split, use a countersink drill bit on the hole. It tidies it up and takes away the damaged wood.** There really is nothing more irritating than drilling two pieces of wood and then finding that the damage done to the wood by the drill means that you can't clamp them tightly together with the screws.

> When you're drilling wood, get into the habit of measuring twice and marking once, making sure both marks are in the same place. If not, re-measure again until you are sure. With a pencil, make two fine lines that cross at the appropriate point. Place the end of the drill bit onto the centre of this mark and start drilling slowly.

> Sometimes, in order to get a screw into a piece of wood, you need a pre-drilled hole; **this is where you make a pilot hole. Make the hole slightly smaller than the gauge of the screw,** and use a hand screwdriver or power screwdriver to screw it straight into the wood.

For tiles

No matter how careful you are, a few tiles will always shatter when drilling. Here are ways to help avoid this:

> **Make a mark on the tile first, using the object you are fixing.**

> **Place two bits of masking tape in a cross over the spot**, and re-mark.

> **Start drilling the hole in the tile with a tile bit.** Allow the drill to rest on the tile at the mark and resist the temptation to press hard. Keep the drill steady and keep it going: don't use the hammer part of the drill or you will smash the tile. When the tip of the bit is halfway into the tile, change it for an appropriate sized masonry bit, then continue to drill slowly and without too much pressure, through the back of the tile and into the wall.

DRILLING OTHER SURFACES

Metal: Please be very careful when drilling metal – **the bits of metal (called swarf) can curl up from the drill bit very quickly and cut deeply**. Protective gloves are a must. Start drilling slowly, increasing the speed and the pressure as you go.

Plastic: Drill plastic or acrylic flat against a piece of wood or MDF. Don't use a high drill speed as the heat of the drill will melt the plastic and weld it to the drill. So go slowly. **Silicone spray may help**. This is a lubricant that encourages the drill to cut the plastic rather than grinding and perhaps shattering it.

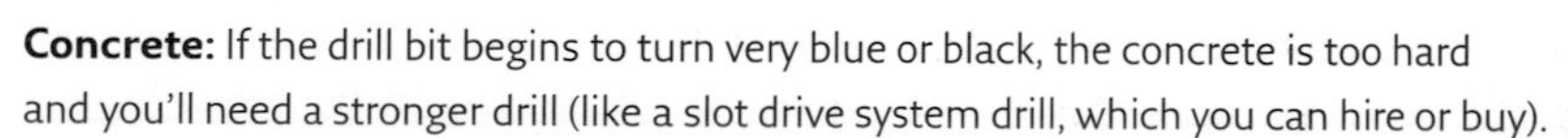

Concrete: If the drill bit begins to turn very blue or black, the concrete is too hard and you'll need a stronger drill (like a slot drive system drill, which you can hire or buy).

Glass: Drilling glass is a specialist task, often using water or oil to aid the drilling process, and I would suggest going to a glass shop for this. If you do try it, drill on a flat surface with a dust sheet underneath to absorb the vibration and to stop the glass from shattering.

TOP TIP: USE A CLEANER

Ask someone to hold the vacuum cleaner pipe right underneath where you are drilling, or secure it to the wall with some Blu-Tack, to save hours of cleaning up. Remember to switch it on!

For plasterboard

There are many types of plasterboard fixings, some of which don't need a wall plug – they are themselves a metal wall plug with a special screw. Otherwise, a normal screw with a plasterboard wall plug is perfectly okay.

> Find out where your studs are by either using a joist detector or **tapping along the wall with your knuckles.** The plasterboard is hollow and gives a deeper sound than the solid wooden joists. If you need to put a screw into the stud part of the wall, drill until you get to the stud then cut a wall plug to the depth of the hole. Insert it into the hole and then the screw will go through the wall plug into the stud.

> To drill a hole in plasterboard, use a masonry drill bit. Mark on the wall where you need your screw to go and place the bit against the mark. **Drill slowly until you go through the plasterboard.** You may find pink or yellow fluff on the bit when you pull it out – don't worry, it's just pieces of the cavity wall insulation. **Pop in the appropriate plasterboard fixing wall plug,** offer up whatever you are fixing to the plasterboard and then insert the screw so that you can attach the object of your dreams.

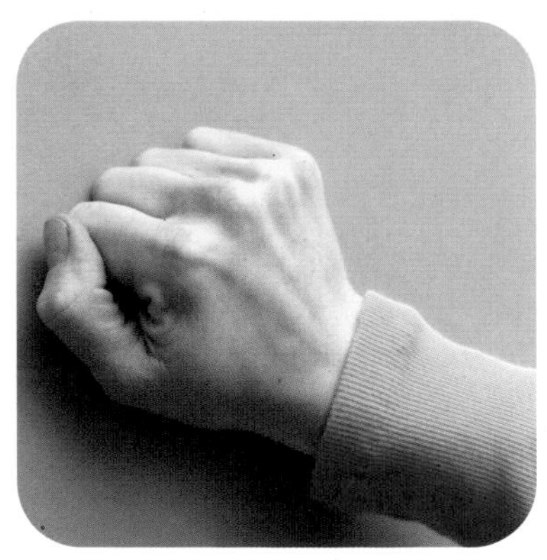

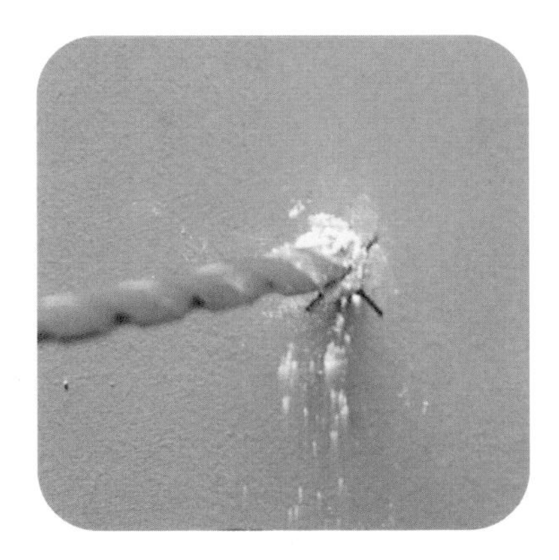

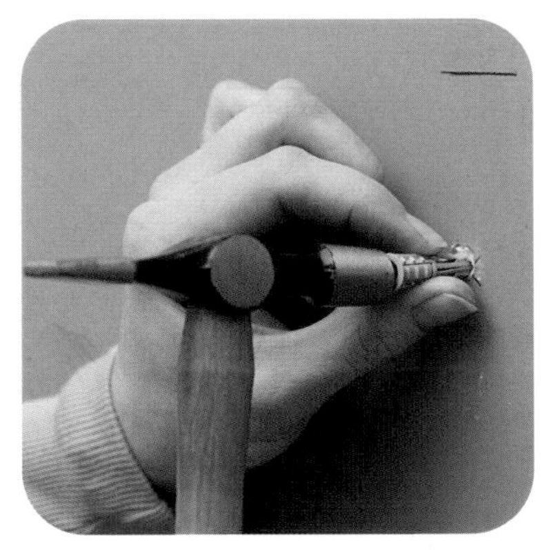

For lath and plaster

Lath and plaster walls are the precursors of the plasterboard now used for internal walls. Laths – narrow strips of wood – are nailed to the studs to provide a supporting framework for the plaster. In older hourses, a mixture of horse hair and cow hair mixed in with the plaster can often be found coating the laths.

> Draw a cross on the wall with the centre at the point where you need to make the hole. Due to the structure of this wall, the point you've chosen will be in one of three places: you could be drilling through the plaster into a lath, a stud or a point between two lathes. Make sure you've got a masonry drill bit and a sharp pointed wood drill bit ready. Start by placing the masonry drill bit on the centre of the cross, and squeeze the trigger gently with your drill on the ordinary setting, as the depth of lath and plaster can be hard to judge.

> If the masonry drill bit meets wood, it will go no further. **Replace it with the wood bit, and drill for about another 50mm (¼in).** If you are drilling into a lath, it will not be any deeper than this and the drill will go straight through to the wall's interior. **Insert a metal or plastic toggle bolt into the hole.** You must then tighten the screw into this bolt; a bar is formed to anchor the bolt to the back of the lath. Make sure that the arms of the toggle bolt catch the two lathes on either side of the hole.

> If the wood continues for more than 50mm (¼in), you have found a stud. In this instance, stop drilling and measure the depth of the hole with a screwdriver. Cut a wall plug to this size and insert it into the hole. You will then be able to insert a wood screw – it will be secure, because it has penetrated the stud.

> If the masonry drill bit goes straight through the plaster to the empty interior of the wall, then you have found a point between the laths and you should insert a metal or plastic toggle bolt into the hole.

SAFETY FIRST

Wear a mask at all times (to stop breathing in all the dust) and goggles (to save eyes from flying bits of drilled debris).

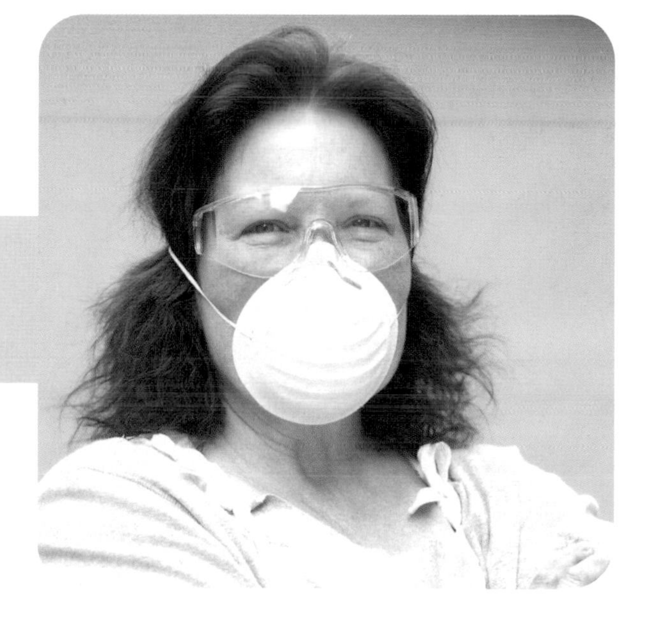

Putting up a shelf

After long deliberation, you've finally decided that you really need a shelf for something specific, like displaying Granny's picture and the vase your Auntie Hilda bought you for your 21st birthday.

How to put up a shelf

Here we've chosen a fantastically simple design of shelf that is made up of only two components: the outer shelf and the inner metal support bar. The support bar attaches to the wall onto which the outer shelf then slides and is locked into place by two screws that are supplied in the pack. This type of shelf is available from many superstores, including Ikea. It comes in two sizes, in a wide range of colours and wood finishes with very tough fixings, and with no visible means of support. I think it is a brilliant design.

TOOLS REQUIRED

- **Shelving system**
- **Hammer drill OR two separate drills**
- **Size 8 wall plugs and 5cm (2in) matching screws**
- **Masonry drill bit size 8**
- **Small spirit level for checking shelf level**
- **Longer spirit level for drawing lines**

1

Take the dimensions of the wall and/or alcove. Measure on the wall where the shelf will go and **mark this height in your notepad** too. Then, in the notepad, draw the oblong shape the shelf makes.

2

Make a note of the full length of the shelf in your notepad and **measure to the shelf's centre, making a mark on the back of the shelf.**

3

Measure to the centre of the wall, making a small mark with a pencil, then measure up the wall to the height where the top of the shelf will go. Where these two marks meet is where the centre mark of the support bar will lie. Put the spirit level on the wall at the mark and **make a line across the wall to indicate the top of the shelf**. Make sure the bubble in the glass phial is exactly in the middle and your shelf will then be level.

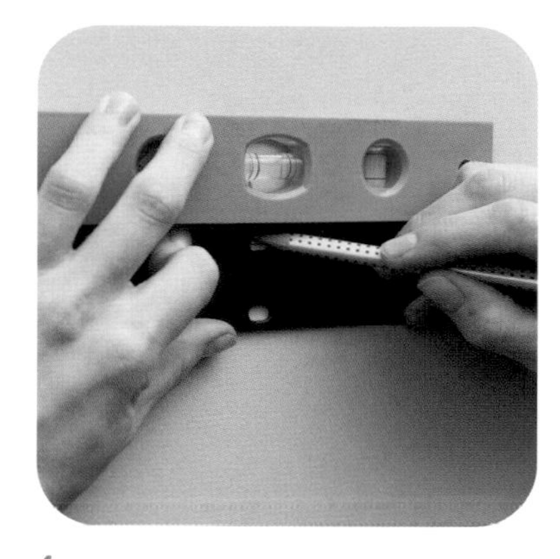

4
Offer up the support bar along the pencil line and **draw a complete copy of the shape of each hole** (run the pencil right round, making a good mark). So the screws don't show on the shelf, make sure you put up the support bar the right way. If the shelf is positioned low down, ensure the holes taking the locking screws are on the bottom of the shelf; if the shelf is high, put them at the top.

5
According to the type of wall onto which you are fitting the shelf, follow the appropriate drilling technique described on pages 52–3. **Lightly tighten a screw at each end of the support bar** so it is straight along the line drawn with the spirit level. Only tighten them when you are sure that the bar is straight.

TOP TIPS: KEEP IT STEADY

Put a strip of masking tape down the back of the spirit level. It will stop it sliding all over the wall.

Putting a large piece of Blu-Tack on each end of the support bar – don't cover any of the holes – will help you to hold it steady as you mark out with a pencil the positions for the screws. Make sure you take off the Blu-Tack before screwing the support bar in place or it could get very messy!

6
Slide the shelf onto the support bar and insert the two locking screws into the small drill holes in the shelf. These will line up with the holes in the support bar, creating a good, strong lock.

Fitting alarms and smoke detectors

Often for insurance purposes, alarms require specialist installation by a registered security company who will then be linked to your alarm and alert the police if they think there is an intruder on the premises or if the panic button is pushed. You should also ensure you have a maintenance contract with the security company for annual testing to ensure the alarm is in continuous working order. Fitting alarms also involves wiring and mains power connection, which must be completed by a certified electrician (see page 76). However, one thing you can install yourself is a smoke detector.

How to fit a smoke detector

A smoke detector is one of the most important things you can install in your house. You can easily do it yourself with screws or strong adhesive; or a fire prevention officer will fit it for you if you are a senior citizen or disabled. The position of the alarm must give you enough time to get out of your home and call the fire brigade before too much damage is done. The instructions within the pack will tell you where best to place the detector. If you are still in doubt, your local fire officer can help.

TOOLS REQUIRED

- **Certified smoke detector from a reputable supplier**
- **Phillips screwdriver**
- **Metal wall plugs (designed for plasterboard)**
- **Solvent-based, direct bond adhesive (optional) - a putty-like substance available in a large tube and applied in a special gun**
- **Low-tack masking top or double-sided sticky pads (optional)**

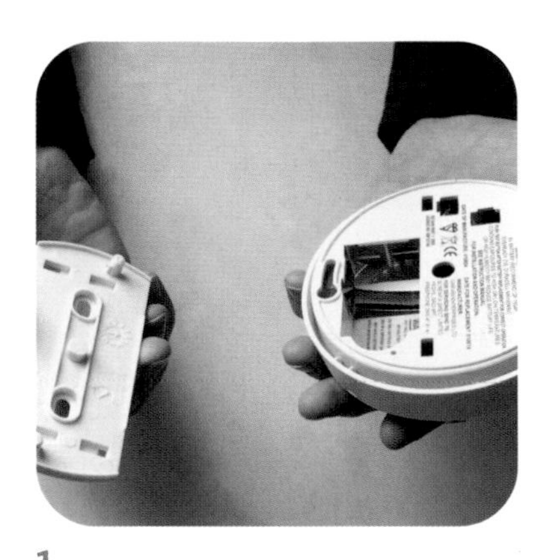

1

A smoke detector comes apart into back and front sections when the two screws visible from the front of the detector are removed.

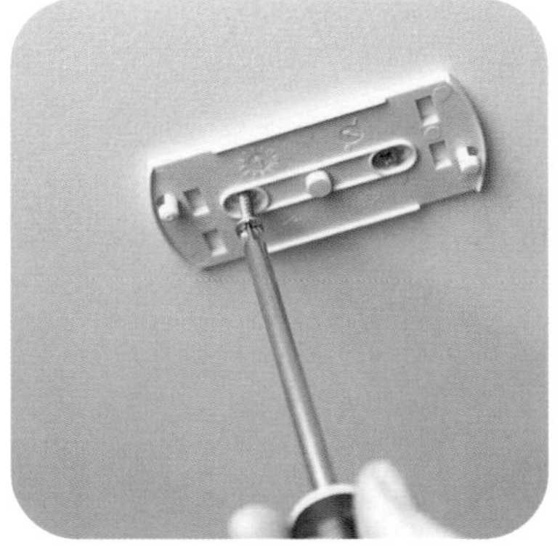

2

Following the Top Tip on page 49 **screw the back of the detector to the ceiling** using the metal wall plugs and a Phillips screwdriver.

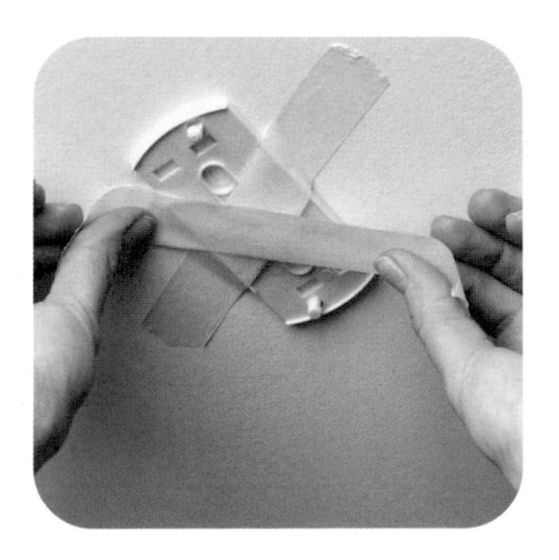

3

If you choose to use an adhesive, it will instantly bond the surface of the smoke alarm to the ceiling. If you are worried that the glue won't be strong enough, you can also **criss-cross low-tack masking tape over the top of the fixing plate.**

4
Alternatively, in the centre of the alarm **place a couple of white double-sided sticky pads** and between them and the adhesive you should have a firm hold.

5
Ensure the battery is in place and test the detector according to the manufacturer's instructions.

6
Screw the front section of the smoke detector to the backing plate. Your smoke alarm is now ready to save the lives of yourself and your family – not to mention Auntie Hilda's budgie!

SAFETY FIRST

Regularly test batteries to ensure they are in working order (do this every three to six months).

Fit your own alarm box

Fitting a false alarm box to the outside of your house is something you can do yourself. Most manufacturers will give simple instructions for fitting one, but as it will be placed high up on the outside of the building it should be fixed with a strong exterior adhesive. Check out the choices at your local DIY store.

> If you have to climb a ladder to fix the alarm box – which, let's face it, is quite likely – please follow the safety guidelines on page 19.

> Such a false alarm box will provide a deterrent but only if it is an accurate copy of an existing alarm in production. Thieves in my mind are stupid – but not that stupid.

Hanging pictures and mirrors

The first thing you need to decide is where to hang your mirror or picture – it's something you should give a bit of thought to. The only laws are the laws of the spirit level, the tape measure and your own eyes – there's no point hanging a mirror so that you can only see the top of your head!

How to hang a picture

When deciding where the bottom of the picture should be, think about what you might have in front of it, especially if hanging it over a mantelpiece – I usually allow a 5–7.5cm (2–3in) gap, but use common sense (there's no point having a huge clock obscuring the best part of a picture). Remember that if your mirror or painting is heavy, you'll need a sturdy wall to hang it on. The information given to the right explains how to hang a picture; the principle is exactly the same for a mirror.

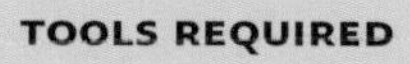

TOOLS REQUIRED

- **Strong tape measure**
- **Pencil**
- **Electric drill and selection of drill bits**
- **Phillips screwdriver**
- **Selection of wall plugs and flat-headed wood screws**

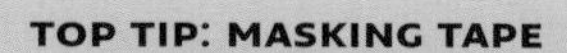

TOP TIP: MASKING TAPE

If you are worried about making marks on your walls, place a piece of low-tack masking tape where the mark will go and then mark the masking tape.

1

Once you have decided on the space that suits you best, measure up from the floor or mantelpiece and make a mark for the bottom of the picture (or see Top Tip below). Measure the height of the picture and **mark the wall the same distance away from the bottom mark and as close as possible to the centre point.** This will give you an idea of where the top of your picture will be.

2

Measure the back of the picture along the top and find the centre, **marking it with a pencil.** Note down the distance from the edge of the centre point on the back of the picture together with all other measurements. You then have a written reference for the next task.

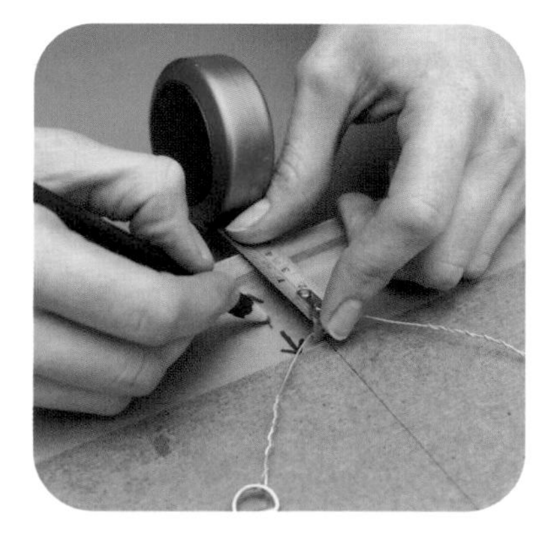

3

Put the end of the tape measure on the wire at the back of the picture and **measure from the top of the wire to the top of the picture.** Note down this measurement. Measure carefully right across the wall (or mantelpiece); note down the measurement and make a pencil mark in the centre.

4
Using the measurement from Step 2, measure down from the top mark and make a mark on the wall. This is called the 'hook height' and is where the wire hangs from the lowest part of the hook. A mirror's hook height may differ (see Top Tip above). Depending upon the type of wall on which you are hanging the picture, **follow the appropriate drilling and wall plug technique** (see pages 52–3).

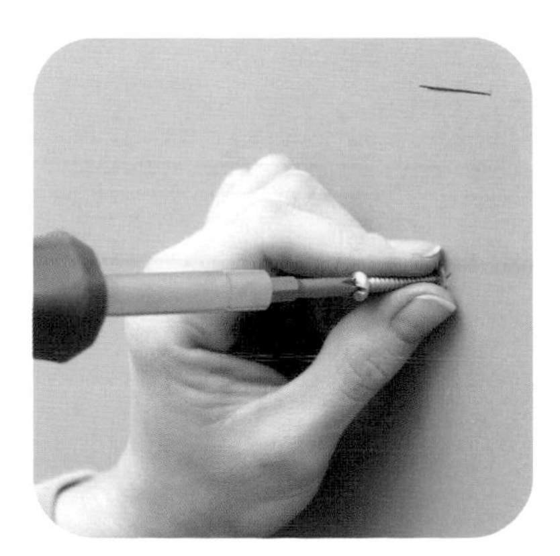

5
Always use **flat-headed wood screws** so the wire or chain will not slip off.

TOP TIP: MIRRORS

To take the hook heights for a heavy mirror, mark its centre and then hold up the wire or chain so there are two points from which it will hang (you can do this with the mirror on the floor but allow for the wire tension when it's hanging). Mark the measurements from the centre to each hook height on the mirror back and on the wall. Hang the mirror from two large screws in wall plugs.

Hanging hooks and pegs

Look to doors and walls for extra storage space. If you hang a hook on the back of a door, drill a pilot hole and use an appropriate screw and plug. In a hollow door, a door plug is the essential first step.

How to make a peg hanger

A row of sturdy wooden dowels can be easily incorporated into any solid wall – you can never have too many places to hang things.

TOOLS REQUIRED

- **Wooden dowels**
- **Spirit level**
- **Joist detector**
- **Electric drill and masonry drill bit**
- **Wall plugs and screws**
- **Adhesive**

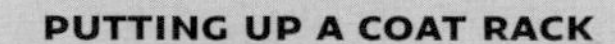

PUTTING UP A COAT RACK

Putting up a coat rack inside the front door is most practical. If you have children, place one at their height, too.

Most DIY stores sell wooden or steel plaques with four to six pegs on them. These do not come with screws or wall plugs so buy whatever you need to suit your wall. Mark where you want the coat rack to go, using a spirit level to draw a line the length of the rack. Mark the first hole directly onto the line and drill on that mark. Follow the Top Tip on page 49 for ensuring an accurate fit.

1
Mark where the first peg will go and **use a spirit level to draw a line** on the wall so that all subsequent peg marks line up. Then, with the cross centred each time, draw two lines the width of the wooden dowel. This will be an accurate guide to where the drill bit will cut the hole.

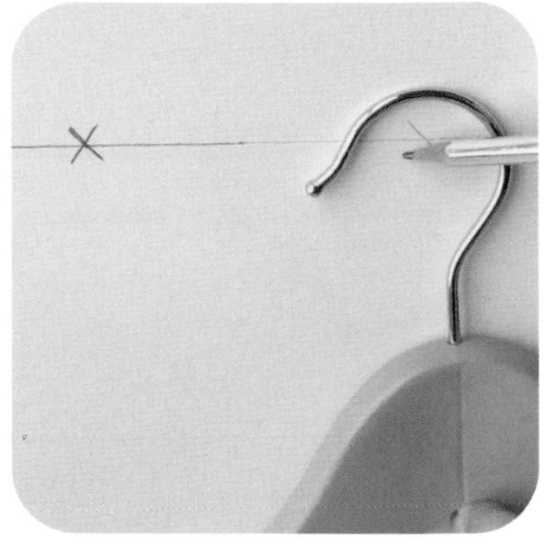

2
If you are fitting a series of pegs, ensure they are **spaced sufficiently for half a coat hanger to fit comfortably** (25–30cm/10–12in) or just the distance that looks good.

3
Drill a hole 6–8cm (2¼–3¼in) deep and at a slight angle. If you are hanging more than one hook, ensure they are all at the same angle by **making a small template from cardboard** with the angle that the drill will cut into the wall.

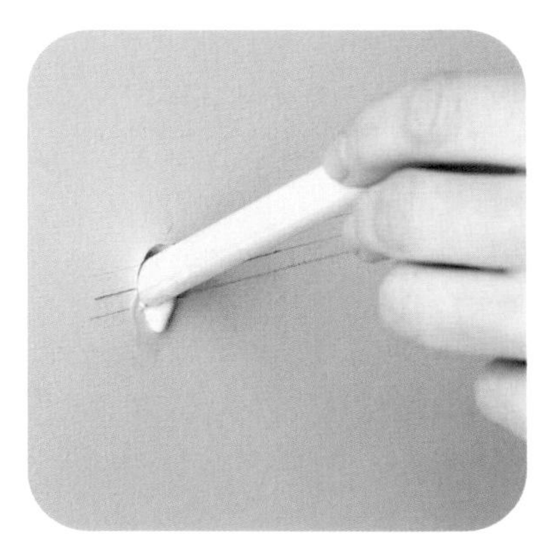

4
Once you have made the hole, **half fill it with the adhesive and insert the dowel.** If some of the adhesive comes out, just wipe it clean with a damp cloth.

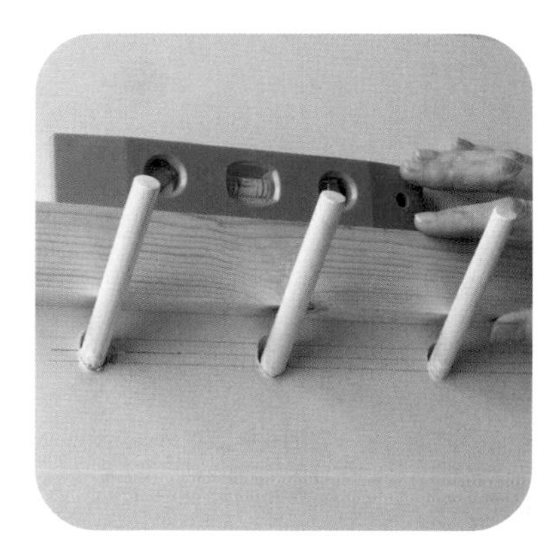

4
Lay a piece of wood across all the pegs to ensure they are level. Fill any gaps above them with no-sand filler, then leave for 24 hours to set.

ATTACHING A CEILING HOOK FOR A LIGHT FITTING

To find the centre of the ceiling, tap a small panel or dressmaker's pin into each corner of the room at ceiling height. Take a cotton thread from one corner to the one diagonally opposite, and then repeat with the other two corners. The centre of the room is where the two threads meet. Mark it with a pencil.

Identify the location of the joist above the ceiling plaster. To do this, first tap the ceiling around the centre mark. It will sound hollow until you reach a joist, which will provide a higher-pitched solid sound. Confirm the location of the joist with a joist detector.

The hook must be attached to the exact centre of the joist and the light fitting's saddle must be fixed as close as possible to the edge of the joist. To check which way the joist runs, use a very fine, old wood drill bit and drill a series of small holes where you think the joist runs. Drill another row of holes near the centre the other way to see how wide the joist is. Hopefully the room centre is just to one side of this joist so the wire or cable can be directed to the fitting straight under the saddle and the ceiling plate will not have to be messily chased into the ceiling plaster.

When attaching a large screw hook for a light fitting, drill a pilot hole to make it easier to screw in the hook and to save damaging the joist. Follow the appropriate drilling technique for wood and plaster to fix the hook in place (see pages 50 and 52) and remember that if you are fixing a saddle hook, the screws will be positioned further down the length of the joist.

Hanging curtains and blinds

Metal and wooden curtain poles have completely taken over the market with the result that while the white plastic rails we are so familiar with do exist, there aren't so many around. There is an enormous range of poles to choose from, mostly with matching finials and tiebacks.

How to put up metal or wooden curtain poles

Putting up metal or wooden curtain poles is very similar to fixing plastic curtain rails, except that they are usually held in place by decorative brackets rather than screw blocks. The kit should also include end stops and large curtain rings. Before you start, draw the window on a piece of paper and work out where you want the new pole to go. The only rule is the rule of your own eye – 'I want it there!' When it comes to handling a stainless steel pole, it can be a good idea to wear cotton gloves to prevent getting mucky finger marks all over the rail.

TOOLS REQUIRED

- > **Curtain pole, including brackets, end stops and rings**
- > **Tape measure**
- > **Pencil**
- > **Spirit level**
- > **Screwdriver**
- > **Electric drill and masonry drill bit**
- > **Wall plugs and screws**

1

Mark the length of your curtain rail above the window. The curtains should sit square and overlap the window at the top, bottom and sides – they will then look more elegant and keep out draughts and light effectively.

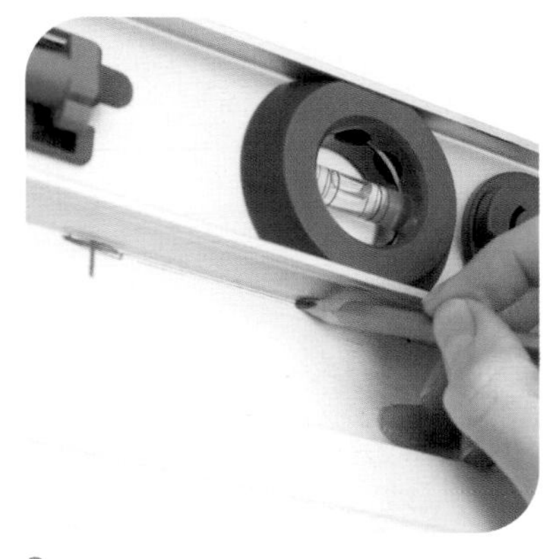

2

Mark where the brackets will go, making sure they are evenly spaced. If your rail has joins, place a bracket beneath each one. Using your spirit level **draw a line between two of the brackets**; this will ensure your rail will be straight.

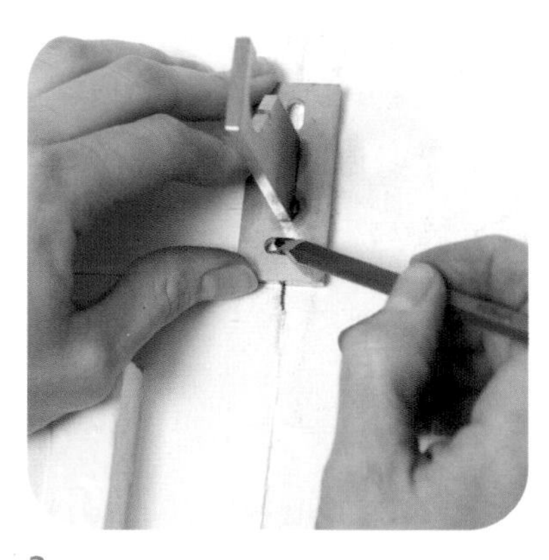

3

Using one of the brackets as a template, **mark through the screw holes** then drill, plug and screw the bracket into place.

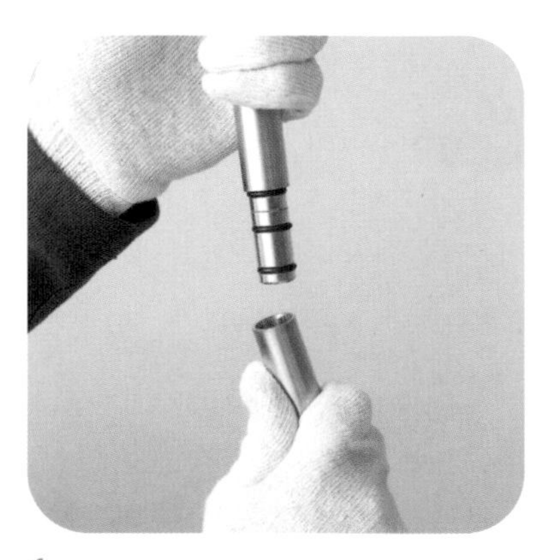

4

Connect the two bars of curtain rail **by inserting the smaller connecting bar** between the two.

5
Now count the correct amount of curtain rings needed for your curtain and **slide them onto the pole.**

6
Place the curtain rail onto your brackets and secure by **screwing the small fixing plates onto the brackets.**

TOP TIP: BAY WINDOWS

Metal rails can be bent to fit a bay window. However, make sure your brackets are secured at both ends of the rail, in the centre of the rail and at the corners where the rails bend.

PUTTING UP PLASTIC CURTAIN RAILS

Plastic rails are designed to be attached to the top of the window or to the wall using screw blocks, which also hold the rail in place. These usually come with the rail, along with screws, end blocks and connectors for the curtains themselves.

Plastic rails usually come longer than you will need so you may have to cut yours to an appropriate length. If this is the case, use a junior hacksaw and a cutting block to do the job.

Mark and attach the screw blocks to the wall as for the pole brackets to the left. If you are attaching the blocks to the window frame, use a bradawl to mark the hole before drilling.

With some designs it will be necessary to tilt the rail upwards to fix it onto the screw blocks: rest the rail on a ridge in the blocks and pull down and push at the same time to click into place. Attach the end stops, and now you are ready to hang your curtains.

How to attach a roller blind

A typical roller blind kit consists of a plastic roller with two end caps, two support brackets and a pull cord, plus the blind itself. They come in several widths and you will need to buy one that is wide enough so that the blind will overlap the window at both sides. If it is wider than you need, it is easy to cut the blind and roller to the right length as long as the blind is made from non-fraying fabric.

TOOLS REQUIRED

- > **Roller blind**
- > **Tape measure**
- > **Junior hacksaw**
- > **Cutting block, such as a mitre block or straight combination cutting block**
- > **Bradawl**
- > **Screwdriver**
- > **Electric drill and masonry drill bit (if fixing the rail to a wall)**
- > **Wall plugs and screws (if fixing the rail to a wall)**

1
Measure the width of the space where the blind will be. Then **measure the width of the blind plus the end fittings.** The difference between the two is the amount you need to cut off the blind and roller.

2
Some 90% of roller blinds are attached to the window frame. For perfect screwing, **make a hole with a bradawl or drill a pilot hole.**

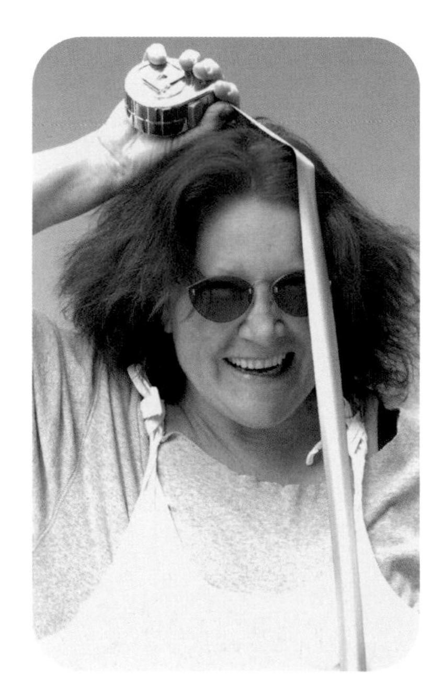

3
If you are going to fix the roller blind to a wall, plaster or brickwork, resist the temptation to use the screws in the pack and go for a screw that is at least 2.5cm (1in) longer than the supplied screw. Mark where the holes are in the brackets on the window frame or wall and **drill the first hole, put in the wall plug and screw** and then mark out the second hole and – by Aunt Hilda's budgie – you have a perfect fixing.

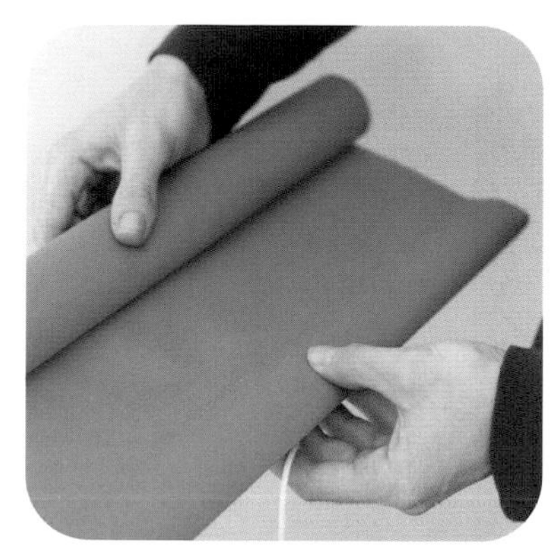

4
Before putting the rolled-up blind into the fixings, attach the pull cord fitting to the side of the pole that you want it, and decide whether you want **the blind to roll down the back** or the front of the roller. If it is at the back, it will sit snugly against the window frame, eliminating most of the light. (You may want to use a pelmet to hide the roller.)

5
When fixing the second fitting bracket **use a spirit level to ensure a straight blind**. If, however, it still looks crooked, the window itself may not be straight, but the blind should still be fixed level or it will not work properly.

6
Insert the cross-shaped opening of the spring at one end of the blind into the bracket (the orientation of the cross is unimportant).

7
At the other end of the blind, **align the slot on the bearing with the edge of the bracket** and push the bearing into the bracket until a 'click' is heard. Finally, insert the plastic covers over the mounting brackets.

How to attach a Roman blind
With its pleated folds, a Roman blind is a softer alternative to a roller blind, but you will find that it fixes to the window frame or wall just as easily.

TOOLS REQUIRED

- **Roman blind**
- **Tape measure**
- **Wax crayon or pencil**
- **Spirit level**
- **Electric drill and masonry drill bit (if fixing to an outside wall)**
- **Wall plugs and screws (if fixing to an interior wall)**
- **Screwdriver**

TOP TIPS: PERFECT FIT

If slotting the headrail on proves to be difficult, you could try to slightly loosen the fixing screws.

To remove the blind at any time, push a flat-bladed screwdriver up between the headrail and the back of the mounting brackets and lever away from the wall. Then push the blind up and off the brackets.

1
Measure the width of your blind and mark the measurements on the window frame or wall above the window, depending on where you want to fix your blind.

2
Insert the fixing brackets into the back of the head rail and use your tape measure **to ensure they are clipped evenly along the headrail.**

3
Once happy with your bracket positions, note down the distance between each one and, using one of the brackets, **transfer the measurements** onto your initial markings over the window.

4
You should now have a row of marks above your window, so get your spirit level and **draw a straight line** through all of them.

5
Using one of the brackets as a guide, drill and fix a wall plug at each bracket position. Then, making sure that the brackets are the correct way up (this one had a protruding edge for the blind to rest on), **screw all the brackets into position**.

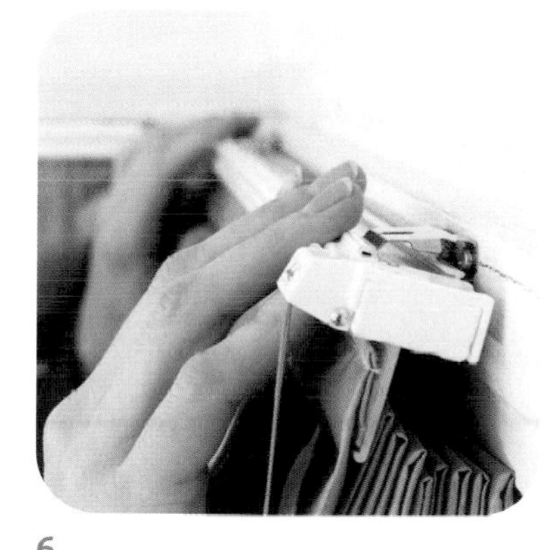

6
Finally, **slot the head rail onto the fixed brackets** and Bob's your uncle (and Hilda's your aunt). Before you first use the blind, raise and lower it three times. Then raise the blind to its top position in four separate steps, dressing the folds into position each time. Leave fully raised for 24 hours so the pleats retain their shape.

The wonder of flat packs

You might have been to Ikea or maybe you have mail ordered a wardrobe and it has arrived in one or two very flat packs. Most people find the prospect of putting together a flat-pack piece of furniture extremely daunting, but once you've cracked reading the drawings that come with the instructions (as sketchy as they at first seem), all the information you need really is right there in front of you.

Be ordered and logical

Stay calm and study the drawings carefully, then do the following: **familiarise** yourself with all the parts the manufacturer has supplied; **identify** the top and bottom of the pieces; **order** everything so you can follow the steps in the drawings logically. When unpacking, resist the temptation to screw up all the packaging and dump it in the bin. Instead, take the packaging to another room and store it until you know that all your pieces are present and the parts are perfect: you might need to return the item and so need the packaging.

Look after your flat pack and it will look after you

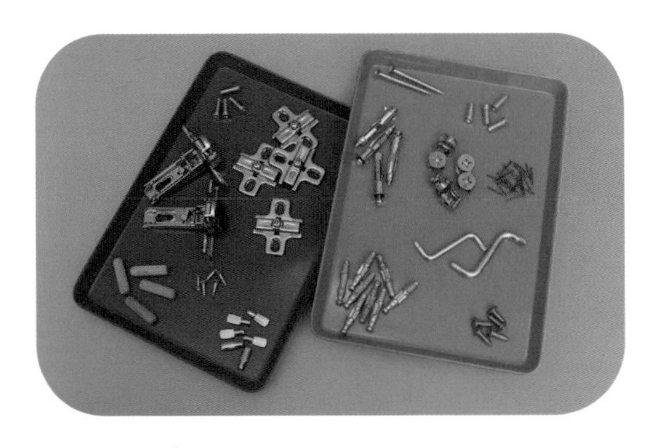

> Before buying a piece of flat-pack furniture, keep in mind that you have enough space and ceiling height to erect something on the floor and then stand it up when you've finished.

> If you're not going to erect a flat pack piece straight away, store it flat on the floor or you will bend all the pieces and you will never get it together.

> **Use a tray or a shoe box to hold the fixings** – this makes life so much easier.

> If you have a wooden floor, lay down the packaging to save your floor and to prevent the sides of the piece of furniture from scratching.

> Always work flat on the floor so that bits can't fall on your feet or get broken by hanging off a table.

> Ensure all the holes are drilled properly in your flat pack before you start.

> Check you have all the tools you need before you start: key essentials include an electric screwdriver or driver drill with a drill bit the same size as any Allen key provided in the flat pack, a rubber-headed hammer or mallet, and a small, very sharp chisel.

> When you look at the parts you have taken from the box, do yourself a big favour and with a roll of low-tack masking tape, mark out on each piece what is the top, bottom, side, front, back, inside and out. This saves hours of rearranging and taking pot luck.

> When using an electric screwdriver or driver drill, use the driver on the lowest setting. If the drill stops and makes a clacking noise, set the drill a little higher and continue until the screw or the bar goes in – but only just, the screw must stop as soon as it is completely in the wood.

> Never over-tighten the screw or bar as you may quite seriously damage either the screw or the piece of flat pack you are working on.

TOP TIP: BE ORGANISED

If you can, separate all the pieces into different bowls or boxes so it's easier to find the piece you want. As they start to be used up, a feeling of satisfaction creeps over you.

FLAT-PACK FIXINGS

Long fixing bolts: Quite thick and used with an Allen key for fixing parts together. They go directly through two pieces and lock them together. To fix in place you should be able to use the drill driver on a low setting with the drill bit that is the same size as your Allen key.

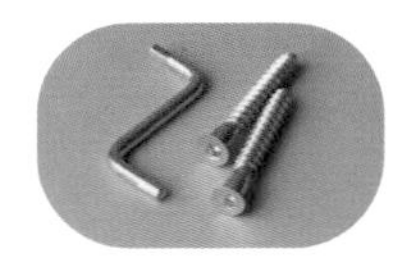

Wooden dowels: Usually come in two sizes, the smaller sizes for tasks like building drawers and the larger ones for the main body. They are always placed in pre-drilled holes.

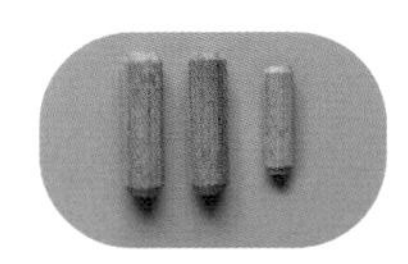

Shorter, thinner bolts (locking bolts): Quite a fat head and used to screw into panels, as indicated. They stand proud of the piece when the next part of the unit is joined on. The bolt is visible through a round hole, which is where a locking disc is inserted.

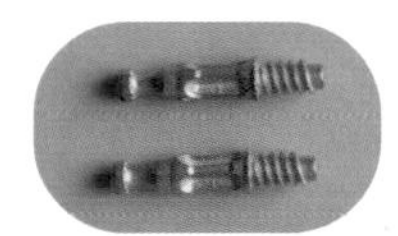

Circular locking disc: Looks like two discs joined together to resemble a metal plug. The side of the plug that disappears into the wood will have a gap in it, which sits over the locking bolt. When the disc is turned with a screwdriver, the disc catches the bolt and locks it firmly into place. You may or may not hear a click but you should not be able to turn the locking disc any further. If it resists being turned back, you have a firm fixing and your flat pack pieces should not come apart.

Assortment of ordinary screws: Applied where indicated, either with a screwdriver or a drill driver. Remember to check the torque of the drill so that the screw only just goes in – you can then tighten screws by hand.

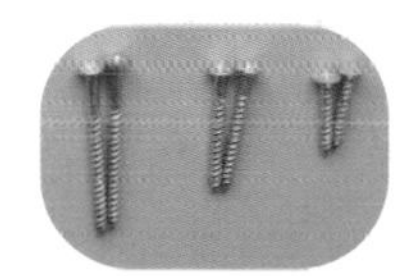

Little nails and/or tacks: Usually for fixing the backs on your piece of furniture. This is a very important part of the construction as these little nails keep the whole thing square. I always have a box of spare tacks – I put a tack in every 15cm (6in) to make it more secure.

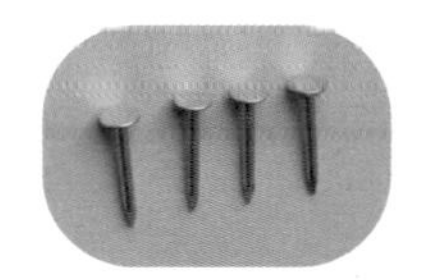

Door catches: Can be a nightmare, especially when magnetic. The best way to deal with them is to make a mark on both the door and the door jam at the same time, and then attach the catches. The flat-pack manufacturer may have given you little dents as guides, but check first that they match.

How to put together a flat pack

Here are instructions for making a simple chest of drawers, which gives you most of the techniques needed to make any flat pack. You will be provided with a helpful book (some without words!). Read it again and again – and then once more, for luck.

TOOLS REQUIRED

- > **Flat-pack chest of drawers**
- > **Pencil**
- > **Phillips screwdriver**
- > **Flat-headed screwdriver**
- > **Hammer**
- > **Rubber hammer**

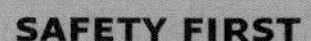

SAFETY FIRST

Most manufacturers of flat packs provide the means to secure the piece of furniture to a wall. This is especially useful if all the drawers or doors are open at once, as the chest could easily topple over. Mark on the wall where you want to attach the stay, screw it into the wall using a washer and poke it through the hole at the back of the chest. Screw to the inside top. Now you can't topple it!

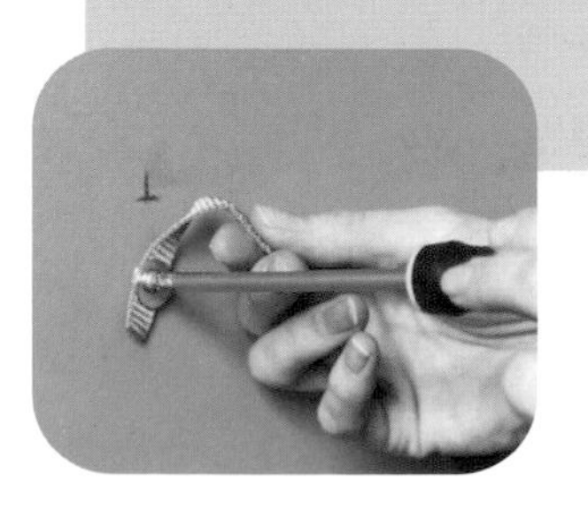

1

First things first. Take everything out of your package and **lay it out like an exploded diagram.** Work on a soft surface so you won't scratch or break anything as you put it together. Now check everything is there. Go through that helpful book.

2

The top and bottom of the chest is joined with both wooden dowels and long fixing bolts (see page 69). Push the dowels into the holes indicated in the diagram in your helpful book. **Push the parts together.** They may need extra help with that ever-so-useful rubber hammer.

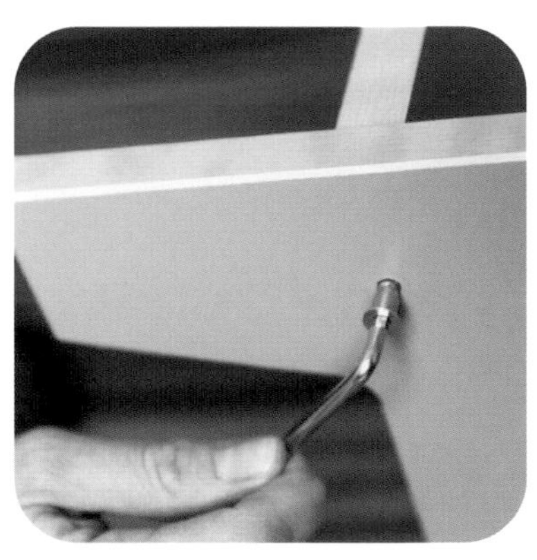

3

Join the sides to the top and bottom pieces. For this you will use those long fixing bolts and the Allen key provided. The bolts will go **directly through the two pieces,** locking them together.

4
Put the backing onto the chest. This is usually a thin piece of hardboard and is attached with simple tacks. **Hammer in a tack every 15cm (6in)** to make it more secure.

5
Now it's time to make the drawers. These use shorter locking bolts, dowels and circular locking discs (see page 69). **Screw the locking bolts into the fronts of the drawers** and insert the dowels into the drawer sides. Push together the two pieces.

6
Slide the base of the draw into the grooves on all three sides. This is quite a thin piece and should slide in quite easily. Then push in the back piece, screw and, using your rubber hammer, bang in the bolts.

7
Here's where we use those locking discs. Push them into their holes. The side of the plug that disappears into the wood will have a gap in it, which sits over the locking bolt. **Turn the disc with a screwdriver,** the disc will catch the bolt and lock firmly into place.

8
Attach the knobs provided using the screw supplied or use a knob or handle of your own if you want to personalise your chest.

9
Screw the sliders onto the drawer with a Phillips screwdriver. Slide the drawers home and now you have a beautiful chest of drawers for when Auntie Hilda comes to stay.

How to attach hinges

If you are assembling a cupboard or wardrobe with doors, please don't be afraid of hinges. They come in two parts: one part fits snugly to the door in a purpose-made circular hole. The other fits into the matching places on the inside of the of the wardrobe or cupboard wall. Make sure the arrow is pointing in the right direction (which is usually out towards you) and then by turning different screws you can ensure the door is straight and you can prevent any rubbing.

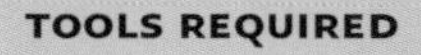

TOOLS REQUIRED

- > **Assembled flat pack**
- > **Flat-pack hinges**
- > **Screwdriver**

TOP TIP: WARDROBE DOORS

To make long doors on a wardrobe close properly, place a piece of thin cardboard on the inner bottom of the wardrobe and stand the door on this before you tighten the screws on the hinges, from inside the wardrobe. The door will then open and close without scraping on the bottom of the wardrobe. When fixing the other door, leave the first door open – it would not do for your partner to come home to find you locked in the new wardrobe.

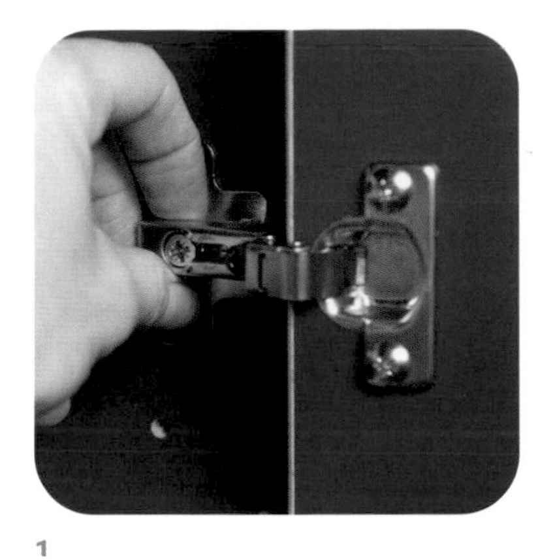

1

There will be at least two hinges, to be spaced regularly along the door and wardrobe wall and screwed into place. Once you have done this, check the arrows on the underside of the hinge are pointing in the right direction and **then lap the long part of the door hinge over the adjoining part,** which will click together. There may be a screw to tighten too.

2

To then move the door up or down, turn the screws in the two long holes in the part of the hinge that goes on the inside wall of the wardrobe or cupboard.

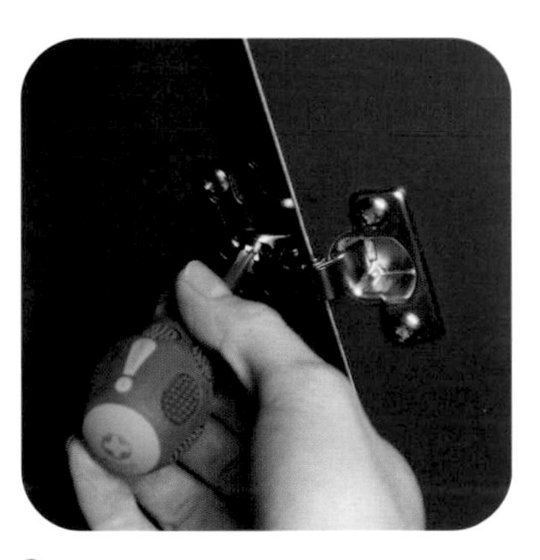

3

To align the doors so there is a neat but straight gap between them, turn the grub screw that sticks out in the middle of this part of the hinge. Turn to the left or right depending on how the door needs straightening. The fitting at the top of the door pitches the top to the left or right, and the fitting at the bottom pitches the bottom of the door to the left or right.

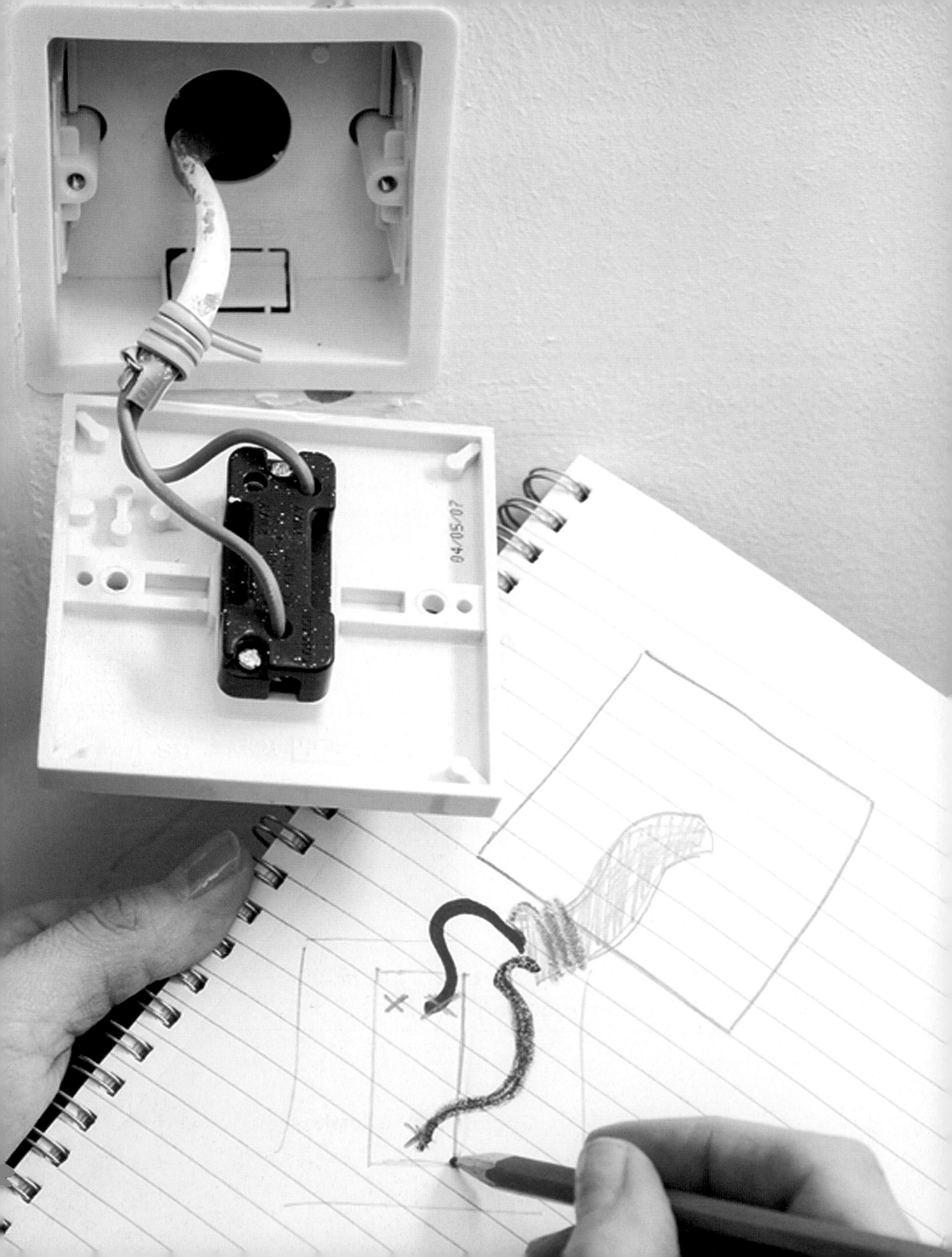
04/05/07

CHAPTER TWO

Wire it

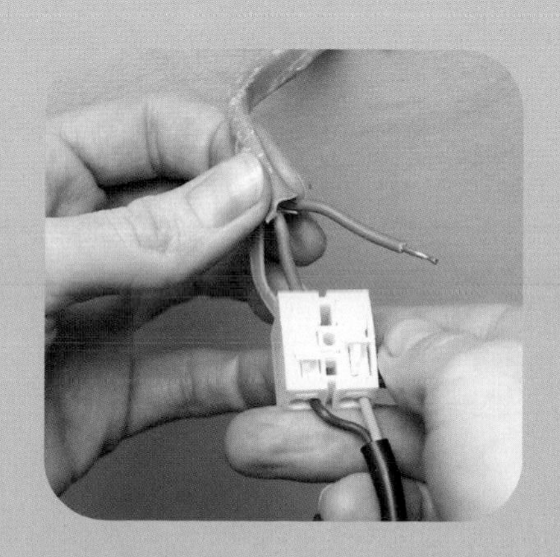

Learning about your fuse box

This is the one chapter where I can't stress strongly enough that if you feel at all uncertain about a job, you should get a professional in to do it instead. Electricity CAN kill and WILL kill, and faulty wiring can cause fires. However, it's really useful to understand the basics, and with just a little know-how you can make sure that your home is safe from electrical problems.

NEW ELECTRICITY REGULATIONS

From 1 January 2005 electrical installation work in England and Wales must meet the requirements of a new section of the Building Regulations, Part P. Similar regulations apply in Scotland and Northern Ireland. There is a legal requirement for you to notify your local Building Control department regarding all major electrical installations, including work in your kitchen, bathroom, utility room and outdoors, and to have such work carried out by a competent electrician. However, you can still do certain minor repairs, replacements and maintenance work, such as replacing socket outlets, switches and ceiling roses, or make other alterations to an existing circuit except in bathrooms, kitchens, utility rooms or outdoors. For full details, and especially if you are in any doubt about what you are able to do yourself, contact your local authority's Building Control department. See also: www.partp.co.uk; www.odpm.gov.uk/electricalsafety; www.scotland.gov.uk/build_regs, and www.dfpni.gov.uk/buildingregulations.

All the wiring in this chapter falls into the first category above, which means you can do it yourself and you don't have to notify your local authority's Building Control Department before starting it. However, if you have any concerns about doing a job, get a qualified electrician to do it.

SAFETY FIRST

Always wear rubber-soled shoes when undertaking any projects that involve electricity.

If you come across wiring that looks suspect to you in any way, call an electrician and get it looked at.

When you're using power tools, never trail the flex across the floor where you or someone else could trip over it, ripping the plug from the socket. Apart from potentially causing an accident at the time, it can damage the equipment, the plug and the socket, and could eventually lead to a fire.

When you are using appliances that could put you at risk of an electric shock, such as power tools or garden tools, fuses are not enough to keep you safe. A circuit breaker or residual current device (RCD) is a life saver if you accidentally cut through a cable or if the wiring in the equipment is faulty. It protects you when, for example, two bare wires touch and create a fault. Some sockets have internal RCDs, or you can purchase an RCD adaptor and plug it into a socket before connecting the tool - which I think is much better.

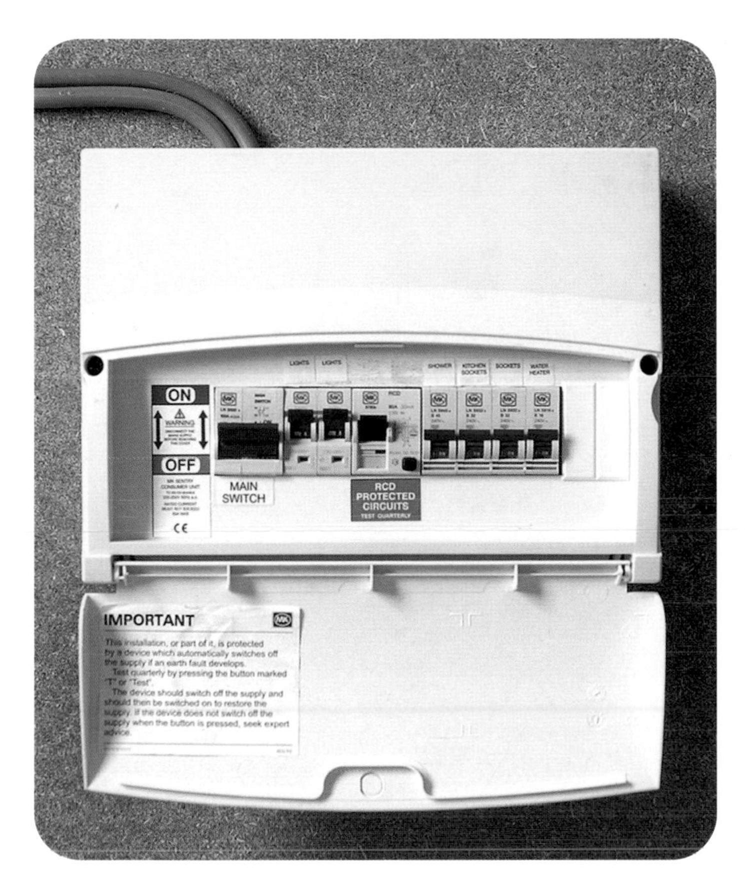

Know your fuse box

On page 13 I have already described the purpose of your fuse box and if you followed my advice, you will have already found yours and added that information to your House Bible. Most modern fuse boxes are **'consumer units'** and within them, the mains current is split to feed the different circuits in your house, with a miniature circuit breaker (MCB) guarding each one. These MCBs take the place of the old-fashioned fuses.

It isn't possible to 'blow' an MCB. Instead, more normally, a switch automatically trips, cutting off the electricity, and once you've sorted out the problem, all you need to do is switch it back on again. In older-style fuse boxes there are no switches, instead a fuse wire blows and needs to be taken out and replaced (see overleaf). **If you are at all in doubt as to what type of fuse box you have** and whether or not you can re-wire a fuse, check with a qualified electrician.

TOP TIP: MAKE ACCESS EASY

If you do get a new fuse box installed, please make sure it's easily accessible - in other words, not on the floor or so high up that you can't get to it without giving yourself a hernia! Regulations state that it must, however, be child proof either with a cover or by fitting it within its own lockable cupboard. A good way of disguising it is to put it under the stairs or build it into a radiator cover on hinges for easy access, but make sure it isn't in a place where it will get bashed by moving furniture.

Faulty electrics

If you own your home and your building survey said your electrics were in any way faulty, or if your fuse box or any other part of the wiring looks old and dodgy, get a qualified electrician to check it out and see if anything needs to be replaced. You may want to get an older-style fuse box replaced with a modern one for greater convenience, even if it is still in good working order. If you are renting, it is a legal obligation of your landlord to ensure the wiring is up-to-date and working effectively. I am always amazed by how many fuse boxes don't indicate what each fuse/MCB is for. Take time to work it out, and label each one of them so you'll always be able to find them in an emergency.

TOP TIP: GET A TORCH

Always keep a working torch as close as possible to your fuse box, as well as replacement fuse wires or cartridges. Don't keep candles or matches near the fuse box, however, because there is a danger of them combusting. Keep torches in the bedroom and the kitchen as well, for those nights when a fuse goes.

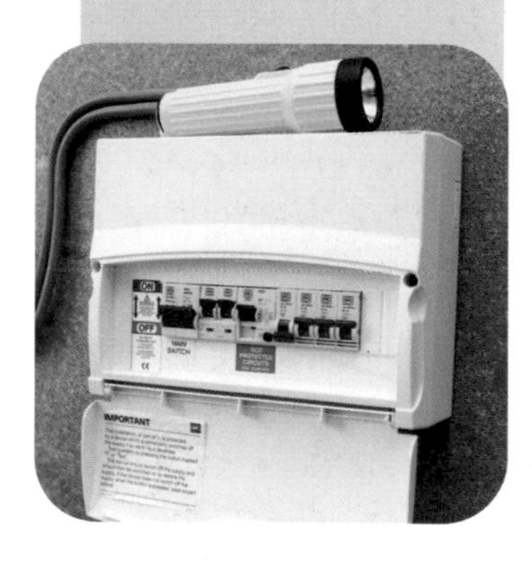

How to find out what each MCB switch is for

This information is only suitable for modern, 'consumer unit' fuse boxes because it involves switching each MCB off and on again. If you have an old-style fuse box, follow the same procedure but take the fuse cartridges in and out.

TOOLS REQUIRED

> **Rubber-soled shoes – always wear these for jobs that involve electricity**
> **A torch**
> **Pack of labels, e.g. address labels**
> **Pack of coloured sticky spots**

SAFETY FIRST

If you live in a converted flat and almost everything goes off when you turn off the master switch, but one or two lights or sockets remain on, this means that they may have been left on the original circuit rather than the one for your flat – this is very unusual, but also very dangerous, so you should get an electrician to sort it out as soon as possible.

1

Put on all the lights throughout the house. Plug a piece of electrical equipment into a socket in each of your rooms. **Identify your master switch.** This is the biggest switch in the fuse box, or more likely a lever. To confirm you've got the right one, switch it off and check through the house to make sure that nothing is still on. Then switch it on again and label it.

2

Switch off the first switch in the fuse box. Go around each of the rooms working out what has been switched off by the MCB you've chosen – for instance, first floor lighting or kitchen sockets.

3
Mark the appliances and light switches that correspond to a particular MCB with a sticky spot of the same colour.

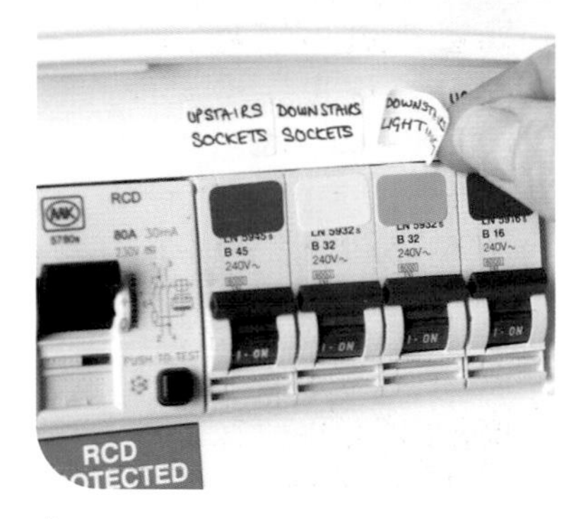

4
Label the fuse box to match. Repeat this exercise with each switch in turn until you've labelled them all.

5
When you've finished, there might be two extra MCBs that don't control any of the lights or sockets. The one marked with the highest amperage, 30 amps or above, is your cooker MCB (or, if you have one, an electric shower, which has a minimum of 45 amps) and, if there is another one, it is probably your central heating fuse at 20 amps or more. **Label these MCBs too.** Go back around the house switching off those things you aren't using and removing the sticky labels!

WHAT TO DO IF A FUSE BLOWS

A fuse will blow as a safety precaution in your circuit if it is overloaded. Sometimes this occurs because of an external event, such as lightning causing a surge of electricity coming into the house. This will usually shut down the whole board. If this happens, it is simply a matter of switching the master switch back on again.

First check if the fuse has gone in the plug by testing with a new one (see page 80). If this isn't the problem, return the equipment to the manufacturer or ask a service engineer to repair it. You will also need to check if the MCB or fuse has blown. In the case of an MCB, switch it back on again. If you have old-style fuses, read on.

Turn off the main switch on the consumer unit and as your fuse box is already beautifully labelled, you will instantly be able to identify which fuse needs attention. If it is a cartridge fuse, replace the cartridge with a new one and check to see if the circuit works. On a blown rewirable fuse, the wire will usually be broken. Make a sketch showing which parts of the fuse the existing wire is wound around. Then remove the wire gently with a small screwdriver and replace with a new length of the correct type, leaving it slightly slack between the terminals.

Changing plugs and sockets

These days it's a legal requirement for electrical appliances to be sold with a plug supplied, so you won't need to wire a plug as often as we used to in the old days. However, there are always times when it's necessary to tackle this basic task – it's simply a matter of matching colours to screws.

Electrical colour coding

All the flexes on your electrical equipment are insulated with a plastic cover. Beneath this cover there are usually three wires: a live wire, a neutral wire and an earth wire. (Some older lamps do not have an earth wire.) These wires, in turn, are insulated to prevent them from touching and causing a short circuit. The plastic insulation is colour coded to show you which wire is which. The colour coding for flex changed some time ago but the same colour change has only happened recently for cables. The chart below indicates the old and new colours. The instructions opposite refer to the new colours. If you are wiring an old plug, substitute the new colours for the old.

ELECTRICAL COLOUR CODING FOR CABLES

	Live	Neutral	Earth
Old colours	Red	Black	Green
New colours	Brown	Blue	Green and yellow stripes

How to wire a three-pin plug

If a plug becomes damaged, then as long as your equipment is still alright, you can change the plug by following these instructions. They will also help you to change a fuse if the old one blows. Remember to change the fuse for a similar rated one or else the equipment will continue to blow... and blow... and blow.

TOOLS REQUIRED

- **Notebook and pencil**
- **Wire strippers**
- **Electrical screwdriver**
- **Three-pin plug**
- **Correct amperage fuse for the appliance (usually given on a label on the flex or on the manufacturer's instructions)**
- **Box for all the bits and screws**

TOP TIP: MAKE A CONNECTION

If the wire is not showing at the end where it will go into the fixing, strip back the insulation by cutting off a small amount of plastic cover with wire strippers. This exposes the wire and allows it to make a connection.

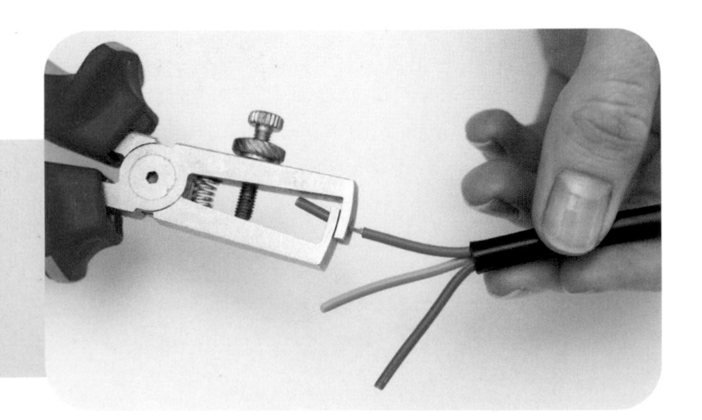

1

Keep your notebook by your side and make sketches of what you are doing. Hold the old plug with the three prongs sticking up in the air. In between all three there will be a screw. **Remove it with your electrical screwdriver** and put it in the box. Then carefully take apart the two halves of the plug.

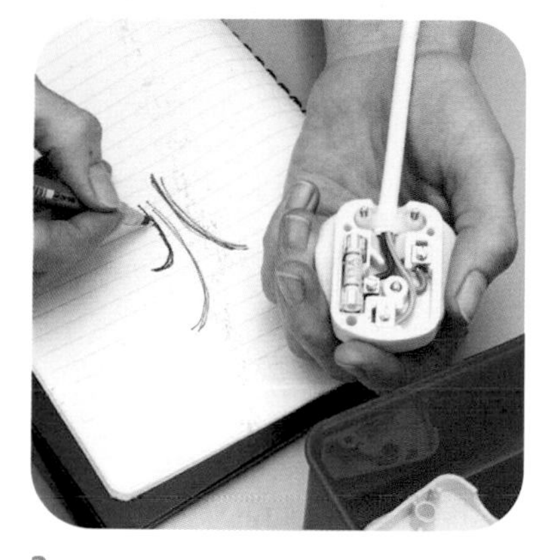

2

A flex bar with two tiny screws keeps the flex in place. The flex then splits into three parts. The brown live wire connects to the fuse cartridge; the blue neutral wire goes to the left, and the green and yellow earth wire is secured at the top. **Draw a diagram to show which colours go where in your plug.**

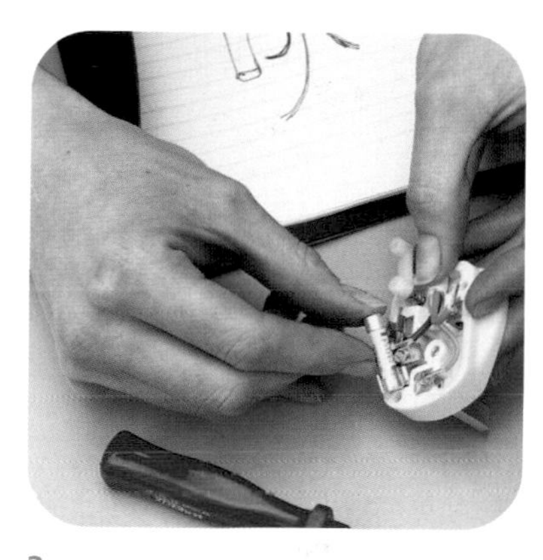

3

With your electrical screwdriver, take out the fuse cartridge. Remove the screws securing the bar and each of the three smaller wires to release them from the plug. Take care not to let the rest of the plug fall apart at this point – it easily can.

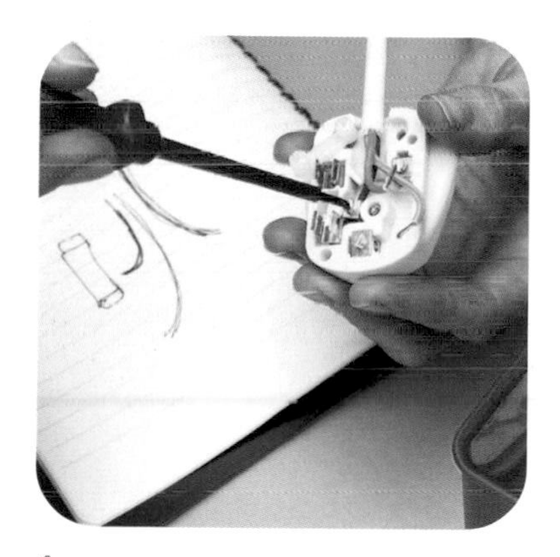

4

Discard the old plug and open the new one. Ensure bare wire is showing at the end of each piece of coloured insulation (see Top Tip). Put the flex where the flex bar will lie and connect the live wire next to the fuse, as in your diagram. **Undo the screw and insert the wire** – you may need to take out the fuse. Tighten the screw and replace the fuse.

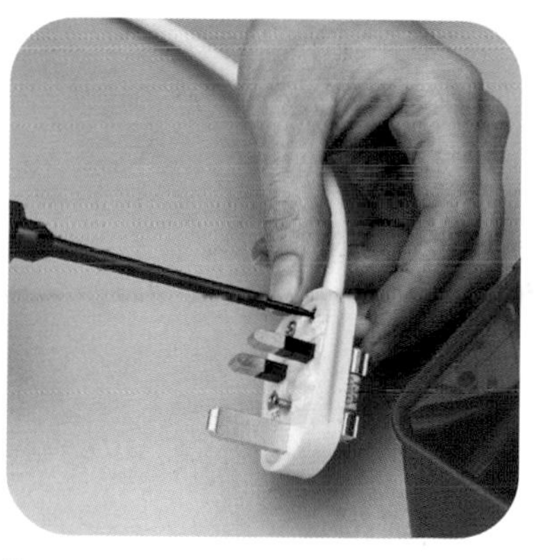

5

Connect the neutral and earth wires to their respective fittings. Make sure there is no bare wire showing when you tighten the terminals. **Remove the flex bar and then replace it, screwing it over the flex.**

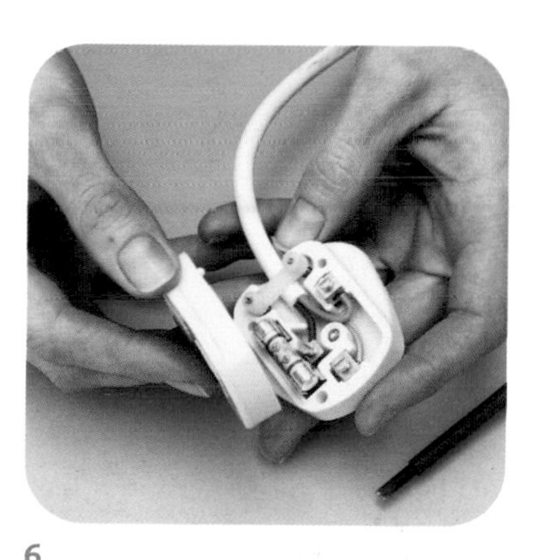

6

Then put together the two halves of the plug, screw, tightening securely. Now check that the appliance works. If not, the most likely mistake is that you've forgotten to put the fuse back in!

How to replace a socket

The most likely reason for replacing a socket is that it's old and broken, and if your home has a number of sockets in poor condition, you should probably get an electrician to check the electric circuits. However, if you're confident that your wiring is essentially sound and you want to remove and replace an existing socket, it's a reasonably straightforward job.

The first thing to do is TURN OFF THE ELECTRICITY, or 'pull the switch'. This phrase comes from the old-fashioned type of master switch that took a lot of effort to pull – my dad used to delight us when he did this by shaking as if he was being electrocuted. Mum would just say, 'One day it will be the real thing and no-one will take any notice of you,' call him a silly old fool and walk off.

TOOLS REQUIRED

- Rubber-soled shoes
- Torch
- Note pad and pencil
- Small and large electrical screwdrivers
- Electrical tape
- Earth wire cover
- Socket face plate
- Corresponding back box (optional, see opposite) (make sure that you have the dimensions when you buy it, or do the job in two halves so that you can take the old one with you)

SAFETY FIRST

Whenever you're doing a job that involves turning off the electricity at the fuse or the master switch so that you can work with the mains wiring, make sure that everyone who might have access to these switches knows about it and, if necessary, tape it down and add a label warning people not to switch it on.

Remember to turn off the electricity at the master switch.

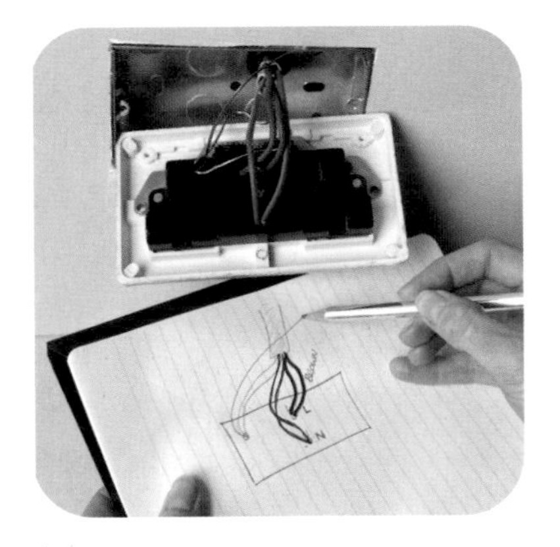

1

TURN OFF THE ELECTRICITY AT THE MASTER SWITCH. Undo the two holding screws on the face plate and pull it away from the wall. Behind the face plate is a back box. The wires from the mains come out of the back box and connect to fixings on the back of the face plate. These fixings enable the wires to connect to the prongs on your plug when you plug it into the socket. **Make a diagram of where each wire goes.**

2

Usually there will be two wires of each type coming out of the back box. In each pair, one brings the electricity into the socket and the other takes it on to the next part of the circuit. Unscrew the fixings on the back of the face plate and **release the wires before removing the face plate completely.**

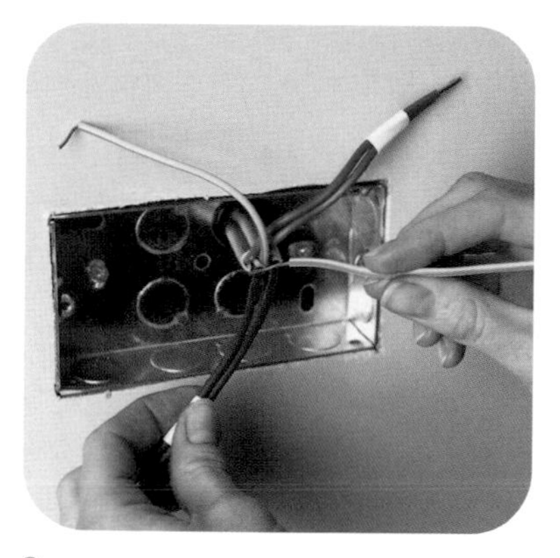

3
If there is a bare earth wire, cut a piece of earth wire cover to the right length and **slide it onto the wire** (see also the Top Tip, below). If you're worried about the pairs of wires getting separated, tape them together with electrical tape, but be very careful not to cover the ends where they will make the connection.

FITTING A NEW BACK BOX

The back box is fixed to the wall by two holding screws. Check to see whether it is intact. If it is loose or cracked around the screws, it is better to replace it - otherwise, if it is intact and you are changing the face plate for cosmetic purposes, you can go straight to Step 4 and fit the new face plate. To remove the back box, unscrew the two holding screws and pull it away from the wall, unthreading the wires as you go. The new back box should come with instructions, so READ THEM CAREFULLY. Usually, this will involve breaking the plastic or punching out the metal to make holes for the screws and wire to go through.

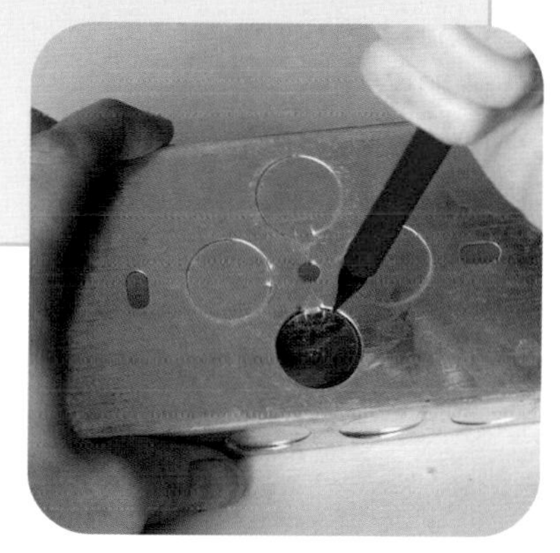

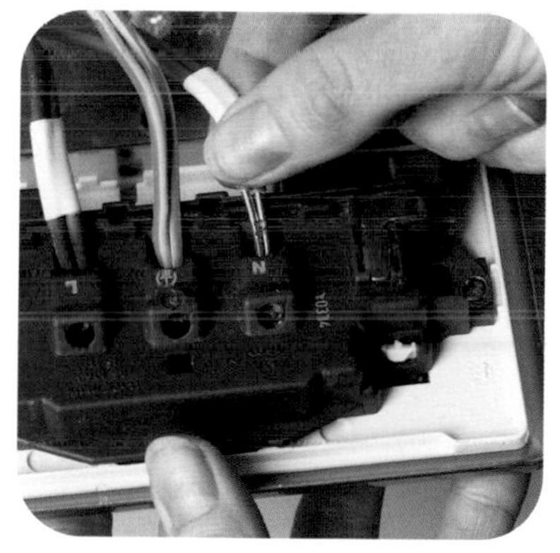

4
Now, following the wiring diagram you made in Step 2, **connect the wires to the fixings on the back of the new face plate.** Make sure there are no bare wires showing after tightening the connections.

5
Check that your wires are in safely and tightly by giving each one a little tug. **Secure the face plate to the wall by tightening the two holding screws.**

TOP TIP: COVER UP

Sometimes the wiring in a socket or plug hasn't been done quite as thoroughly as it should have been, with perhaps the earth wire being left bare. If you come across this, always cover the earth with a piece of earth wire cover (see Step 3) to prevent it from touching another wire and causing an earth fault.

Fitting lights and switches

One of the most important elements in your home is lighting. If you carefully choose your lights to complement the decorating, not only does it set the mood, but your two-up, two-down terrace will become a palace. With a central pendant or group of inset halogen downlights, all wired to a central dimmer switch, the Monet that Auntie Hilda gave you for your 30th birthday will be lit to perfection. It may be a repro, but what the heck? It's beautiful and it sets off the colours of the room so well.

Lighting options

Ensure your lighting is as flexible as possible, so that you can vary it to suit the mood, whatever the occasion. In addition to fixed lights on the ceiling, you can choose from track lighting, up- and downlights and smaller table and desk lamps to dot around the room. Just be aware of the scale of the room when you are placing them.

THE DIFFERENCE BETWEEN BAYONET, SCREWCAP AND HALOGEN BULBS

It may be easy to change a light bulb, but everything is more difficult if you're not familiar with it – I had a cry for help from one of my senior citizen clients when she couldn't get the bulb out of the lamp her daughter had given her for her birthday. The source of the problem was that she was trying to take it out as if it was a bayonet when in fact it was a screwcap, and she'd never come across one before.

Bayonet fittings are the most common bulb fitting in this country. They have a plain end with two metal prongs sticking out of the fixing on either side. In the bulb holder, there are two 'P'-shaped grooves cut into the metal. Slide the prongs on the bulb into the long groove of the 'P'-shape, feeling the resistance of the springs inside the fitting. Then twist the bulb slightly clockwise so that the prongs go into the loop of the 'P'-shape – they'll lock as soon as you release your hold on the bulb.

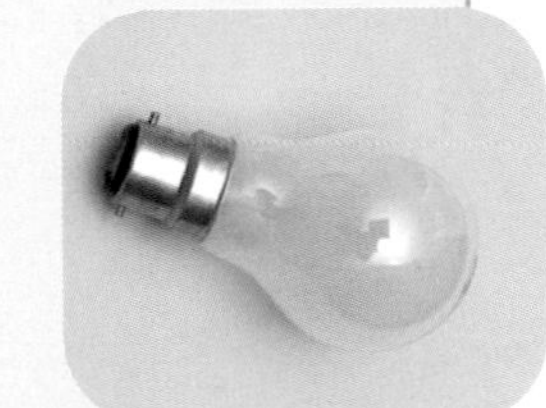

The screwcap bulb is exactly what it says – instead of the prongs, there's a screw thread, allowing you to just screw in the bulb. Wipe the thread with a clean soft cloth before screwing it in. I usually spray mine with a little silicone spray and then wipe it dry – this lubricates it and resists water.

Halogen is a low-voltage system that was developed way back for commercial use. It created such a lovely light that it was further developed for our homes – lucky us! The only problem with halogen lighting is that it gets extremely hot, which is good if you have a halogen cooker but not so good if there are curtains nearby, so be careful where you install it.If your halogen bulb has just blown, get it replaced as soon as possible and try not to use the lights around it until you've replaced it – you'll reduce the life of the other bulbs by overloading the circuit. Try not to touch halogen bulbs with your fingers, as your fingerprints will cause them to run hotter and will reduce their lifespan – use a cloth or tissue.

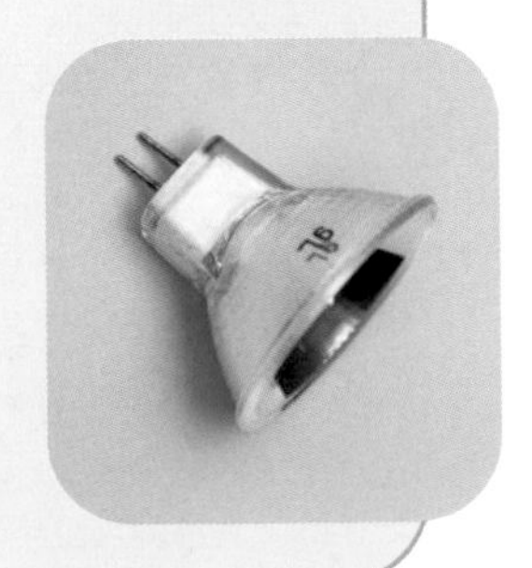

WHAT TO DO IF CHANGING A LIGHT BULB DOESN'T WORK

Every now and again when you replace a light bulb you'll find that the new one doesn't work either, meaning that you'll need to find out what else might be wrong.

First make sure that you haven't just been unlucky with the new bulb by testing it in a lamp holder that definitely works. If the bulb works in the lamp holder, you probably have one of two problems:
> The light fitting is broken, either where the bulb is screwed in or where it connects to the mains in the ceiling rose, in which case see page 86.
> The light switch isn't working, in which case see page 88.
> If the fitting is freestanding, the fuse might need changing, in which case see page 80.

As it's more common for a light fitting to fail than the switch, you should try that first.

Lighting up your cupboards

Have you ever spent hours searching through your wardrobe for that little black number or that suit for meetings, and it was like looking for a black cat in a coal cellar on a dark night? I even resorted to using a torch once. Well, your fashion decisions could become a lot easier with just a trip to your local lighting supplier to get the right device. Some plug into the mains, meaning that you will need to make a hole in the cupboard. Others are battery operated.

The light should be attached in such a way that **when you open the door, it switches itself on and when you close the door, it switches off.** There are many brands on the market with very good operating instructions – read the instructions thoroughly, and if you don't understand something, then phone the helpline number on your appliance or go back to the shop and ask them about it.

SAFETY FIRST

Never install a halogen bulb in a cupboard. They get so hot that one in a confined space could set your possessions on fire.

How to replace a light fitting

The light fitting is the whole of the unit that connects the bulb to the wiring in the ceiling or wall, with the connection usually concealed by a plain circular box or an ornamental ceiling rose.

Light fittings might need replacing because they are broken, or because some of the fancier light shade arrangements include the whole of the light fitting right up to where the electricity connects with the mains cable. To remove or install the fitting, you'll need to replace the whole lot. Here we show the simplest kind of ceiling rose. You may find one with more wires, but just follow the same steps, noting down how each wire is connected, and you shouldn't have any problems.

TOOLS REQUIRED

- > **Rubber-soled shoes**
- > **Torch**
- > **Note pad and pencil**
- > **A step ladder of the right height**
- > **Medium electrical screwdriver**
- > **Very small electrical screwdriver**
- > **Hammer (optional)**
- > **Earth wire cover**
- > **A new light fitting**
- > **A large gin and tonic for when it's finished, as a prize**

1

Read the instructions on your new light fitting, making sure that you understand them. TURN OFF THE ELECTRICITY AT THE MASTER SWITCH. Make sure you position the stepladder so that you don't have to lean forwards or backwards, or stretch upwards, to look straight at the fitting. **Unscrew the ceiling rose anticlockwise.**

2

If this doesn't work, take the non-business end of the larger screwdriver and tap firmly all around the base of the piece of plastic and try again. Once you've detached the cover, it should **slide down the flex, revealing the back plate attached to the ceiling.**

3

The wires in the cable are **joined to the wires in the back plate by connection blocks.** Look at how the wires from the cable go into the connection block. There should be a live wire, a neutral wire and possibly an earth wire (see the table on page 80).

4

Make a diagram of the way each wire goes into the connection blocks. If there is an earth wire and it's bare, cover it (see page 83).

5

Loosen the tiny screws holding each wire in their respective connection block and then carefully pull out the wires.

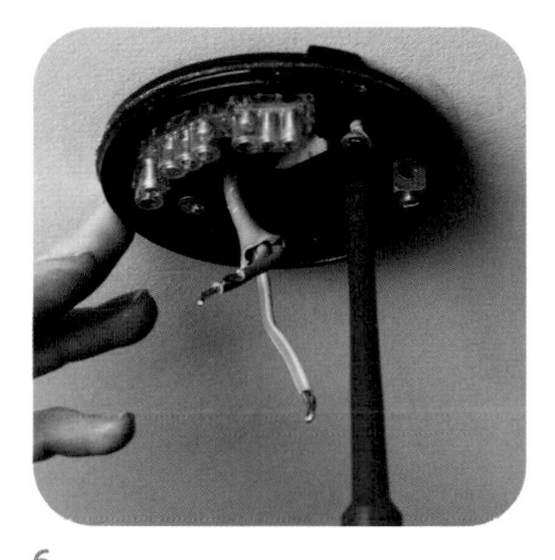

6

Unscrew and remove the back plate unless your new fitting requires one, in which case leave it where it is. Read the instructions on your new light fitting. Also check them against the diagram you made of the old fitting in case some lazy person ran out of the right colour of wire and used a different colour instead.

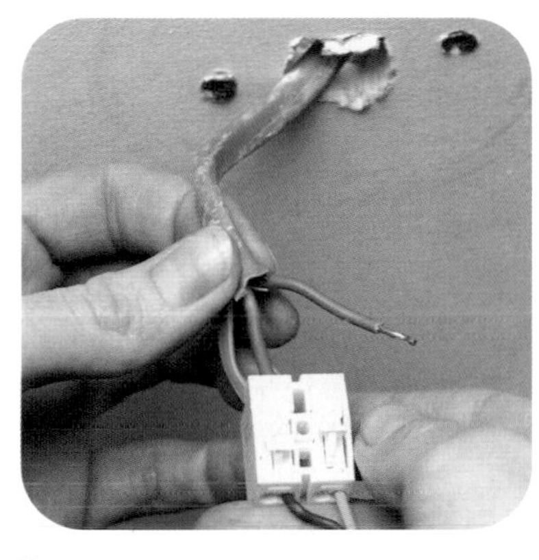

7

If everything makes sense, **insert the live wire(s) into the correct holes in the new connection box** and tighten the screws. New fittings don't generally require an earth wire, in which case, if you have one, simply tuck it out of the way.

TOP TIP: TWIST THE WIRES

New wires on fittings come with a tiny speck of solder to keep all the fine bits of wire together. If you find that it has worn down and looks like a bunch of grass, all you need to do is twist it between your fingers and turn the strands against themselves.

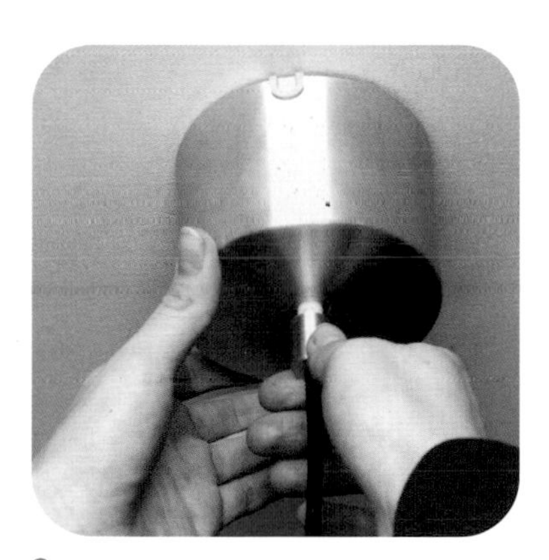

8

Follow the instructions to assemble the fitting, turn on the electricity and check your new light fitting works.

How to replace a light switch

You might need to change a light switch because the bulb isn't working or perhaps you just feel like a change – the old one may be chipped or covered in paint, or you may want to install a dimmer switch.

Sockets and light switches are very similar in construction, so if you can change one, you can change the other. The most important thing is that before you do anything else, you TURN OFF THE ELECTRICITY AT THE MASTER SWITCH.

TOOLS REQUIRED

- **Rubber-soled shoes**
- **Torch**
- **Note pad and pencil**
- **Electrical screwdriver**
- **Sticky or masking tape**
- **Earth wire cover**
- **Insulating tape**
- **Wire cutters**
- **New light switch**
- **Corresponding back box (make sure that you have the dimensions when you buy it, or do the job in two halves so that you can take the old one with you)**

1
The switch that you're going to replace should have two screws holding the face plate to the back box. The back box will either stick out from the wall or be embedded in it. **Undo the screws and fasten them to the face plate with sticky tape.**

2
At the back of the face plate you'll see two wires attached to the plate by their screws. Identify them using the colour-coding table on page 80. Modern back boxes are usually made of plastic, so wrap the third wire, the earth, around the cable. If the back plate was metal, attach the earth wire as in Step 5.

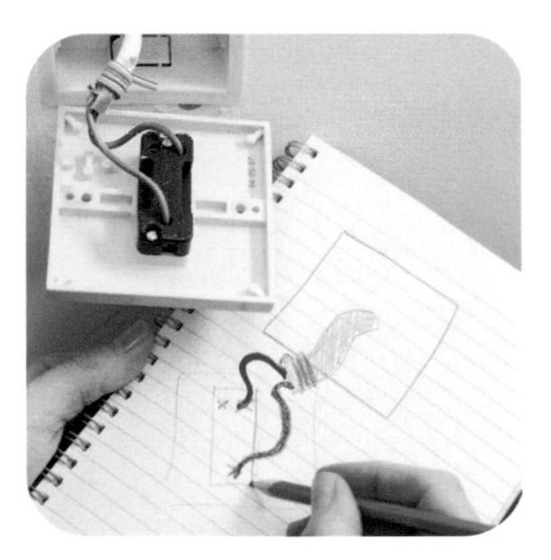

3
Make a drawing of the wires, showing which colours go where.

TWO-WAY SWITCHES

If you are installing a two-way switch, wire each of the switches as shown here. The first switch has more wires because it is attached both to the cable from the light and to the cable linking the two switches, whereas the second switch only connects to the linking cable.

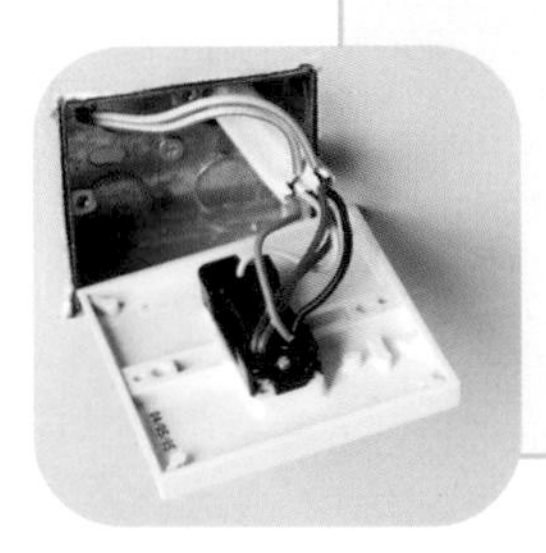

4

Remove the screw holding the wires in the fixings and release them so you can remove the face plate. The wires will now be sticking out of the back box. If the earth wire is bare, cover it with a small piece of earth wire cover (see page 83).

5

Examine the back of the face plate of your new switch. Using the instructions and your diagram to work out which wires go where, thread them in and tighten the screws. Check that the wires are tightly in their fixings by moving them with the screwdriver or give them a gentle tug. Because a metal front is being used here, **the earth wire has to be attached to the face plate.**

6

Place the face plate onto the back box and either **use the old screws or the new ones to screw the face plate back on.** It's normally better to use the new screws, but if the old ones were in keeping with the rest of your switches and they fit, it's okay to keep them. Turn the electricity back on. If the new switch doesn't work, turn off the master switch again and ensure all the wires are tightly secured.

DIMMER SWITCHES

Dimmer switches are a boon – you'll need the light in your sitting room on full blast if you're doing something complicated but, on the other hand, if you come home from work with a headache, the last thing you want is a bright light. The solution is to change the main light switch for a dimmer switch, but do be aware that some types of halogen bulb can be damaged by dimmers.

CHAPTER THREE

Plumb it

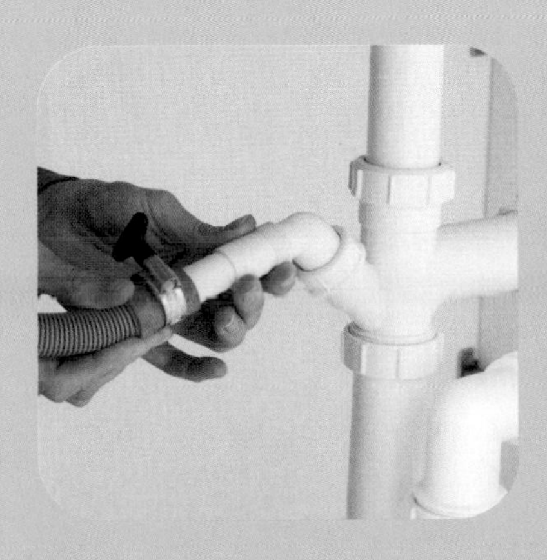

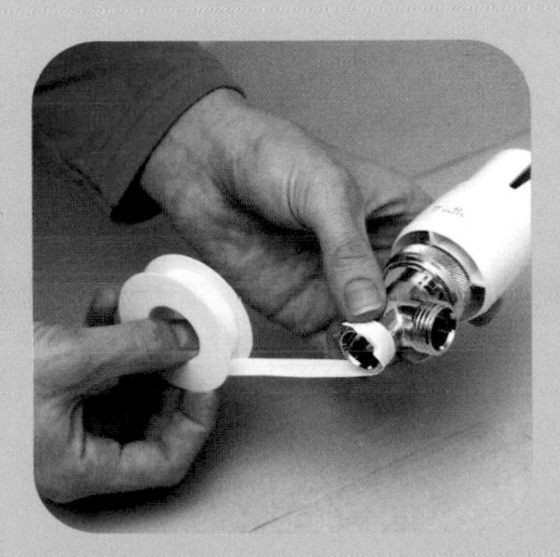

Establishing the cause of a problem

We rely on mains water for washing, cooking, drinking and keeping warm – what on earth would we do without it? On the other hand, water is at the root of some of the nastiest and most expensive problems a homeowner can face, whether it's a burst pipe in winter or that worrying damp patch on the wall.

Check it out

Whatever else you do, DON'T PANIC. Opposite is a checklist that I've compiled to help you keep your head when everything seems to be going wrong. Sometimes the most frightening problems can turn out to have a really simple cause, which is easy for you to fix once you know how. And if it does turn out that you need to get the experts in, it helps if you have some idea what the cause of the problem might be, so you know who to call and can feel more confident when discussing how to put it right. If the problem relates to damp or condensation, see pages 200–1.

Turn off the water

Before you start any plumbing job, it is essential that you turn off the water at the mains. You may need to do this in an emergency, so it's best to know how to do this even if you aren't planning to do any plumbing.

> To find the main stop cock see page 12. If you've already compiled your House Bible you will, of course, know exactly where the stop cock is already.

> To turn off the stop cock, turn the valve in a clockwise direction. If it doesn't turn easily, lubricate the spindle with a little penetrating oil.

TOP TIP: START EARLY

If you can avoid it, never start a plumbing job at 4.30 in the afternoon. You may need to buy a new part or even call the plumber, and you won't be popular if you've taken the sink apart and the water has to stay off all night.

DIAGNOSTIC CHECK LIST

Symptom	Likely problem	What to do
Pipes and taps are banging and water spurts out when you turn on the tap	Air lock in the pipes	See page 101
Tap drips even when it's turned off	Calcified, worn or slipped washer in tap	Replace the washer – see page 100
Slow emptying of sink or bath	Blocked pipes	See page 104
Water tank/toilet flush not working	Stuck or broken ball valve	See page 108
Water has risen to the top of the toilet bowl	Blockage in U-bend or sewage pipe	Unblock the toilet – see page 107 – or call a drain cleaning company
Big drips or puddles under the washing machine or dishwasher	Split waste hose or inlet pipe	Replace the waste hose or inlet pipe – see page 103
Overflow pipe is constantly dripping	Stuck, broken or calcified ball valve in a toilet or tank	Clean or replace the ball valve – see page 108
Water is spilling from the gutter or drain down the outside wall	Blocked gutters	Clean and unblock the gutters – see page 107 – or call a roofer
Nothing happens when you flush the toilet	Broken siphon	Replace the siphon – see pages 108–9
Heating suddenly goes off	It's been set on too high for too long, the pump has burnt out or there's no water in the system	Turn temperature down a little and reset – see page 96 Turn off the boiler and call the plumber
Radiator is colder at the top than at the bottom	Air bubble in radiator	Bleed the radiator – see page 96
Radiator is cold at the bottom and in the middle	Possible corrosion	Call the plumber to chemically flush or replace the radiator
Radiator stays the same temperature all the time, even when you adjust the thermostat at the bottom	Thermostat valve is stuck or broken and needs to be replaced	Replace the thermostat – see page 98

Repairing a burst pipe

If you've got a burst pipe, you'll usually know about it! One of the timber merchants I work with – and he should have known better – was using a nail gun to put down a solid wood floor in his dining room, and he shot one of the nails straight through a hot water pipe. The damage cost him a fortune, and his wife didn't speak to him for days. But you could also end up with a leak for less exciting reasons, such as corrosion or cold weather, and it can cause no end of trouble if you don't sort it out quickly.

How to do an emergency repair

Even if you decide to call out a plumber to repair the leak permanently, it's very useful to know how to mend a leak in an emergency, so that you don't end up with the water off all weekend or paying emergency plumbing rates. Emergencies are also the time when you'll be really glad you found out where the stop cock is, and that your tool kit is stocked with everything you need.

TOOLS REQUIRED

- **Epoxy resin**
- **An old piece of cloth to use as a bandage**
  OR
- **A temporary pipe cover**
- **A screwdriver**

Remember to turn off both the water and the boiler.

1

TURN OFF THE WATER AT THE MAIN STOP COCK. Turn off the boiler – if you leave the water and boiler on while the central heating system runs dry, you'll blow out the boiler pump, which will turn a small emergency into an expensive repair job. **Place a container under the leak** and drain the radiator system (see page 97).

2

If you're using resin, **spread it over the leak as instructed on the tube,** and bind it into place with the piece of cloth, knotting it tightly.

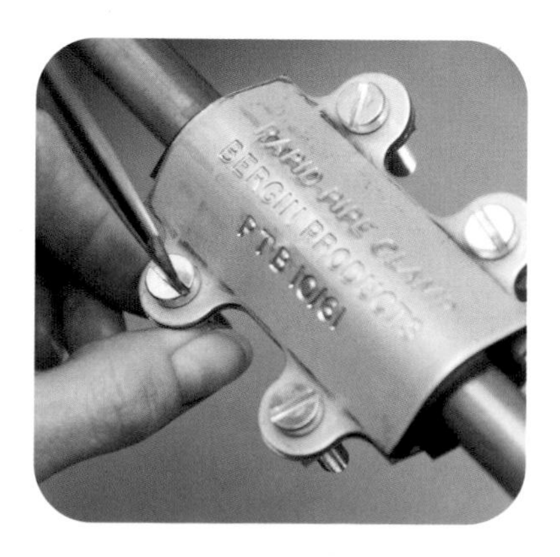

3

If you're using a temporary pipe cover, **use the screwdriver to screw it onto the pipe** as instructed on the packet. Refill the radiator system (see page 97). Now you can get on with your life for a day or so, until you have time to Do It Properly (see opposite) – or the plumber arrives.

How to make it permanent

You've sorted out the immediate problem and saved yourself a lot of money and hassle, and now it's time to make a repair that will last. You'll need to buy some supplies before you begin, so make sure you're fully prepared.

TOOLS REQUIRED

- **Junior hacksaw**
- **Replacement pipe, long enough to replace the faulty section, and the same width and material (copper or plastic). Your plumbing supplies shop will cut it to the right length for you, so ensure you take the measurements with you.**
- **Two push-fit connectors, the same size as the pipe**
- **If your pipe is plastic, you'll also need two pipe inserts to go with the push-fit fittings**
- **Plastic sandwich box or similar**

1

TURN OFF THE WATER AT THE MAIN STOP COCK. Drain the central heating system (see page 97). When the system is dry, **use the hacksaw to saw through the pipe on either side of the leak.** Attach each push-fit connector to the piece of replacement pipe until it clicks twice. Use the new piece as a guide for how much existing pipe to remove from the system.

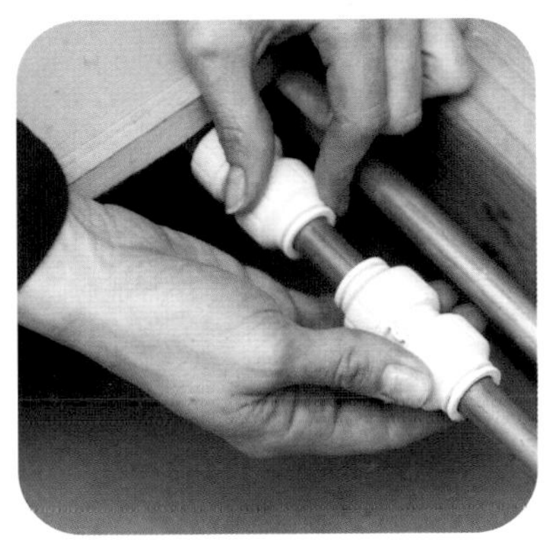

2

Insert the new pipe into the space you have just created and **slide the push-fit connectors in place.** If your pipe is plastic, push the pipe inserts into either end of the new piece of pipe. Place the push-fit connectors onto either end of the original pipe.

3

Place the plastic sandwich box under the mend to catch any leaks, just in case this should happen when you are checking your repair. Refill the radiator system (see page 97). Stand back and admire your handiwork!

TOP TIP: PLASTIC vs COPPER

Plastic pipes in lofts can end up being destroyed by hungry squirrels, and the damage can be horrendous. If you ever get a new central heating system installed and there's a loft involved, Do It Properly and get copper pipes.

Repairing radiators

Central heating systems are fantastic. I remember as a child waking up in winter with my twin sister in a house without it – we used to giggle because the water vapour that formed when we breathed made it look as if we were smoking, and our Dad would have killed us if we ever did that for real. It was an old Victorian house with windows that rattled when the wind blew, and ice formed on the inside of the windows. These days I'm lucky enough to have modern central heating, but I always make sure I get the most out of the system, knowing what a difference it makes.

What to do if your central heating fails

It's not just a particular law that says that your heating is most likely to fail on the coldest day of the year – sometimes having it on at full blast all day can cause it to cut out. So before you phone the plumber and land yourself with an expensive call-out charge, try turning down the thermostat by about five degrees and pressing the reset button. After about half an hour, the system should start running again.

SAFETY FIRST

Don't turn the bleed key by more than a quarter turn at a time (see below), or you'll risk the bleed valve shooting out along with a spurt of water, which may also cause a flood.

TROUBLESHOOTING: BLEEDING A RADIATOR

If you have a radiator that is colder at the top than at the bottom, then the problem is usually an air bubble trapped inside. This can easily be sorted out by 'bleeding' the air out of the radiator. This is one of the few plumbing jobs that you can do without turning off the water at the mains first – but you must still make sure you know how to do this in case of emergencies.

The only tools you'll need are a small metal key called a bleed key, which you can buy from a plumbing supplier or hardware shop if you don't already have one, and an old piece of cloth to put under the radiator to catch any drips.

On one end of the top of the radiator, you will find a small nut. **The bleed key should fit snugly over the nut.**

Make sure the cloth is in place under the nut and **turn the key anticlockwise by a quarter of a turn at a time** until you feel and hear rushing air.

DO NOT keep turning, but hold the key in that position until drips of water start to come out.

Tighten the nut again by turning the key clockwise.

Wait an hour or so and check the radiator to see if it is working better.

How to drain and refill a radiator system

Many plumbing jobs involve draining the central heating system of water before you begin. It's really quite simple to do, so don't let it put you off tackling the job.

The first thing you need to do is find the drain cock on your central heating system. This is not the same thing as the stop cock. It resembles a tap and will usually be close to the boiler on the return pipe. Failing this, try the pipes close to the last radiator in the system or near to the back or front door.

TOOLS REQUIRED

- > **Garden hosepipe**
- > **Adjustable spanner**
- > **Bleed key**

TOP TIPS: BE PRACTICAL

Before starting any plumbing job, make sure you've found your nearest plumbing supplies shop in case you have to pop out for a part in the middle.

If you can't find your drain cock and you have a storage tank in the roof, you can stop water entering the central heating system by raising the ball valve in the tank. Place a piece of wood across the tank and tie the ball valve to it with string.

1

If you have a feed-and-expansion tank (see page 16) and a storage tank, each will have its own stop cock. As well as turning off the main stop cock, **turn off the stop cocks on all tanks in the system** and turn off the central heating boiler.

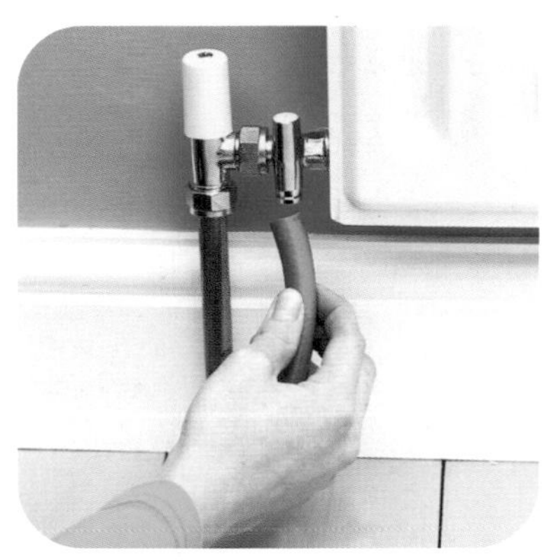

2

Attach one end of the hosepipe to the drain cock. Place the other end through an external door, into a drain outside. Using the adjustable spanner, loosen the square nut at the top of the drain cock, but don't take it out. Then wait for every last drop of water to drain out of the hosepipe.

Work through all the radiators in the house from the top to the bottom, opening the bleed valves in each one with your bleed key. This will allow any water trapped in the radiators to drain out of the system through the hosepipe. Now that everything's empty, you can start your repair. Once finished, close the drain cock and all bleed valves. Remove the hosepipe, emptying any water into the drain. Turn on the water at the main stop cock and any tanks. As the water flows back to the radiators, trapped air prevents it from entering. Turn on the central heating and then, starting at the bottom of the house, bleed the radiators (see opposite).

How to install or change a radiator valve

At the bottom of each radiator there are valves at either end which control the flow of hot water into and out of the radiator, usually with an adjustable valve at one end and a fixed valve, which can only be adjusted with a spanner, at the other. Sometimes the adjustable valve is controlled by a thermostat.

If you have a radiator which isn't heating up properly but is the same temperature from the top to the bottom, or if you've already tried bleeding it but found that there was no air to let out, then the chances are that the adjustable valve is stuck or broken and needs to be replaced. I recommend that you replace it with a thermostat valve, even if the previous valve was of a different kind, as it gives you much more control over the temperature of individual rooms.

TOOLS REQUIRED

- **Adjustable spanner**
- **Wire wool**
- **New radiator thermostat valve**
- **New connector to join new valve to radiator**
- **PTFE tape**

TOP TIP: USE A SUPERSTORE

For specialist parts, the big plumbing superstores are excellent. Don't be put off by the fact that they're aimed at the trade – the shop staff and even the plumber standing next to you in the queue may be happy to give you advice.

A thermostat valve allows you to have the ultimate in control – and save money.

1

Drain the radiator system (see page 97). Use the adjustable spanner to unscrew the nuts to either side of the existing valve. **Start by unscrewing the nut next to the valve.**

2

Unscrew the nut below the valve and then you can remove it. The radiator will still be fixed to the wall by its brackets.

3

Sometimes you may find that a replacement valve won't fit onto the old connector, in which case **remove the existing one.**

4
Remove any existing tape from the end of the central heating pipe and **clean it with wire wool** to make sure the new fitting slides on easily.

5
The thermostat valve should come with a new cap nut and an olive. The cap nut connects the valve to the central heating pipe, and the olive looks like a copper wedding ring and makes a watertight seal. **Slip the cap nut over the end of the pipe and put the olive on top of it.**

6
Wrap a piece of PTFE tape over the thread on the thermostat – again, this is to make a tight seal and prevent the radiator from dripping.

7
Attach the new connector to the radiator and then put the new valve on the radiator pipe, **lightly screwing the cap nut over the bottom of the valve.** Don't tighten it fully at this stage.

8
Attach the connector to the valve and **tighten the nuts with your spanner.** Refill the system (see previous page) and be ready with your spanner in case some water drips and you need to tighten the nuts a little more.

Repairing taps

Once, at a meeting of my local Women in Business group, I was asked what I would say to a stranger stuck in a lift with me before I forced my business card into their shaking hand. All I said was 'Irritating drips?', and the whole group fell about laughing. It made me realise that we all suffer from this problem every now and again, and it's usually all down to a faulty washer in a tap.

How to change a washer in a tap

Fixing a tap that constantly drips is one of the simplest and most satisfying jobs a novice DIYer can do – it's so easy to end the water torture once you know how.

When you turn on a tap, a rubber washer is lifted to let the water into the spout. Then, when you turn it off again, it lowers to seal the gap once more. If the washer is faulty or has been dislodged, then it allows water through constantly.

TOOLS REQUIRED

- **Screwdriver**
- **Chamois leather**
- **Adjustable spanner**
- **Notepad and pen**
- **Wrench (optional)**
- **Pliers**
- **A set of washers of different sizes**

A dripping tap needn't be an irritant: it's easy to replace the washer.

1

Turn of the water at the stop cock. Put the plug in the sink, making sure it's in firmly. Remove the hot or cold sign on the top of the tap. Look inside the tap and you'll see the retaining screw. Choose the right screwdriver from your tool kit and **unscrew it in an anticlockwise direction.**

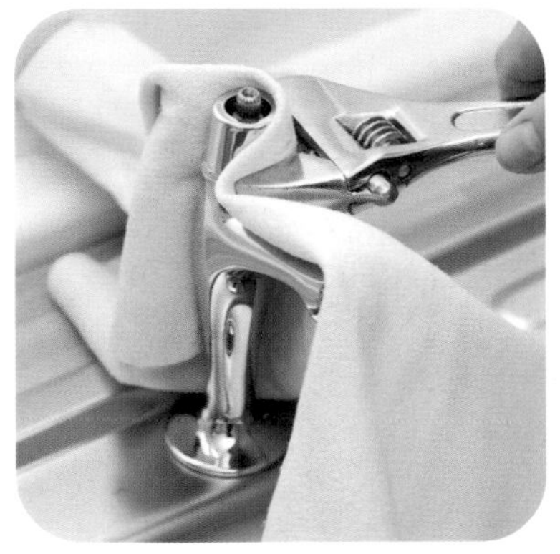

2

Now you can take the handle off the tap. Then wrap the chamois leather around the body cover to protect the chrome, and **remove it using the adjustable spanner.**

TOP TIP: USE YOUR NOTEPAD

Whenever you're doing a job that involves taking something apart and putting it back together again, write numbers on your notepad and place the first part that comes off on number 1, the second on number 2 and so on. Then reassemble the parts in reverse order.

4
Remove the headgear nut with the adjustable spanner. If it's really tight, wrap the chamois leather around the base of the tap and use the wrench to hold it firm while turning the spanner. Another trick is to tighten the headgear nut slightly to dislodge any calcified deposits before loosening it.

5
Once the headgear nut has been unscrewed you can remove the whole fitting. Now you should be able to see the washer. It may be released by a button, **or by a nut that you need to unscrew with the pliers.** Remove the old washer with a screwdriver.

6
Insert the new washer and reassemble the tap by replacing the parts in the opposite order to that in which you removed them. Turn the water back on and watch with amazement as your tap works perfectly – the feeling of power is immense!

TROUBLESHOOTING: AIRLOCKS IN PIPES

If your pipes and taps are banging and screaming and the water spurts out when you turn on the tap, you probably have an air lock in the pipe. The easiest way to get rid of the air lock is to use a tap to clear it:

Single taps: Connect the hot and cold taps with a piece of pipe and turn the cold tap on fully. The pressure of the cold water should force the air back up the hot water pipe to the tank, releasing the air as a bubble, which will rise to the top and escape.

Mixer tap: Holding a thick rag over the spout of the tap, turn on the hot tap very slightly. Keeping a tight hold of the cloth, turn the cold tap on fully. The same result should occur.

Installing kitchen appliances

Why call out a plumber for a job that you can easily do yourself? As long as your house or flat already has the right plumbing pipes, you can install a new washing machine or dishwasher using just the tools in your tool kit.

How to install a washing machine

These instructions assume that the appliance will be plumbed in next to the kitchen sink. If your washing machine or dishwasher is installed elsewhere in your house or flat and there are no pipes close by, turn to a plumber for professional help.

TOOLS REQUIRED

- **Newspapers**
- **Scissors**
- **Adjustable spanner**
- **Butterfly clip or circlip**

Perhaps not too surprisingly, on all water valves, red equals hot water and blue equals cold – but it is always best to check. Turn on the hot tap and feel if the pipe gets warm.

1

Cut some newspapers to the size of the base of the washing machine and **lay them on the floor underneath it.** In the future this will help you to see whether there are any leaks and where they are.

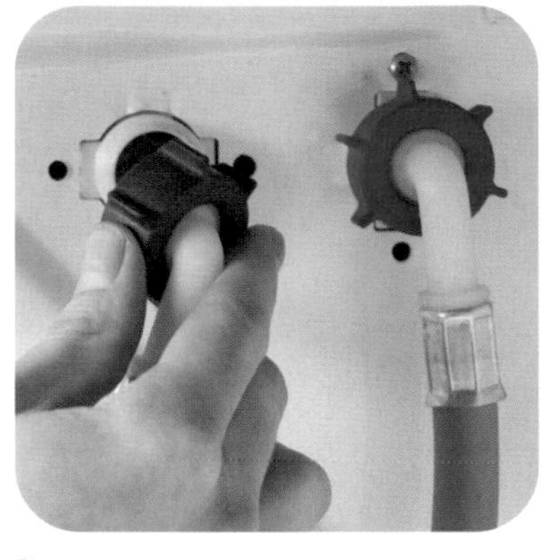

2

Your machine should have two inlet valves on the top back, one for hot water to be delivered into the machine (denoted by the red valve) and the other for cold water (the blue valve). There should also be two pipes that fit onto these inlets, and a ribbed waste hose, usually running from the bottom of the machine, to take dirty water away again. **Screw the pipes onto the inlet valves.**

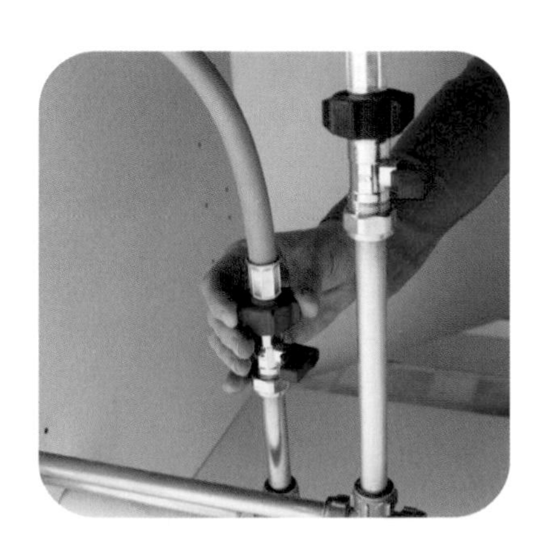

3

Under the sink, you will find two pipes, one with a red valve at the end and the other with a blue valve. Take the red pipe from your washing machine and attach it to the red valve under the sink. Tighten the nut with a spanner. **Repeat this step for the blue valve.**

4
Where a washing machine is installed away from the sink, you will find an open-ended pipe **into which you just pop the waste from the washing machine.**

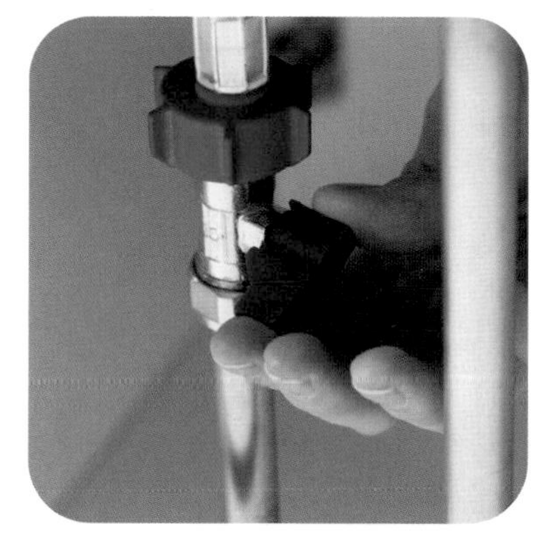

5
Turn on the cold water inlet valve under the sink with a quarter turn. Check at either end for leaks, and tighten the nuts with your adjustable spanner if necessary. Repeat the same process with the hot water inlet valve. Plug in the machine and run a rinse and spin cycle, making sure the waste hose and inlet pipes do not leak.

6
Use a spirit level and the machine's adjustable legs to make sure it is level – you'll slowly destroy the bearings if it isn't. Now you can put all that dirty laundry into the machine and put your feet up while technology does the job for you!

TROUBLESHOOTING: REPLACING A DISHWASHER'S WASTE HOSE

Big drips or puddles under the dishwasher are usually caused by a split waste hose (or 'bottom hose'), which can easily be replaced. Check for this as soon as you see any water on your newspaper, because it can cause a great deal of damage. This is where the newspaper under the machine will really help (see opposite) – as well as providing early signs of leaks, it will help you to locate the split. If there isn't any paper, rusty or chalky marks on the pipes are a giveaway, as well as drip marks on the floor.

Once you've located the split, turn off the valve at the end of the hose furthest from the appliance. Use a spanner to unscrew the nut, circlip or butterfly clip that keeps the hose in place and remove it. Take it to your plumbing supplies shop to match it to a replacement, **and tighten the nut to secure the new hose before turning the valve back on.**

Clearing blockages

Slimy things that lurk in the 'U'-bend or bottle trap under the sink can cause nasty smells and make us ill if we are not careful. It is easy to be clean, but not so easy to control what happens down the plug hole. Whether it be the kitchen sink, the bathroom basin or the bath, things just get stuck, and for every bit that gets lodged, something else sticks to it, which then gets gluey with oils and fat and – hey presto! – we have a bunged-up pipe and a very nasty smell. You can purchase all sorts of clever things to stop bits from going down the sink – use them, the more you can do the better.

Blocked sinks

The most common blockages are caused by hair and fat mixed together. Even chemicals can't destroy hair, so you need to keep it out of the drains. Fat congeals around the hair, making a horrible blockage. When my sister and I did the dishes as children, our parents always told us to transfer any oil to a particular tin, and when it was full Mum hung the fat block for the birds from the scrawny little tree in the garden – it saved Dad from a horrible job unblocking the sink.

> If you have a sink plunger, **place it over the plughole, holding a rag over the overflow** to stop the air from escaping.

> If you don't have a sink plunger, fill the sink with water, and, **holding a rag over the overflow with one hand, take the plug out of the sink and place the heel of your other hand over the plug hole.** Pump up and down a few times until you feel or hear the blockage clear, and then let the water out in the normal way to see if it runs freely.

> If the sink is still blocked, try using a chemical unblocker.

SAFETY FIRST

Do NOT use more than one different chemical unblocker to try to clear the same blockage – the chemicals within them can react with one another and are dangerous.

How to fix a blocked sink

If the plunging methods described on the left don't work, it is time to tackle the waste trap beneath the sink. Before you start, make sure you warn anyone who might want to use the sink that you are doing this! My Dad had a habit of 'tinkering', as my Mum put it, and this did not always fit in with Mum's agenda. On one occasion, her particular agenda was to do the washing up, which meant that she poured a very cold cup of tea down the sink. She had no idea that the reason Dad was under there was that he was taking the waste unit apart. The conversation that followed was quite surreal and he had a bruise on his head for weeks.

TOOLS REQUIRED

- > **Rubber gloves**
- > **Bowl or bucket**
- > **Wrench**
- > **Auger (optional)**

1

Before you start taking the plumbing apart, **have a good look at the pipes under the sink** and draw what you see or take a photograph with your digital camera or phone. This will help to guide you when you come to put everything back together again.

Remember to tell everyone who lives with you that you are taking the sink to pieces and NOT to run any water!

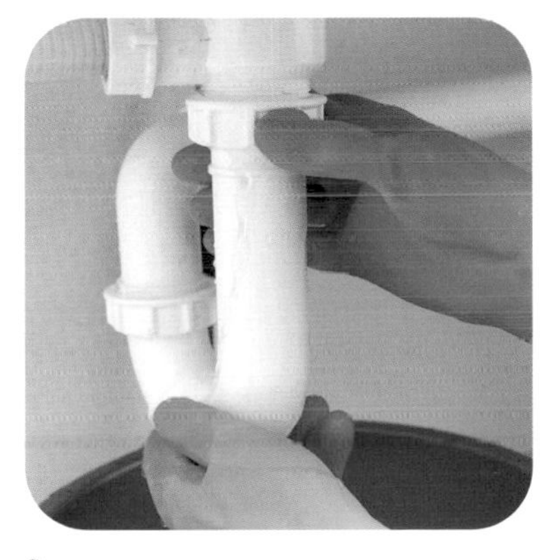

2

Place the plug in the plug hole and put the bowl or bucket under the waste trap ready to catch the contents of the blocked sink. **Loosen the large plastic nut at the top of the waste trap** (you might need to use the wrench if it is too stiff), turning it in an anticlockwise direction. Repeat with the nut at the other end of the trap.

3

Pour the contents of the waste trap into the bowl or bucket. You might also need to rinse the trap – if so, make sure you remember to use another sink or basin!

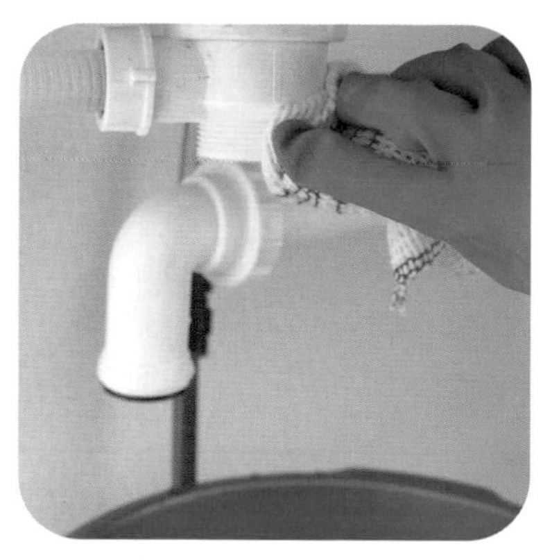

4
If the top of the waste trap was leaking as well as being blocked, **dry the screw well with a cloth.**

5
Then apply some sealant around the thread – don't squeeze too much onto the fitting.

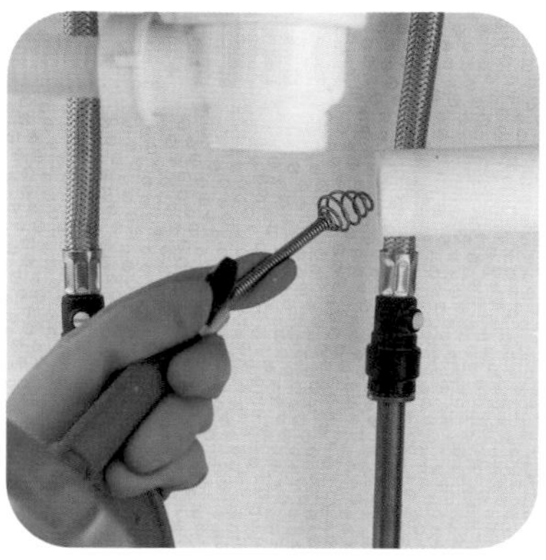

6
If there was no blockage in the waste trap, **use an auger to explore the recesses of the exit pipe.**

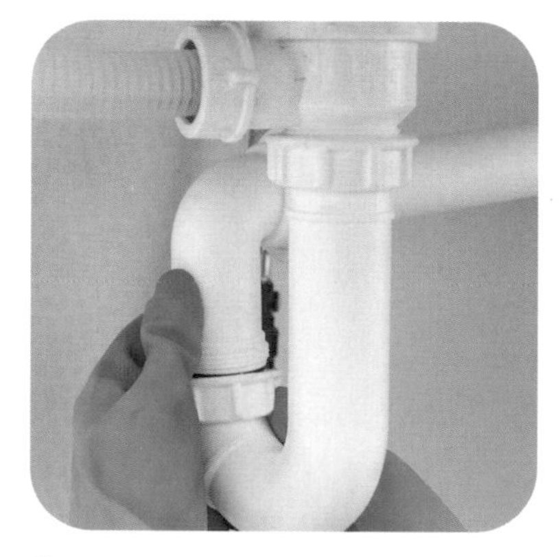

7
Reassemble the waste trap, first tightening the top plastic nut **and then the smaller one behind.** DON'T FORGET TO DO THIS! There is a rubber washer with the larger plastic nut – make sure it is positioned so that the wedge end faces away from the nut. Turn the water back on and check the system to ensure the blockage has gone and there are no leaks.

Blocked toilets

We all love the telltale signs of the blocked toilet, when the water has risen to the top of the bowl and isn't going anywhere. Here's how to sort it out without too much mess or heartbreak.

TOOLS REQUIRED

- > **Rubber gloves**
- > **Bowl or bucket**
- > **Jug**
- > **Cooper's plunger**

TOP TIP: BLOCKED GUTTERS

Check and clean the gutters once a year, as soon as the trees have lost all their leaves - if these are swept into the gutters, the water will overflow and pour down the wall. Another cause of guttering blockages can be rubble left over from roofing jobs - always make sure that the gutters are cleared whenever any work is done on your roof or those of your immediate neighbours. It's amazing how many people don't have drain covers for the top of the down pipes - they're very cheap to buy, and without them, you'll end up with a drain full of leaf compost and possibly the start of permeating damp (see page 200).

1

Pull on your rubber gloves and find yourself an old container that you can throw away. **Scoop out some of the water from the toilet into the container,** and pour it down an outside drain. Try to dislodge the blockage with a few sharp plunges of the toilet brush.

2

If it still won't budge, you need a Cooper's plunger, or a home-made equivalent. A real Cooper's plunger is like a large sink plunger with a flat piece of rubber end. Again, **try to dislodge the blockage with a few sharp plunges.**

3

To make a plunger, **insert the head of an old-style mop in a tough plastic bag** and seal with duct tape. Plunge away and then flush the toilet a few times to make sure the blockage has completely gone. If this doesn't work, get the professionals in - the methane in the sewers can knock you unconscious if you start trying to take the system apart or, even worse, it will explode!

Fixing flushing problems

Wherever there is a tank in your water system, there is usually also a ball cock or – to call it by its proper name – a ball valve. It's the ball that sits at the end of a lever and floats on the surface of the water, regulating the flow in and out of the tank or toilet cistern. It's important to maintain and check your tanks regularly, so that you may be forewarned of potential problems before they happen, as any faults can cause leaks or damp problems.

TROUBLESHOOTING: BALL VALVE PROBLEMS

If no water is reaching the taps, or the overflow on the outside of your house is constantly running, the chances are that you've got a problem with the ball valve in your storage tank. This can be the beginning of permeating damp, so avoid the damage that it will cause, and fix it now.

Not all central heating systems have a storage tank, but those that do usually have it in the loft. Your tank should be covered to prevent any creatures getting in, and if it isn't, the problem may be that the ball valve is caught up on something like a dead pigeon.

Animals aside, check the ball for calcified deposits or leaks. Moving it up and down will release it if it is just stuck, and if this doesn't help, remove it and wash or replace it. Different ball valves are attached to the system in different ways, but it is usually very simple to remove and replace them.

If your ball valve needs replacing, take the old one with you when you go to buy the new one, and show it to the assistant – you will then ensure that you get exactly the type you need. Keep the old one until you know that the new one is working.

Regularly checking the level of the water in the feed-and-expansion tank can prevent expensive problems from occurring. It could be happening because the ball valve isn't moving freely, in which case, remove, wash and replace it and then check that it is functioning properly.

How to fix toilet flush problems

If you flush the toilet and nothing much happens other than the sound of rushing air, you have a problem with the siphon in the cistern. It could be the siphon itself, the diaphragm inside it or even just a washer – it's a simple job to find out which and replace whatever has gone wrong.

TOOLS REQUIRED

- **Notepad and pen**
- **Wrench**
- **New siphon or diaphragm – you're best off buying these once you've discovered the problem and can take the old ones to the shop with you**
- **New washers bought with the siphon or diaphragm**
- **PTFE tape**

Remember to turn the water off at the stop cock!

1
Empty the cistern and the pipes that feed it by **holding up the valve while you flush the toilet** several times. The siphon is the inverted U-pipe in the middle of the cistern. Release it by using a wrench to undo the big plastic locking nut that clamps the siphon to the base of the cistern. Hold the nut on the other side of the siphon and it should come apart quite easily. Sometimes, a modern cistern is installed as a unit and is impossible to take apart, in which case you might have to buy a whole replacement.

TOP TIP: KEEP NOTES

As you take the flush mechanism apart, make a note of what went where and in what order, so that you don't get confused when you're putting it back together again.

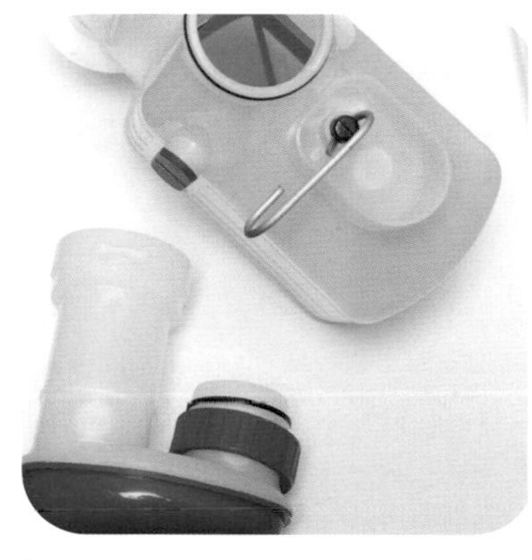

2
Remove the siphon and look to see whether it's the siphon itself that's broken or whether the diaphragm inside is split. Take the unit to your plumbing supplies shop to get the correct replacement.

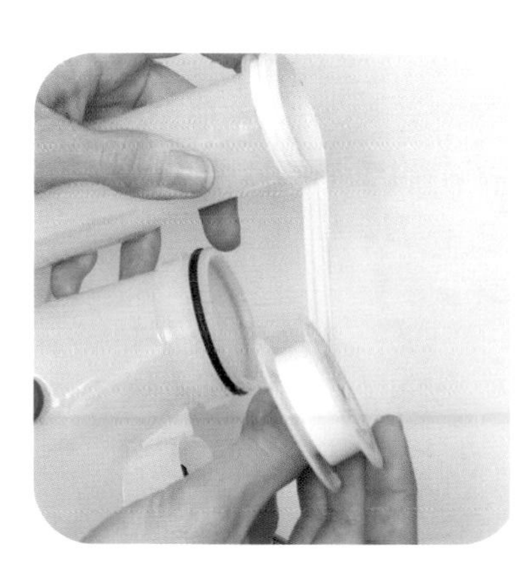

4
Reassemble the unit in the same way that you took it apart. Before you replace the plastic locking nut, **wrap a piece of PTFE tape around the thread** for good luck. Once everything is back in place, turn the water back on and check that the cistern does not leak from the nut at the bottom.

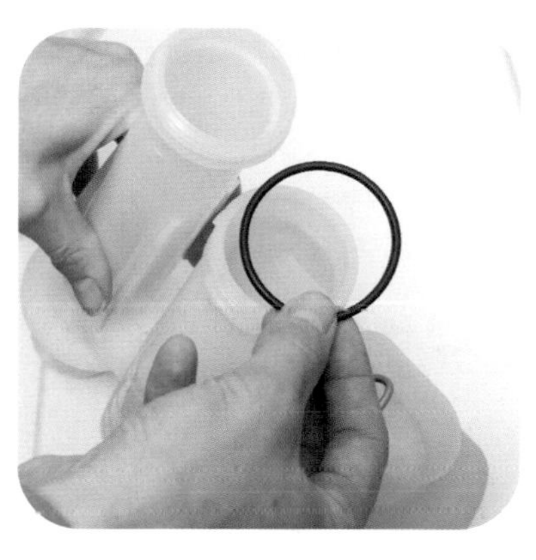

3
If the washer has perished, **replace it with a similar-sized one.**

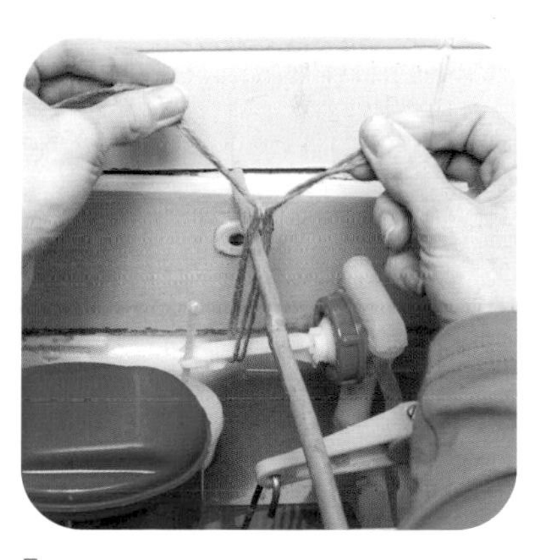

5
If the cistern does leak, **lift the valve to stop more water coming in and tie to a chisel or stick placed across the cistern**. Flush the toilet several times to empty the cistern, tighten the nut, and then untie the valve to let the water back in. Check on the leak to see the job has been done successfully!

CHAPTER FOUR

Tile it

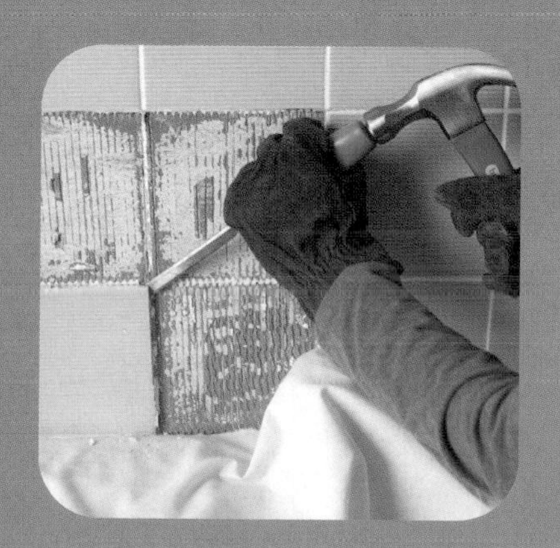

Understanding the basics of tiling

When tiles are laid and grouted properly, they look fantastic, but all it takes is just the slightest deviation from perfection and they look horrid. Whether you fancy doing a Gaudi or just a cheap white tile job from the local superstore, you only need a few simple rules to make the difference between tiling happiness and a very permanent eyesore. This chapter looks at silicone sealant as well as tiling – the two always go together if you are going to have a leak-free system.

SHOPPING LIST

Before buying your tiles, run through this checklist of things you'll need for almost any tiling job. However, you'll need extra tools and materials for many jobs, so make sure that you also read through the whole chapter thoroughly and work out exactly what you need.

> **Tiles**
> **Grout**
> **Tile adhesive**
> **PVA**
> **Paintbrush**
> **Paint scraper**
> **A piece of timber 5mm (¼in) thick, about 10cm (4in) wide and 100–180cm (3–6ft) long**
> **Spirit level**
> **At least ten soft cloths**
> **3 buckets or containers**
> **Tile spacers**
> **Small adhesive spreader**
> **Grout float**
> **Grout protector**
> **Silicone sealant**
> **Sealant carrier or gun**

THE DOs OF TILING

✓ Do measure the area that you're going to tile in advance, and always measure twice to check that you have the right measurement – or more times if your measurements disagree.

✓ Do tell the shop assistants what type of area you're going to tile and where they will be set. It's possible that you've fallen in love with the wrong tiles. Do also take their advice on which adhesive, grout and grout protector you need to use.

✓ Do work out how many tiles you need for the job when you're choosing your tiles in the shop. It's an easy multiplication, but if you're unsure of the results, always ask the professionals in the shop – I'm in awe of how quickly they tell you how many you need.

✓ Do buy a few tiles extra, if you can afford it, to allow for damage.

✓ Do clean as you go. Adhesive, grout and silicone sealant are all a nightmare to remove once they've started to dry (see page 122).

✓ Do tile the room before you install a new bathroom suite, and if you're tiling a room with an existing suite, where possible ease the wash basin and toilet cistern away from the wall and tile behind them.

✓ **Do use a gauge rod to plan your work (see page 117).**

✓ Do use the correct tool for spreading adhesive – anything else and you will get an uneven tile surface.

✓ **Do put adhesive on the tiles** rather than all over the area you're going to tile – you never know when the doorbell might go, stopping you in the middle and causing the adhesive to dry without the tiles in place.

✓ Do remove every loose piece of paint and paper from the area you're going to tile (see page 114).

✓ Do leave 8–12 hours between stages to allow for drying.

✓ Do fill the bath or sink before sealing it with silicone – this pulls it away slightly from the last row of tiles and makes sure that you have the best possible 'squeeze and stretch' seal.

THE DON'Ts OF TILING

✗ Don't skimp on preparation.

✗ Don't try to rush the job – it isn't worth it, as wonky or badly cut tiles stick out like a sore thumb and will make your house harder to sell. Allow three days overall, however small the job – you need to allow for drying time between stages.

✗ Don't tile on top of wallpaper. Strip the wall to the plaster and apply a coat of PVA to seal it; the PVA will also give the wall a key for your adhesive.

✗ Don't skimp on sealant – it's the only way you'll get a flexible, waterproof seal.

✗ Don't tip tile adhesive or grout down the bath, sink or shower outlet – you'll block the drains.

✗ Don't let anyone use the bathroom or shower while adhesives and grout are drying.

✗ Don't let water get anywhere near your tiling job, other than your damp cleaning rags, both while you are working and for 24 hours afterwards.

✗ **Don't tile right down to the sink, shower or bath edge – you need to leave a space for the silicone sealant.**

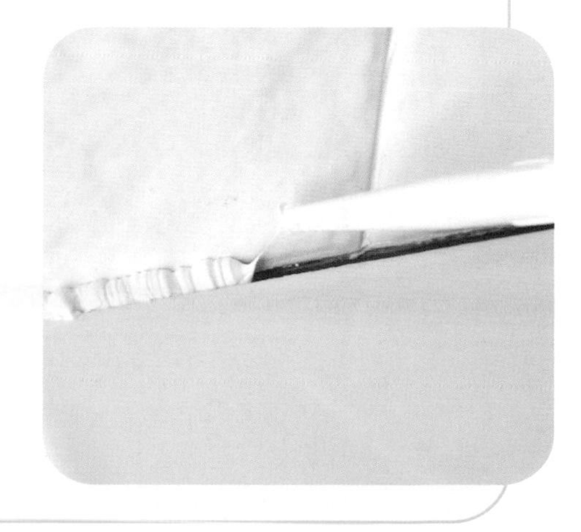

Removing tiles

You've chosen your tiles, you've bought your grout and adhesive, and you're ready to begin. Let's start with 4 sq m (4 sq yd) of tiles on a single wall behind your bath. I'm going to take you through the whole process, from removing old tiles and preparing the surface, through the tiling itself and keeping your tiles clean, to tidying up at the end. All these stages are equally important if you want to Do It Properly and end up with a job that you're proud of.

How to take down the old tiles

Here's a cautionary tale: you're sitting in the bath with a hammer and a blunt chisel and the first tile you hit comes off a lot faster than you ever expected. It crashes into the side of the bath, breaking a huge hole in the surface, and the nice bath you had at the start is nice no longer. Let's find out how you could have avoided that.

TOOLS REQUIRED

- > **Large pieces of old rubber-backed carpet or thick rug**
- > **Duct tape**
- > **Dust sheet or old bedsheet**
- > **Hammer**
- > **Chisel**
- > **Paint scraper, or a piece of acrylic from your bathroom supplies shop**

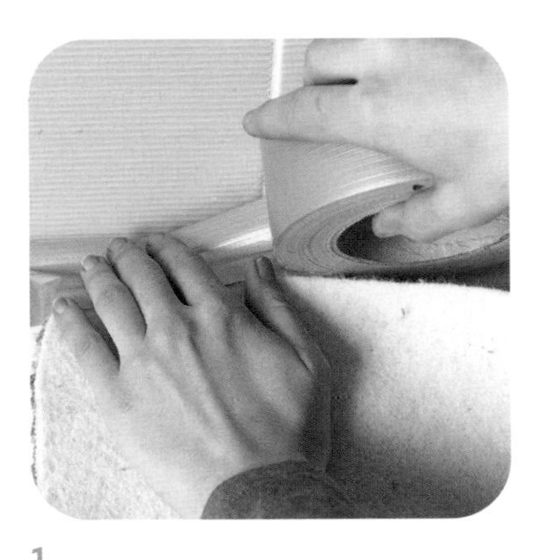

1
Tape a length of the carpet or rug, fluffy side down, to the bottom row of tiles so that it covers the edge of the bath.

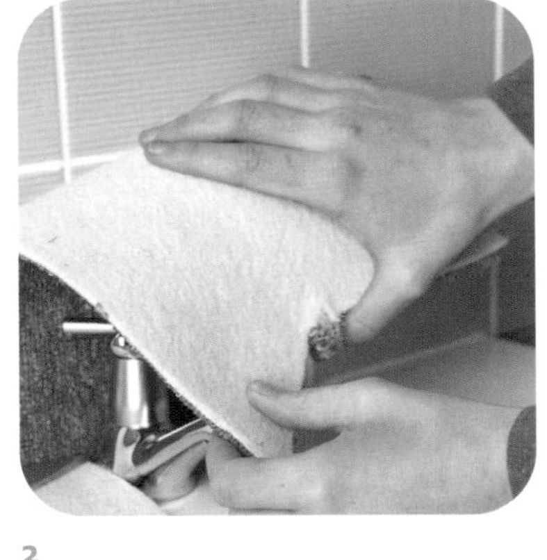

2
Tuck another piece of carpet over the taps and tape it to the tiles or the bath. Lay a third piece of carpet in the bottom of the bath.

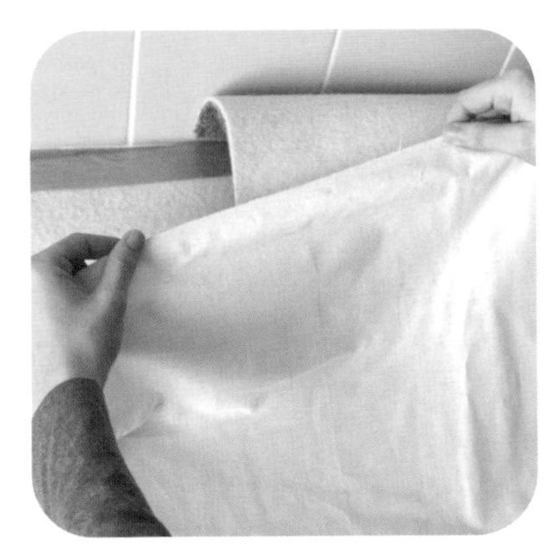

3
Then, and only then, **place a dust sheet or an old bedsheet to cover everything** including the carpet, and tape it down.

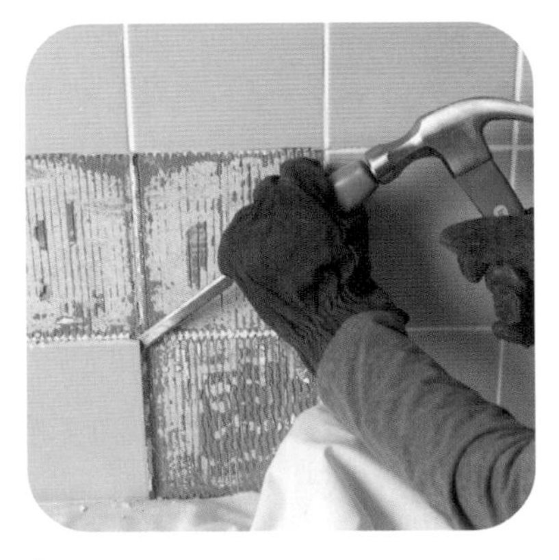

4
Knock the tiles with the hammer and **lever off with the chisel,** letting them fall on the dust sheet.

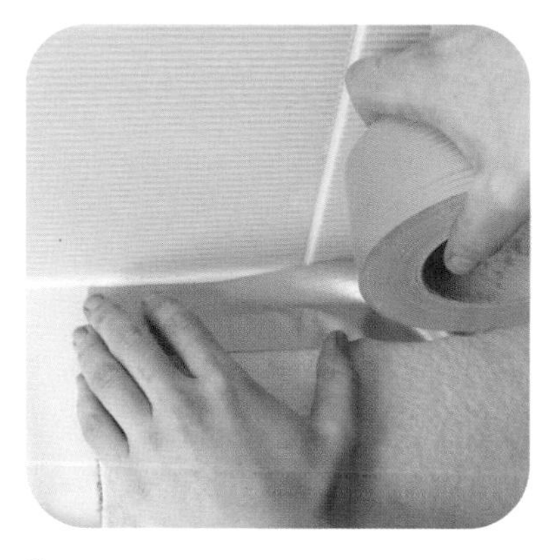

5
When you get to the row that the tape is stuck to, **peel back the tape and then stick it to the edge of the bath**. Remove the final row of tiles.

6
Using a blunt chisel, **remove as much of the silicone sealant as you can manage** between the tiles and the bath.

7
When no more will come off, **switch to a paint scraper with a sharp blade**, but be very careful not to scratch the bath. If you have a plastic bath, a piece of left-over acrylic from your bathroom supplies shop may do a better job as plastic on plastic is less likely to scratch.

8
Peel back the tape and roll up the dust sheet, wrapping up all the broken tiles and dust inside. Then remove the pieces of carpet leaving your bath clean and unspoilt. Don't move onto the next stage of preparation until you've cleaned up all the rubbish.

TROUBLESHOOTING: PREPARING A SURFACE TO BE TILED

Preparing the wall is one of the most important parts of tiling, because if you don't have a sound surface for the tiles to stick to, you'll find that they won't stay on the wall for very long.

Remove every last piece of grout, adhesive, paint or wallpaper until you are right down to the plaster.

Paint the wall with a 50/50 mix of water and PVA. This is called priming – it provides a key for the adhesive to stick to. Let it dry completely.

Now you are ready to start tiling.

Setting out tiles

If tiles are applied badly, they look bad. In fact, they look worse than bad as any deviation from perfect will forever jar. Please take your time when setting out tiles – use your gauge rod and mark where the tiles will fall, especially where they start and finish. It is all-important that you do your prep work and that you have very flat walls to start with. Then follow the few simple rules on these pages and you will have tiles you can be proud of rather than regarding them as a dismal failure.

How to set out tiles

The gauge rod is the key to setting out tiles so follow the steps on this page and all will be well. If you want to use different colour tiles, once you have marked their positions with the gauge rod – and before tiling – paint the wall with different colours of emulsion to get a really good idea of the finished effect.

TOOLS REQUIRED

- **Tape measure**
- **Spirit level**
- **Pencil**
- **Notepad**
- **Gauge rod**

TOP TIP: EYE LINES

The first job is to walk into the room you want to tile and notice where you look at first. The corner that you instantly see is the one that most needs to look right, so this is the corner where you need to have whole tiles going from the corner upwards and outwards in straight lines. This is where you should start the job.

1

Draw a sketch of the wall in your notebook. Measure its width and height and mark these measurements on the sketch. With your tape measure, find the approximate centre of the area you are planning to tile and **draw two lines in pencil that meet at this point, one horizontal and one vertical**. Then, starting at this central line, use your gauge rod (see below) to mark where the edge of each tile will fall for the first horizontal row.

2

If you find that the last tile in either direction will need to have more than a third cut off it, **adjust the central line and use the gauge rod and pencil to mark out the new position of the tiles**, if possible allowing for whole tiles in the corner that you identified as the first place you see when you walk into the room.

3

Now that you've marked out the position of the first tiles on the wall, **draw all the tiles in your notebook**. If your tiles are patterned or you're using more than one colour of tile, you can also use this sketch to plan which tiles go where. Work from your sketch as you do the tiling.

MAKING A GAUGE ROD

A gauge rod is a piece of timber 50mm (2in) thick, about 10cm (4in) wide and 100–180cm (3–6ft) long, depending on the size of the space that you are tiling. It is used to measure the distances in your room to work out how many tiles will fit in each part and where they will go.

Lay the rod flat on the floor and place a series of tiles next to it along its length, separated by spacers as they would be on the wall. **Use a pencil to mark the position of each tile on the rod.** For rectangular tiles, mark the horizontal lengths on one side and verticals on the other. You can then place the rod against the prepared wall before you start and mark the position of each tile on the wall, both vertically and horizontally.

Cutting and shaping tiles

Cutting tiles has been made much easier by the vast number of electric cutting machines on the market. You can buy or hire them, and there are some especially designed for the novice, which are so good that I use them professionally. The best kind are powered by electricity and have a continual supply of water to the cutting wheel to keep it cool and stop bits of tile and dust from flying around. Make sure the water reservoir is topped up.

CUTTING TILES

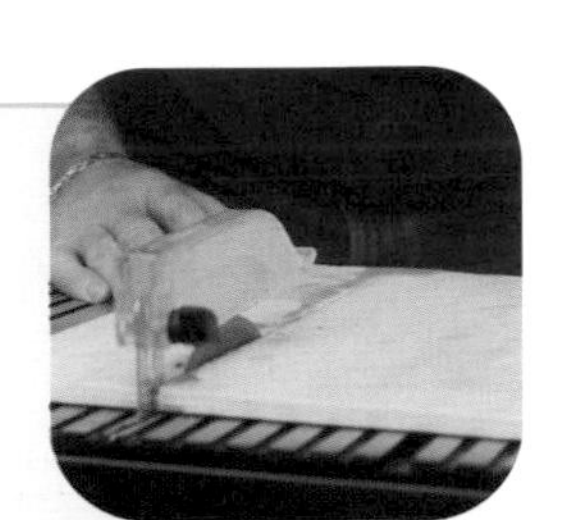

Use the wet tile cutter lying flat for straight cuts. Where edging tiles turn a 90-degree corner, it looks fantastic if you cut the edges of both tiles to a 45-degree angle so they can meet in a perfect join. To do this, tip the tile cutter to the correct angle, **most modern tile cutters have an attachment for tipping**. If the cut edge isn't perfectly straight, sand it with fine WHITE sandpaper. It looks pretty wonderful, even if I do say so myself.

It's even possible to cut a hole in the centre of a tile for a pipe emerging from the wall. **Use a tool called a carbide grit hole saw, which attaches to your drill**. Resist the temptation to use the hammer setting – it will do exactly the same thing as a hammer and smash your tile.

Floor tiles are made of harder materials than wall tiles, so if you're planning to lay some, mention it to the shop assistant when you're hiring or buying your tile-cutting machine. If you need to make holes in them, you'll need a slot drive system drill, which will drill through floor tiles like a knife through butter.

TROUBLESHOOTING: FALLING TILES

Tiles usually fall off the wall because there's water behind them due to cracks, poor silicone or grout or, unfortunately, from a leaking pipe. Worst of all is subsidence, which is when the wall itself cracks and moves, but in most cases water will be the culprit.

Try pulling all the tiles off the wall and if the tiles are in good enough condition to go back up again, clean all the adhesive off the back by soaking them in warm water with washing-up liquid. Place on a flat soft surface before scraping the backs with a blunt chisel or narrow screwdriver. Be careful of your hands as tools can cut and bruise.

Make sure that you also clean the wall properly, right down to the plaster, and prime it with PVA – it's probably the lack of PVA that caused the problem in the first place (see Troubleshooting, page 115).

How to cut and shape tiles

When there are small areas to fill there are several ways of cutting a tile. For lines that aren't straight, use a nibbler, and to make straight lines use a scorer and metal rule. Always wear protective gear when cutting tiles: goggles and mask

TOOLS REQUIRED

- Goggles
- Mask
- Chinagraph pencil
- Nibbler
- Tile file
- Sandpaper (optional)
- Scorer
- Metal rule

SAFETY FIRST

When cutting tiles, always wear goggles or specially designed glasses to protect your eyes from flying tile fragments.

1

If you need to remove just a part of a tile, say, for example, to fit around a socket, use a handy tool called a nibbler. Using the chinagraph pencil, draw a line on the tile for where you want to work to and **then start 'nibbling' away.**

2

Continue to remove small pieces of tile until you have reached the marked line.

3

The edge of the tile won't be a smooth finish after you've used the nibbler so **use the tile file to remove any rough pieces.** You can also use coarse sandpaper to finish the edges.

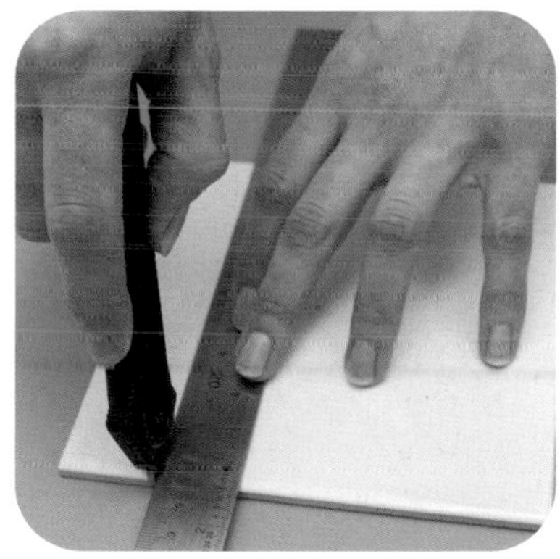

4

If it's a straight edge that you require, a simpler way to cut the tile is by using a scorer and metal rule. Place the ruler on the line where the cut is to be made **and score deeply alongside it.** The tile should break neatly into two pieces.

Applying tiles

Most DIY books include pictures applying adhesive to a wall and then placing tiles onto the adhesive. This is not the best way to do it if you're a beginner – you never know when you might need to clean something up, resulting in you letting the adhesive dry while the tiles stay in their box.

How to apply tiles

Now that you've prepared your surface (see pages 115 and 116–17), you can enjoy the fun part of the job.

TOOLS REQUIRED

- **Tiles**
- **Bucket of clean warm water**
- **Tile adhesive**
- **Small adhesive spreader**
- **Your sketch of the wall**
- **Tile spacers**
- **3 containers (see page 123)**
- **At least 10 soft cloths**
- **rubber hammer or mallet**
- **piece of wood**

1

Wet the tiles by putting **the whole box in a bucket of clean warm water**, then take them out and leave them to drain. The adhesive will take longer to dry, but the adhesive will stick to the tile better, the tile will slide more easily if you need to adjust it and you'll get a perfect fix.

2

Spread the tile adhesive evenly over the back of a tile. Doing it this way means that you can concentrate on one tile at a time. If it isn't even, the tile will tilt fractionally, and this tilt will reflect light, drawing attention to its wonkiness.

TROUBLESHOOTING: PREPARING A WALL ABOVE A BATH THAT ISN'T LEVEL

Drill holes in a length of 5cm (2in) wide wooden batten about every 50cm (20in) and use the holes to mark the wall for drilling. The batten needs to be straight and the top one tile's height above the edge of the bath. **Drill holes, insert wall plugs and then fix the batten to the wall.** Mark out the position of each tile on the batten with the gauge rod and **start tiling.**

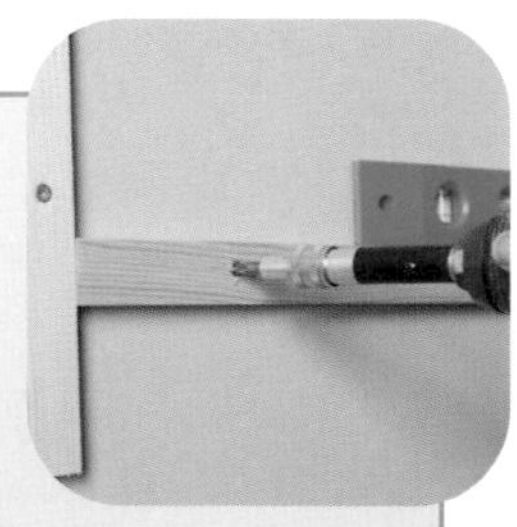

Leave the tiles to dry out for 24 hours, and then unscrew and remove the batten. Try to remove the wall plugs. If they're stubborn and they're sticking out of the wall, use a fairly blunt chisel and a hammer to cut off the tops so you can tile evenly over them. Then fix the first row of tiles to the wall in the same way as in Step 3, cutting them accordingly. Leave the tiles to dry for 24 hours before grouting them.

3
Place the tile on the wall in the position you've planned for your starting tile. This will be in the corner that you see first when you come into the room, and immediately above the bath if you have a level bath, or above the batten if the bath wasn't level. If you are tiling immediately above the bath, **break one arm off a cross-spacer to form an upside-down 'T' shape** and place it against the wall on top of the bath at the point where the first tile and the next one will meet. This will give you room to put the silicon sealant between the tiles and the bath, right at the end of the job. If you are tiling above a batten, you will do this step later.

TOP TIP: LEAVE TO DRY

Never drill through freshly laid tiles – give them 24 hours to dry first

4
Clean any adhesive off the front of the tile (see page 121). **Take a whole cross spacer and put it onto the top corner of your tile** on the side next to where the next tile will go, and repeat the process again, aligning the second tile snugly against the spacer and the batten or bath.

5
Continue with spacers and tiles **until you have a complete row.**

TOP TIP: LEVELLING TILES

Smooth down the tile to make it perfectly level. If you find that you've applied some tiles unevenly, hold a piece of wood against the tiles and tap lightly with a rubber hammer to level them out. Remember that you can only do this while the adhesive is still wet.

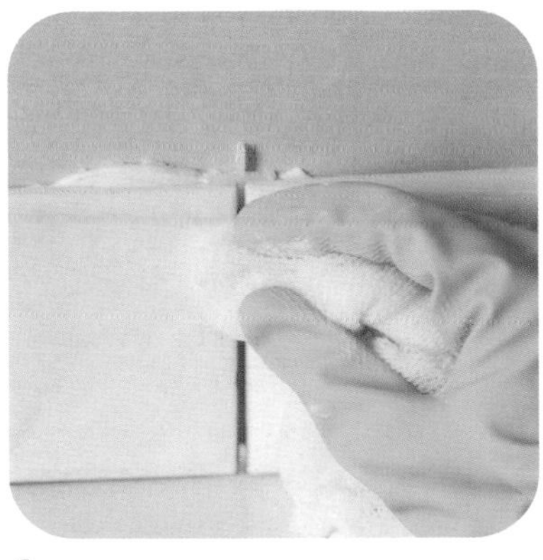

6
Then do a mega clean until there isn't a speck of adhesive anywhere, and continue with the next rows, until you've finished the whole wall.

Using grout and silicone sealant

Now it's time to grout, which is then followed by the application of silicone sealant. This is used around baths, sinks and the base of the toilet to stop water from leaking into the walls or floor. Without it, you'll have problems with damp or even rotting wood (see page 200).

TROUBLESHOOTING: GROTTY GROUT AND SPOTTY SILICONE

Grotty grout and spotty silicone – these are the terrible twins that invade your bathroom. Why oh why does the grout or silicone go black and spotty? Why does the grout fall out from between the tiles? And why do the tiles fall off the wall? Water does the most damage when it seeps through the silicone sealant around the bath. Because you usually can't see it, by the time you find out, it's done a lot of nasty stuff.

Silicone: This is quite difficult to get rid of, but a paint scraper does the trick, though it will damage the bath if you aren't very careful, especially if it's plastic. **If possible, buy a small hand-sized piece of acrylic – plastic against plastic is less likely to do any harm.**

Clean out the silicone with a chisel for as long as you can and then change to a paint scraper and keep going until every speck of spotty sealant is off.

Clean the area with methylated spirits and a paintbrush together with a soft lint-free cloth. Be careful with meths, as it can stain the grout, and don't use white spirit as it contains oils and has the opposite effect to the one you're looking for. Once the area is totally clean and free of dust, proceed with the silicone.

I've never used sealant remover so I've no idea whether it works. It seems to me like another noxious chemical that we should avoid if possible – elbow grease is perhaps the best solution.

Grout: Rake it out with a blunt chisel or narrow screwdriver. Scrub with bleach and a brush, getting out as much dirt as possible. Then rinse it off, leave to dry and paint with 50% PVA and 50% water. Give it time to dry out again and paint with grout protector.

If the grout or silicone goes orange, this is a fungus that is carried in water and soap – in fact, that insignificant tablet of soap is the biggest killer of grout and silicone around. All you really need to do to get rid of it is to use an eco-friendly bleach and scrub the tiles and grout until they sparkle. If you notice while you're cleaning it that some of your grout is soft, take it out and re-grout as explained on page 124.

If your grout or silicone turns black, this is usually due to bacteria living off soap in the water, creating more bacteria, and starting to destroy the grout or silicone. Remove and replace the silicone as described above. Alternatively, the water may be coming to the back of the tile from a leak. Work out where this is and get it fixed.

How to clean as you go

By now you will be excited about seeing those lovely new tiles on the wall, but it will all be in vain if you don't keep them clean while you're working. Get set up to do a really neat job before you start opening any containers of adhesive or grout.

TOOLS REQUIRED

- **3 buckets or equivalent containers**
- **At least 10 soft cloths**
- **Warm water**

BUYING GROUT

You can buy grout and adhesive separately, or you can get a large tub of dual-purpose ready-mixed grout and adhesive. This means that you don't have to mix it in small batches as you would for grout alone. I usually allow one medium-sized tub for one box of standard-sized tiles.

You might want to consider buying a coloured grout. Choosing the colour is a matter of taste. It can lift the plainest tiles, especially floor tiles, and if you have dark tiles then dark grout looks cleaner. The white tile, red grout era is over – it may pop up again, but don't ever use coloured grout on porous tiles, and be careful with it, as it may stain. Make sure there are no drips or splats, and clean as you go.

1

Fill two buckets with warm water and one with the soft cloths. The cloths should be damp but not wet.

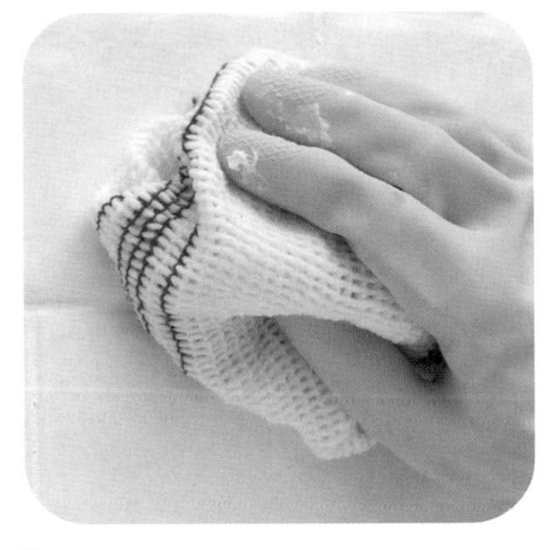

2

Use the cloths to immediately clean up any adhesive or grout that gets on the surface of the tiles or is spilled.

3

Throw the used cloth into the first bucket of water and give it a good rinse, getting rid of as much of the product as you can. Then put it into the clean water in the next bucket – can you see the plot now? – and leave it there. If there's still more to clean up, or for the next spillage, start again with a fresh cloth and repeat the process.

4

When you run out of cloths, rinse them through, squeeze to get rid of excess water and put back into the empty bucket. The first bucket will have sludge in the bottom (even more if you can leave it overnight) – so **tip out the water, scrape out the sludge** and dispose of it in the bin before refilling the bucket with clean warm water.

How to apply grout

Mix your grout in small batches, unless you're using dual-purpose grout and adhesive from one of those ready-mixed tubs. Do around 1 sq m (1 sq yd) at a time, and give yourself the chance to get that right and clean the area thoroughly before moving onto the next section. Now you'll need to use the cloths and buckets of water you've prepared even more than when you were applying the tiles.

TOOLS REQUIRED

- **Grout**
- **Grout float**
- **Multi-purpose cleaning cloths**
- **3 buckets or equivalent containers**
- **Grout protector – this is a clear substance that seals the grout, making it waterproof**
- **Tiny brush the size of a make-up brush or a child's paintbrush**
- **Stiff drink for the survivors**

1

Apply the grout using the grout float, pushing the grout into the holes and away from the surface of the tiles again and again. Grout is the stuff that's going to make your tiles totally waterproof, so you need to pay attention to every crack and space.

2

When you feel like your arm is about to fall off, take your damp cloths and remove excess grout from the face of the tiles (see page 123). **Run the tip of your index finger down the joints to flatten the grout,** then clean your finger and do it again until the grout starts to disappear into the crack and there are no more holes.

3

Polish the surface of the tiles with the clean flat of your hand – I've never found anything as good as a hand for polishing tiles, your skin will pick up every last piece of grout. If any adhesive remains on the surface, remove it with the piece of plastic.

4

Now everything is shiny and clean so leave it for 24 hours and then **apply a grout protector. Paint it on with the tiny brush** and polish it off with a dry cloth. It takes time, but stick with it – you should then have 15–20 years problem-free. Now for that drink!

How to apply silicone sealant

The best type of silicone sealant includes an antifungicide and is marked on the tube that it can be used for baths, basins and sanitary ware. It smells nasty but it's a blessing – it will help you to avoid all the problems with spotty silicone that are explained on page 122.

TOOLS REQUIRED

- **Silicone sealant of the right colour**
- **Sealant carrier or gun**
- **Baby wipes**
- **Clear shampoo or washing-up liquid**
- **Paint scraper**
- **Soft lint-free cloth**

1

Insert the tube of silicone into the gun and have the baby wipes and shampoo or washing-up liquid to hand. **Squeeze the silicone into the crack beneath the tiles along the length of the bath or sink.** Apply even pressure with the gun and keep to a steady pace.

2

If it's a very deep crack, fill it horizontally along the bath and flatten it with the paint scraper. This layer is called 'flat fill'. Smooth the sealant as soon as you can as the silicone will start to go tacky quite quickly. You'll make a mess if you start pulling it around at that stage. Smoothing is easiest if you wet the scraper with shampoo or diluted washing-up liquid.

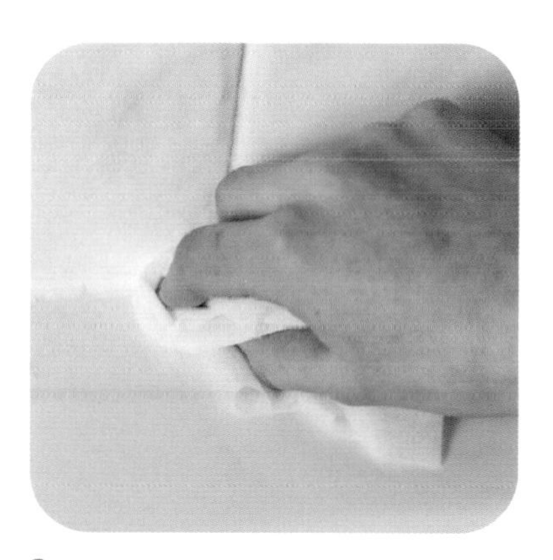

3

If you make a mess, clean it up with the baby wipes, and use them to keep your hands clean too. Once you've applied the flat fill and it's all clean and tidy, leave it for 24 hours to set. Wash the area and pat dry with the soft cloth. For the ultimate seal, run a further thin line of silicone just bigger than a string of spaghetti on top of the original silicone.

4

Dip a finger in shampoo or diluted washing-up liquid and smooth the silicone very lightly, making that familiar concave shape. Leave for 24 hours and rinse. If you didn't get the silicone right first time, you can still add a small amount to make it perfect, smoothing it as before.

CHAPTER FIVE

Plaster it

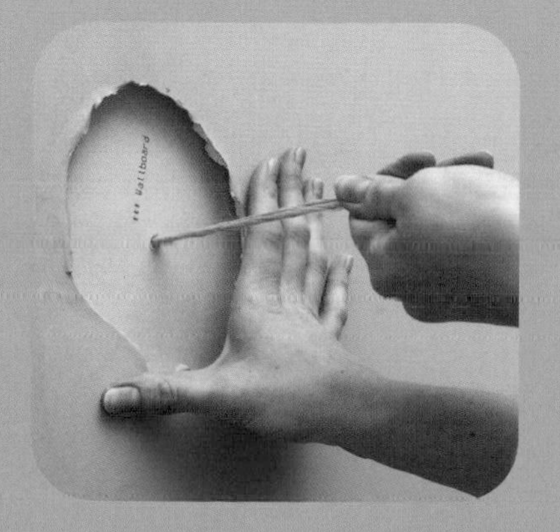

Filling cracks

The main things we'll look at in this chapter are the various ways in which you can repair damage to your walls such as cracks, holes and stains. You should always take cracks in your walls seriously, because occasionally they can be a sign of larger structural problems. Nevertheless, most cracks are harmless and can be rectified much more easily than you think. With the right tools and a few tips, you can work wonders with the cracks and holes in your walls and make them look like new again. In this chapter I look at how to tell the difference between a dangerous crack and a harmless one, and we'll learn how to do what my dad taught me, and I say it every day: 'Let's turn a crack into a smile.'

Looking for problems

Plaster always cracks while it's settling during the months after it's been laid, and even after 200 years houses will sigh a little, move a little and sag a little. Over the decades, the climate changes and the water table shifts, making the clay lose or gain moisture. Timber door frames suddenly decide to shrink, the beams under your floor and in your ceilings twist in hot summers, and yet unless the crack is more than 1.2cm (½in) or is on the outside of the wall, you don't need to worry too much.

GET IN A PROFESSIONAL

If you have a big area to plaster, get in a professional and watch how they do it – but do make sure you get a recommendation first. A really experienced plasterer has been at it for years, day after day after day, and he can do it with his eyes shut.

If you do find a crack on the outside of a wall and it matches one on the inside, that's when you need to take serious action.

> Call a surveyor or architect who deals with this kind of problem. They'll normally attach monitoring equipment to the outside of the building to measure how rapidly the crack is growing.

> The great thing about these professionals is that they should be able to assess what the problem is and where it's coming from in an instant, and can also tell you how to rectify it.

> Don't waste time once you know what to do – if you don't act, you could come home one day to see the back of your house all over the garden.

Some cracks, however, are completely predictable. Let's suppose that you had a wall newly plastered a while back. The builders said not to decorate for about six months until the plaster had settled, so you've done as they said and have waited **while a large crack has appeared across the wall.** For a while it just got bigger, but now the six months is up and it's stopped. It's time to stop living with that funny pink colour and pretending that it's organic and natural – the sooner you've filled in the crack and painted the wall so that it looks like the rest of the room the better. The same applies to all cracks that are 1.2cm (½in) or smaller – filling them is a simple job that you can do every time you decorate.

Products for filling

There are many products for filling cracks, and they're being researched all the time so that we can have fillers that are easier to use, longer lasting, sag-proof (wish I was), even stretchable and able to withstand a little banging and shaking.

> **No-sanding filler:** I use this for most cracks in plaster. It's as light as a feather, and if it's standing out or a bit wobbly, you can easily sand it down. As soon as you start using this filler you'll realise its potential – it's FAB stuff. The supermarket brands are a little cheaper and just as effective. Each filler will have a description of what it's for and ONLY what it's for, so read this carefully – if the packaging doesn't mention the purpose you've got in mind, put it back and keep looking. If in doubt, ask someone, because if it's worth filling, it's worth filling properly, and that's only possible with the right filler. If you've been through every tube and tub and packet of filler in the superstore and you still can't find the right stuff for the job you're going to do, make a call to the manufacturers – they usually have a freephone helpline, which is an invaluable service.

> **Stretchable filler:** You'll need this around doors and windows so that it will move with the door or window. Have you ever slammed a door – let's rephrase that, you would never slam a door – have you ever had a door slam in the wind, making the plaster pop out from around the edge? That means the wrong filler has been used. The stretchy stuff comes in a big tube that you apply with a gun, and for the inside of the building it's usually water based so that you can spread it with a wet finger or a wet continental filling knife. On the outside of doors and windows you need a silicone seal first and then a concrete or mortar filler.

Avoid products you have to mix yourself. They usually set rock solid before you've even finished mixing them, or go crumbly because they've gone past their sell-by date. Whatever type you get, read the instructions, and if you've got a small amount left over, get rid of it – it will only go damp overnight.

TROUBLESHOOTING: RAKING OUT CRACKS

One thing to understand about a crack is that while to you it may look like a miniature crevasse, if you were to look at a cross section on a microscopic slide, you'd instantly see that it's actually more like a mountain split in two! This mistake is behind a lot of problems with filling cracks – if you just fill it in, the filling will stand out like a ridge and look like every other badly filled crack. This is where most of us would throw in the towel and say that it just doesn't work.

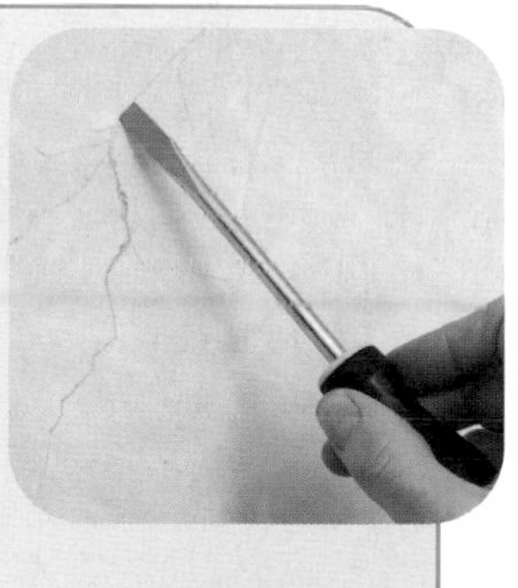

Instead, **start by raking all the flaky bits out of the crack using a blunt chisel or an old screwdriver.** By their very nature, cracks have edges that aren't stable, and so you'll never fill it effectively unless you make the crack wider. Rub the tool you've chosen up and down the crack until you've got rid of all the loose debris.

Then sand down the plaster until it is level with the rest of the wall and take off the rough bits at the edges. Only then are you ready to fill the crack.

Plastering know-how

Back in the old days we started out with wattle and daub, and then we moved on to lime-based plaster with cow hair and horse hair holding it together, sometimes even human hair. Nowadays we have plaster and plasterboard. Plastering is an art, and it's something that you need to develop a feel for.

How to patch plaster

Patching plaster into holes isn't a difficult job, but it is important to stick to a few rules. It's made easier by the modern products on the market – one of the best being ready-made plaster patch, sold in a big tub. It's already mixed, and just needs a stir and, for beginners, perhaps half a cup of water added to the tub, to make it easier to spread.

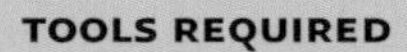

TOOLS REQUIRED

- **PVA diluted with water in equal parts**
- **Paintbrush**
- **Tub of plaster patch**
- **Plasterer's trowel**
- **Tub of plaster skim for finishing**
- **Plaster spreader – this will usually come inside the tub of skim or continental filling knife**
- **Sandpaper**

1

Clean any loose bits of plaster out of the hole (see raking out cracks, page 129). If it can come out easily, it should come out now – you won't get any Brownie points for leaving it there. **Paint the hole with the diluted PVA and leave it to dry completely.** Without this, the plaster will not stick.

2

Stir the tub of plaster patch with a filling knife to a creamy consistency. **Then spoon some onto your trowel,** push the plaster into the hole and slide the trowel away. Don't over fill the hole and don't try to smooth it out – this is the next part of the process. Let the plaster dry.

3

Spread the skim into the hole and smooth it with the spreader. When the skim is dry, sand it down and give it another coat of diluted PVA to prepare it for paint or wallpaper.

TOP TIP: DON'T OVERFILL

Please resist the temptation to over fill. If you have a deep hole, make sure you under fill the first time. Wait until it's dried and then fill again. A continental filling knife is the perfect tool for a smooth finish as it covers the hole completely. You can always sand it down when it's dried.

How to put up plasterboard

Should you need to re-plaster a whole wall, the other option is to use plasterboard. This is wonderfully straightforward, and as long as you take care with the spirit level, it should give perfect results. The small gap between the bricks and the plasterboard even gives you a bit of extra insulation. However, you should never put up a shower on a wall lined with plasterboard, as water can get into the gap and do no end of damage.

The really fun bit is getting all the old plaster off the wall. You could have a plaster-stripping party – it's even better than a wallpaper-stripping party, because you get to let out more aggression. Use hammers, blunt chisels, bolsters, hands, husbands' heads – the fun is endless. Now that's over and done with, paint the whole area with PVA.

TOOLS REQUIRED

- **Tools for getting off the plaster**
- **PVA**
- **Paintbrush**
- **Gypsum adhesive**
- **Large spirit level**
- **Lightweight no-sanding filler**
- **Continental filling knife**
- **Plasterboard cut to the right size**

1
Fix the plasterboard to the wall using the 'dob splat' technique: **place six or eight dobs of gypsum adhesive in strategic points on the wall.**

2
Then splat the plasterboard against them.

3
Using the spirit level, make sure the board is level horizontally and vertically. **Gentle taps will knock it into place.**

4
Fill any joins and cracks with lightweight filler, and sand down the join. Paint the plaster board with PVA. Let it dry, and the wall is now ready for painting or papering. No sweat!

TOP TIP: INSULATION

My office faces due north and is right on an exposed corner. It used to be really cold, even with the heating on, so I backed pieces of plaster board with foil and fixed them to the wall. Now I'm snug as a bug.

Repairing holes in plasterboard

An accidental slip in a roof space can result all too easily in a hole being made in the ceiling. Worry not – it might look unsightly, but it is quite simple to overcome. The same goes for a hole in the wall.

How to repair a hole in a plasterboard wall

If you have made a hole in a plasterboard wall, you won't be able to get behind it to attach a new piece of plasterboard. Instead, you can achieve the same effect using two pieces of wood and a piece of string: simply read on...

TOOLS REQUIRED

- > **2 pieces plasterboard, one the size of the hole, the other 2.5cm (1in) wider**
- > **Stanley knife**
- > **Hammer and nail**
- > **Piece of wood that's wider than the hole**
- > **Piece of string, doubled up**
- > **Chopstick or similar piece of batten (you won't be able to use it again)**
- > **Big tube of high-performance multi-purpose gap-filling adhesive**
- > **Lightweight no-sanding filler**
- > **Plasterer's trowel**

1
Take the bigger piece of plasterboard and hammer a hole in the centre with a nail. Remove the nail and hammer a same-sized hole in the piece of wood. Push the string loop through the hole in the plasterboard and **thread the chopstick through the loop.** Pull the string tight.

2
Apply adhesive on the flat side of the plasterboard and only where it will overlap the hole. Keeping hold of the string, **turn the plasterboard away from you by 45 degrees and slide it through the hole.**

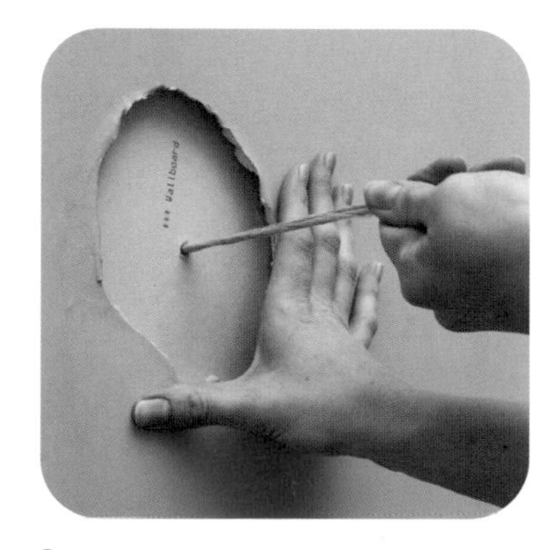

3
Then turn it back again so the adhesive is facing you, **and pull the string so the piece of plasterboard is hard against the back of the plasterboard wall.**

4
Thread the wood onto the string and **knot the string** so the wood and plasterboard are tightly sandwiching the wall.

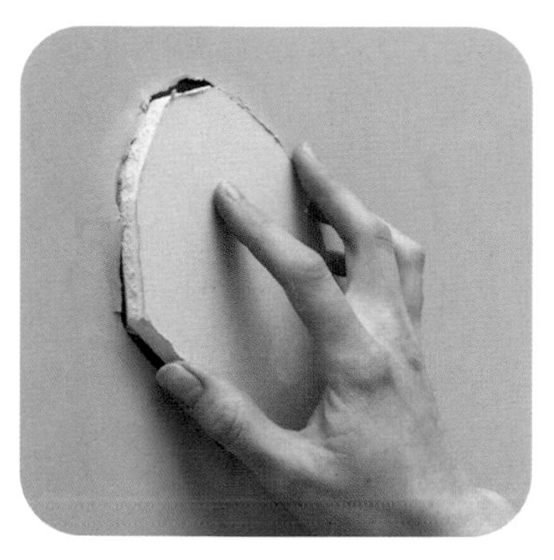

5

Wait for the adhesive to dry. Undo the knot, remove the piece of wood, and push the string into the hole. The chopstick securing it will fall out of the loop into the wall cavity. You can either pull the string out of the hole or push it right through. Take the smaller piece of plasterboard and spread adhesive over the back and onto the edges. **Glue it onto the plasterboard patch.**

6

Fill around the edges with lightweight filler and leave to dry. **With a plasterer's trowel, spread filler thinly across the whole area**. It will set beautifully, and any ridges or bumps can be sanded out. Paint the wall (see page 153) and be proud of yourself.

How to repair a hole in a plasterboard ceiling

Someone has put their foot through the ceiling making a good sized hole - don't panic! It may look frightening, but it's easy to repair.

TOOLS REQUIRED

- **Sheet of plasterboard, at least twice the size of the hole**
- **Stanley knife**
- **Big tube of high-performance multi-purpose gap-filling adhesive**
- **Lightweight no-sanding filler**
- **Plasterer's trowel**

1

Cut a piece of plasterboard so it's a bit bigger than the hole all the way round. Go back up into the loft with your piece of plasterboard and your adhesive, and **stick the new piece of plasterboard over the hole and leave it to dry.** Back in the room below, cut a second piece of plasterboard as close as possible to the shape and size of the hole and glue it to the first piece above before leaving it to dry.

2

Fill around the edges with lightweight filler and leave this to dry. **Use a plasterer's trowel to spread filler in a thin coat across the whole of the area**.

3

Once the thin coat of filler has dried, **sand it down** and then paint the ceiling (see page 152).

PART THREE

THE FINISHING TOUCHES

CHAPTER ONE

Decorate it

Planning and preparation

Auntie Hilda is coming down from Bonnie Scotland for the Easter holidays, and has just phoned to say that she's going to bring some new curtains to brighten up her room. It is looking a bit sad, and I felt so ashamed when she said it that I blurted out, 'Oh, you don't have to worry about that, Auntie! It's already been redecorated and we've just bought new curtains, so please don't drag anything down with you.' (Of course, Auntie Hilda never drags anything. She knows the art of being a lady, and there is always a nice young man around somewhere who can help her with her luggage.)

Now that she's off the phone, I'm left thinking about the horror that is to come, because I've been putting off tackling the dreaded woodchip wallpaper in the spare room for ten years or more. But though decorating properly can feel like a terrible slog at times, there are a few tricks to help make it quite a bit easier, and it's always worth it when you've finished.

Decorating is about allowing yourself the right amount of time to Do It Properly – if you try to rush it, you'll leave the room looking as if it still needs to be decorated, whereas if you take your time, you may never need to work on it again apart from a regular wash and brush up.

Dad always said that there is a correct sequence for every job, and it's just a matter of working out in advance what it is. Once you've done a few decorating jobs, you'll be able to work it out for yourself, but to begin with here is an easy checklist (see right) to lead you through it, which you can adapt to the job you're doing, depending on what needs to be decorated.

This may seem like a long list, but you'll see that some parts only take a short time. Now let's go into more detail about the individual parts of the job.

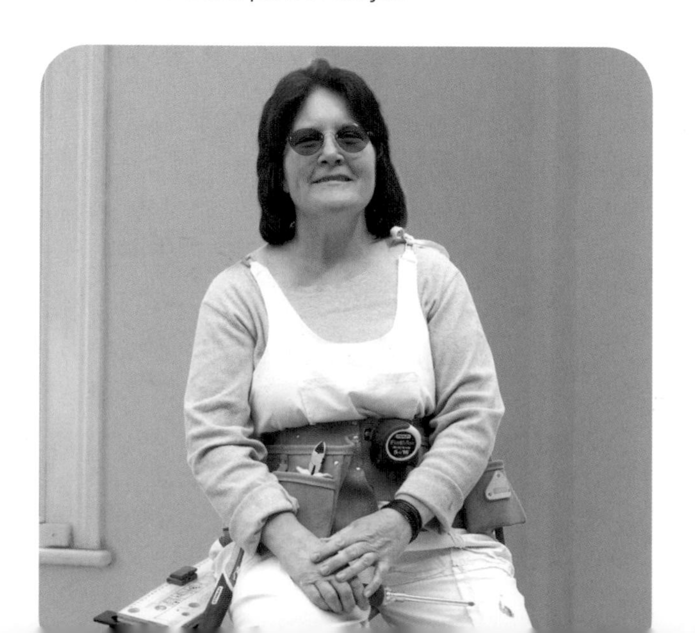

PLANNING CHECKLIST

1. **Clear out and cover up (see page 140)**
2. **Strip the paint and wallpaper (see pages 142–7)**
3. **Fill gaps and patch the plaster (see pages 128–31)**
4. **Wash the skirting boards, frames and other woodwork (see page 192)**
5. **Sand the woodwork, and vacuum up the dust**
6. **Paint the ceiling (see page 152)**
7. **Undercoat windows and doors (see page 154)**
8. **Hang lining and wallpaper (see page 156–9)**
9. **Paint the walls (see page 153)**
10. **Top coat windows and doors (see page 153)**
11. **Vacuum up any debris and paint the woodwork**
12. **Touch up any paint that isn't quite perfect**
13. **Replace sockets, switches, pictures and furniture**

Stripping paint and paper

The quality of your finished surface depends on how well you do the stripping. So take your time as every speck you miss will stick out like a sore thumb in your finish. It is especially important that once you've stripped everything back to the bare surface you then sand the surface thoroughly, starting with the coarsest grade of paper and working through to the finest. The finish will then be silky smooth.

The kiss of life

I recently purchased a beautiful little reproduction table from a car boot sale. It might have been worth something at some time, but it had been broken, scratched, chipped and banged. I immediately saw it in another colour with a paint finish, and after checking with an antique dealer friend that it would never be valuable, I painted it a very pale cream with touches of blue, and it's now in pride of place in my very Swedish bedroom. One of my favourite sayings is, 'There's nothing broke that can't be fixed,' and so if it ain't broke, we won't tinker, but if it is, we'll revive it, give old things the kiss of life, prepare them for another life.

HOT GUN PRECAUTIONS

Paint is not so hard to dispatch these days. There are various chemicals on the market, but they're best avoided. What you really need for stripping paint is a hot gun. It's a bit like a hairdryer but much hotter.

Wear a charcoal face mask, which will deal with the fumes, and if you're stripping something mobile, such as a piece of furniture, take it outside to do if you can. Otherwise, open all the windows, relocate the cat, the dog and the budgie, and take Auntie Hilda with her glass of sherry to another room. Have a big piece of scrap wood ready to rest the gun on when you aren't using it - most hot guns do have stands, but they invariably get knocked over. The gun will usually come with lots of scrapers, some to hold in your hand and others that attach to the end of the gun. These work very well.

I hope you never need this one, but please keep a first aid kit for burns with you whenever you use a hot gun, a soldering iron or a blowtorch.

The second most dangerous thing about using a hot gun, after burning yourself, is shattering a pane of glass with the heat. If you're working anywhere near glass, use a low heat and be very careful.

SAFETY FIRST

Any paint that was bought before 1960 might have lead in it, and using a hot gun on paint containing lead is very dangerous. So if your house dates from before then, be safe rather than sorry and buy a lead testing kit from a paint merchant. If the test is positive and shows that the paint does contain lead, use a prescribed chemical stripper instead. If it's negative, go ahead and use the gun.

Stripping paint off metal

> **A hot gun will remove the years of paint from that beautiful metal Victorian fireplace in the bedroom** – you can actually afford to burn the paint off it, because if the chimney is open, the fumes will go straight up it – but beware of the lead content (see Safety First, left).

> I never cease to be amazed by the delicacy of the designs on these fireplaces. A fireplace looks quite good with masses of paint on it, but once you've removed the paint and **have given it a good scrub with a wire brush,** it can look just amazing.

> **Finish it off with the wonderful polish you can get for black grates.** The more you polish the fire surround, the better the metal will look.

TOP TIP: DON'T BURN

If you're stripping paint close to wallpaper, hold a piece of fairly thick metal between it and the gun while you're working, to avoid setting fire to the wallpaper.

How to remove paint from wood

Always put a hot gun on a low setting so it doesn't burn the wood, and start on a piece that won't be in full view so that if you do scorch it, no one will see, and you'll have a chance to develop your own method of stripping.

Let's take stripping paint from a balustrade as an example. It would be easy to take one look at it and decide that the paint will have to stay there forever. But it isn't that difficult a job. Just remember all those lovely tools that came with the hot gun – the ones you looked at and thought, 'What the heck are they for?' – well, now's your chance to find out! Every tool will have a use, just experiment with them. The banister may look really beautiful when it's stripped. It is almost always made of hardwood, and if you can get all the paint off, you could then sand and varnish it.

TOOLS REQUIRED

- **Goggles and mask**
- **Protective gloves**
- **Hot gun plus all the tools**
- **A 15cm (6in) scraper – this will normally come with the hot gun, and has a range of curves and edges plus a pointed corner for the really awkward bits**
- **Masking tape**
- **Loads of dust sheets**
- **Newspaper**
- **Wooden board for resting the hot gun**

1

Start at the top of the stairs and work down carefully. **Stick masking tape to the edges of the areas you don't want stripped** and cover the edges of your floor below the bottom stair so that the falling melted paint won't burn or stick to anything.

2

You can only strip one long section of a baluster at a time but keep going and you'll be surprised at how quickly the paint disappears. Use the various tools to help you get the paint out of the nooks and crannies of the mouldings in the spindles.

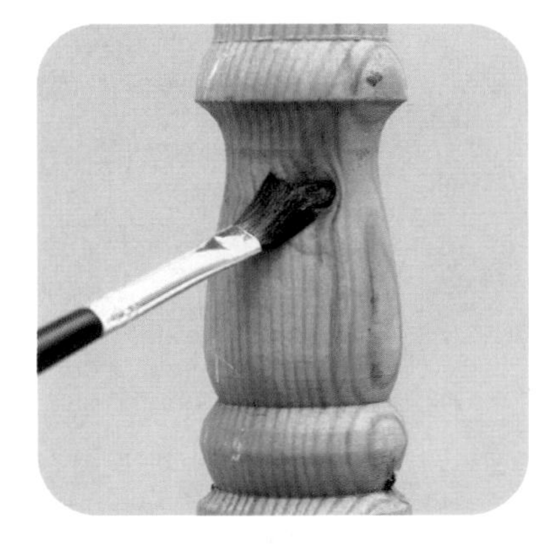

3

Under the paint you may find knots, staples, nails and all sorts of other things that need dealing with. Pull out all the nails and staples (filling the holes if necessary) and **paint the knots with knotting compound** (see page 153). Even when wood is 50 or 60 years old, it can still discolour paint with sap from the knots if you don't seal them.

TOP TIP: CLEAR UP AS YOU GO

Scrape the bits of melted paint into an old tin can and clean the edge of your scraper on it too.

STRIPPING CHEMICALS

If you have very intricate carving on the balustrade and you really can't get rid of the paint with the hot gun, **then use a stripping chemical**, but be very careful. The container will give you full instructions and if you're in doubt, ring the freephone number given. After you've finished with the chemical, clean and neutralise the area as directed by the instructions. This will sometimes be done with a solution supplied with the stripping chemical, and sometimes with vinegar. Never use the chemical in the same session as the hot gun and vice versa, and make sure you are in a well-ventilated room.

Finishing a stripped banister

Now that you have got rid of the old paint, you can wax, varnish or paint the banister.

> **Waxing:** If you want to wax the banister, sand it down until you have a surface like satin. Clean with a tack cloth and then use a soft cloth to rub the wax evenly up and down the banister. Keep buffing with a clean soft cloth. You'll need to do this once a month for at least six months to build up a layer of wax and the most wonderful lustre.

> **Varnishing:** Again, sand, sand and sand. Use your tack cloth to get every minute speck of dust from the surface, then dilute one part varnish with either one part water or one part paint thinner, depending on the instructions on the tin. This weak solution of varnish will penetrate the wood, making a sound start. Then, using the finest sandpaper you can buy, gently sand down the dry surface and apply a coat of varnish straight out of the tin. When it's dry, sand down again and apply a third coat. By the time this dries you should have a surface like satin, as smooth as a baby's big toe.

> **Painting:** Proceed as with varnishing, perhaps applying a second coat of knotting compound after you've sanded the first time to be extra sure. Use your tack cloth to clean up and apply a very good primer followed by an undercoat and top coat.

REPLACING BROKEN SPINDLES ON A BALUSTRADE

Many timber yards have a very good supply of different spindles in stock, and if yours isn't available, it may have a service that will create a new spindle if you give them an old one, or even just a drawing and the measurements. Once you have your lovely new spindles it is time to work out how the old ones were fitted in the first place. Fortunately, some just slip into the top hole once you've got them into the bottom one. Put some fairly thick mastic in the holes before inserting the spindle and clean up any excess before taping the new spindle with masking tape to its neighbours so that it won't slip out while it dries.

How to strip wallpaper

Whatever type of wallpaper you are sripping, follow these steps and it will just fall off. It is especially important to take in Step 1 if it's the dreaded woodchip or anaglypta being stripped. Getting the stuff off the wall doesn't have to be a battle.

Last year, during the hottest weeks of the summer, we stripped the paper from a wall in a 1950s' council flat. There were four layers of paper and two of these had been painted with oil-based paint. While we were working on it, the client was horrified by what was involved. It was the first time I've resorted to having a shandy every lunchtime, but we did it and the photos are in my portfolio. If you saw the job you'd say, 'Nice finish' and nothing more, but the before and after photos tell a different story.

TOOLS REQUIRED

- **Face mask**
- **Electric hand sander**
- **Perforator**
- **2 dust sheets, 1 of which is cut down to measure 1.25 x 1.25m (4 x 4ft)**
- **Spray bottle**
- **Washing-up liquid**
- **Heavy-duty adhesive tape**
- **Wallpaper steamer**
- **Paper stripping knife**

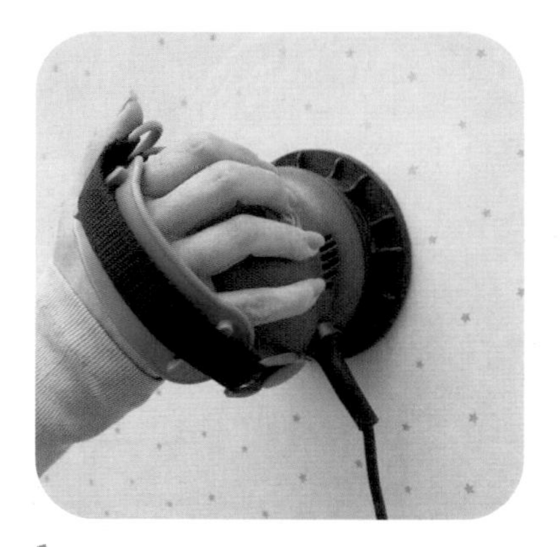

1

Put on the face mask **and go over the wall with the hand sander** – this breaks the painted surface and makes it possible for the steam to penetrate. It'll make loads of dust and mess, so make sure your furniture is protected. If you're removing woodchip, the bits of wood within the paper will start to come off first. You may find there is another layer of wallpaper under the first one and perhaps another under that, but keep going – the more holes you make, the easier it will get.

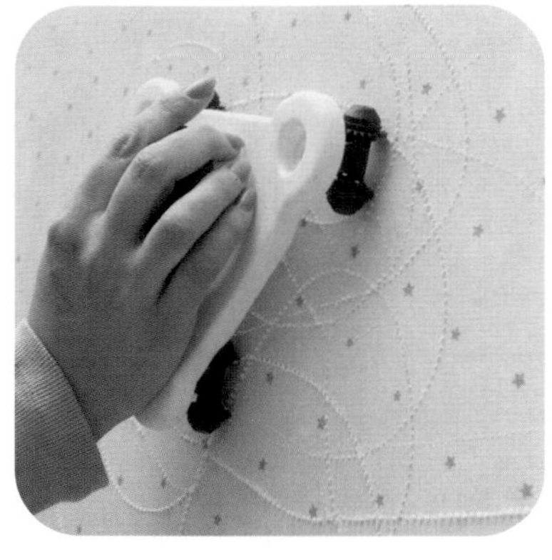

2

Next take the perforator. This is a lovely tool that you can move over the wall in circles. It makes perforations in the paper so that the water and steam will get through.

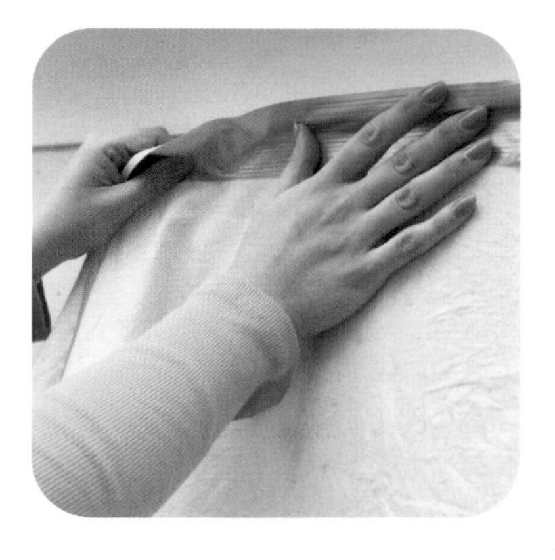

3

Remembering to leave the top edge dry so that the adhesive tape will stick to it, soak the small dust sheet in water until it is wet but not dripping. Fill the spray bottle with water and a drop of washing-up liquid – this will help the water to stick to the wall. Spray the wall all over and **use the tape to fasten the dust sheet to the top of the wall.** Leave it for 20 minutes and then take down the dust sheet and watch the paper peel itself off the wall!

SAFETY FIRST

When you're stripping with water and steam:
*** DON'T spray around light switches**
*** DON'T let water run down the wall into sockets**
*** DON'T spray near light fittings on the wall**
*** DON'T spray near light fittings on the ceiling**

If you think you're going to get in a mess, cover plugs and switches with cling film and masking tape. Roll a dust sheet into a big sausage and push it against the skirting board so that it'll absorb any running water.

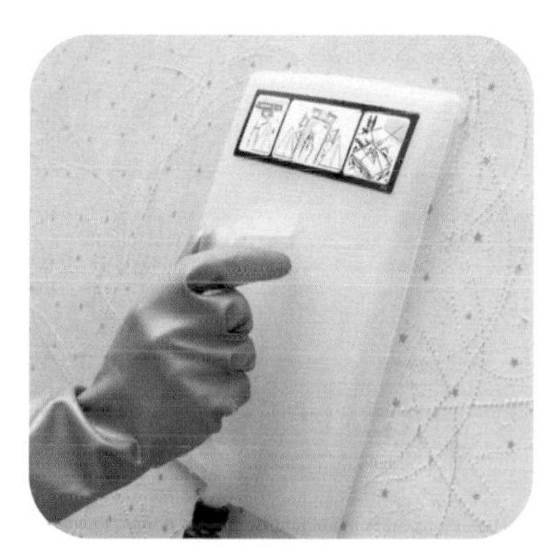

4
Not all of the paper will have come away, so **hold the wallpaper steamer against the paper** to get steam into those perforations, and then scrape away with the stripping knife at whatever's left. Don't hold the steamer to a plaster or bare wall for too long, or you'll blow the plaster and give yourself another job to do.

5
Using the stripping knife, continue until every scrap of paper is off – it's a labour of love. When you think you've finished, wash the wall – you'll discover that you've missed a lot. I'm so glad it's easier than this to get new paper up (see pages 156–9), but if you get all the old stuff off and get it all clean, the new paper will go on like a dream and the finish will be perfect.

SAFETY FIRST

Keep buckets of water handy for cleaning your scraping tools – you can only work efficiently with clean tools. But if you're using a steamer, keep the buckets out of the room while it's switched on.

For the steamer, use a socket in another room on a different circuit and switch off the electricity in the room you're working in.

Preparing different surfaces

Last year I was quoted £2,500 for a spray job on my camper van. I'd done the filling on all the bodywork and I didn't want to pay that much for what I considered to be the finishing touch. So I went to a car paint shop, picked their brains and went home with the proper paint and a tiny roller – and it worked! As long as you do the research and ask lots of questions, you can literally paint anything. The prep work is the important thing, especially a good clean down and then a thorough sanding.

A wall stripped of paper or paint

> Once you've stripped away all the paper, paint and debris from a wall, there's a simple knack to preparing it for painting and this is: fill and paint and fill.

> First, thoroughly smooth the wall with sandpaper. If there are cracks and holes that need filling, use the plaster skim that you may have used to finish off a patching job (see page 130) or a pre-prepared one **to skim over the wall.** Either use the plastic spreader that comes in the same tub to spread it in a thin layer, or use a continental flexible filling knife.

> Once it's dried, give it a little sand with very fine sandpaper and **apply your first coat of emulsion**. This will enable you to see where any remaining marks are, so that you can go over the wall with the no-sanding filler once more using a continental filling knife.

> If the wall still isn't perfect, continue to repeat the same process until you're really happy that it's smooth. Now it's ready for that final, carefully chosen, coat of paint.

A wall covered with old paper or paint

> The surface needs to be free from dust, grease, dirt and flaky bits.

> Take out all the nails and picture hooks, even if the pictures are going to be replaced in the same place.

> Wash the surface with sugar soap and rinse. Let this dry completely and then fill with no-sanding filler, as explained on page 129.

> Leave to dry and then **go over the filler with very fine sandpaper until it's flush with the wall**. If there are loose bits of paper, stick them back down or tear out gently and fill, rubbing down after the filler is dry.

Don't forget the rule when decorating plaster: PVA before filling, PVA before paint, PVA before wallpaper.

A wall covered with new plaster

- **First you'll need to sand it to get off the loose bits,** and then fill any holes with no-sanding filler.
- **Next, prepare it by painting it with a solution of one part PVA to three parts water**. It's a bit messy putting it on, but it stops the plaster sucking up the paint and making it streaky.
- If you don't use PVA, the paint will come off the next time you paint it and make a horrible mess.

TOP TIP: WALLPAPER JOINS

If you have overlaps or bad joins between strips of wallpaper that you're going to paint over, get rid of the excess with fine sandpaper until the wall is flat - this is easier than it sounds. Make sure you load your roller fully with emulsion and no one will ever know that you made a bit of a mistake.

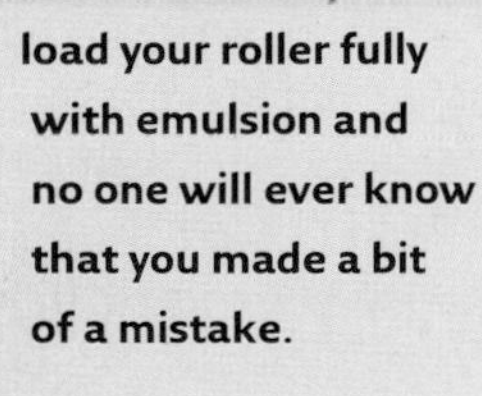

OUTSIDE SURFACES

Masonry: Always prepare masonry with an antifungal cleaner and a masonry primer. If your garden wall cracks a year after painting, it's because it should have received these two treatments.

Iron or steel: Clean the metal with a wire brush, sand off all the rust and then use a rust cure. This is a white liquid that will turn rust back into metal.

Paint the iron or steel with a metal primer, an undercoat and a topcoat - yes, including the rust cure, that's four coats in total I'm afraid, but it's worth it.

Painting

Painting walls is a nice simple job, but how good it will look in the end depends a lot on how well you do the 'cutting in'. This is the process of getting a good straight line of colour along the edges with a brush, whether they are at the top or bottom of the wall, or against a window or door frame. Do this part of the job before you start attacking the walls with the roller, and take your time – it will pay dividends. If your eyes start to hurt or you get tired, go and do something else and come back to it.

Paint choices

Almost any painting job will start with a primer or undercoat, or in many cases both. You then move on to the top coat, which uses either water- or oil-based paint.

> **Primers or undercoats** are for painting onto wood or metal and sealing every nook and cranny. In some circumstances, such as skirting boards and door and window frames, this will be followed up with an undercoat before two topcoats are applied. Plaster also needs a primer, but this is normal PVA rather than paint. Again, this is followed up with an undercoat and one or more topcoats. Deep colours will need darker undercoats than pale colours, and it will usually say on the tin what the correct undercoat is for that colour.

> **Water-based paints** include emulsions for walls, and also acrylics. They have almost no odour, dry quickly and are easy to wash off brushes and rollers with water alone – most of them are really eco-friendly.

> **Oil-based paints** include the gloss paints that are normally used for woodwork within the house. These are a bit smelly, take a long time to dry between coats, and can only be removed with specialist brush-cleaning fluid, but they do have a very hard surface when they're dry.

Whatever type of surface you're painting, do look through all the different types of paint to check whether there's one specifically designed for that purpose – there are so many on the market. For more information, see page 206.

Storing paint

The most important thing when you've finished painting is to make sure that the lid is tightly on the can, and the way to ensure this is to **run wide masking tape around the rim as soon as you open it.** It will keep the rim clean so that you can just take off the masking tape when you've finished, and replace the lid as if the can had never been used before. All paint is best stored at even temperatures – big changes in temperature will change its chemistry, particularly if it freezes, and oil-based paint is flammable. Sheds aren't a great place for storing paint: they aren't warm enough in winter and they are also a fire risk. A garage is better, especially close to the wall adjoining the rest of the house.

TOP TIPS: PAINT QUANTITIES

To work out how much paint you need, multiply the height of each wall by its width to get an area in square metres (yards). There will be a guide on the can saying how much it will cover (see also page 206), though you should bear in mind that this will vary slightly depending on your painting style, and also on the manufacturer and colour of the paint .

Brushes and rollers

The DIY stores are full of clever gadgets for painting, but unless you're proficient you won't be able to use some of the quirkier things. Start out by investing in the basics, and spend a little time choosing the right brushes and rollers to suit the job you're doing (see page 34).

> **Keeping brushes out of the paint can:** My trick to stop brushes from vanishing into the paint pot is to **glue together two tiny plastic plant pots, base to base**, and put that in the can so that you have something to rest the brush on. Other options are jam jars or a thin glass tumbler, but the plant pot solution is the best as it displaces the least paint.

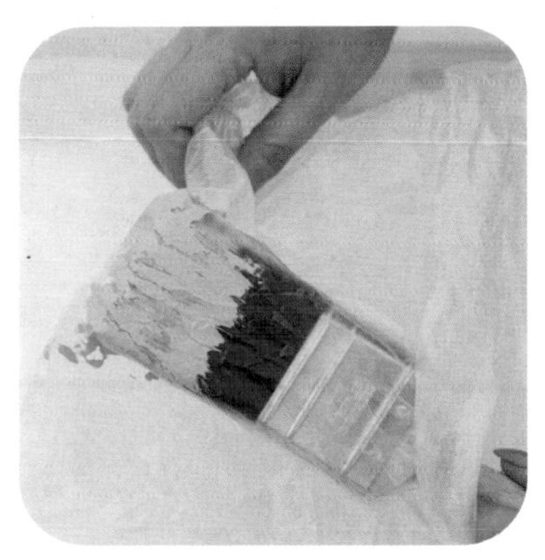

> **Storing brushes and rollers:** While you're working or taking breaks in the middle of a job, it's best to **place your brushes in a plastic bag to stop them from drying out**. With rollers, slide them off the handle and leave them in the can if the can is big enough, and if you need to stop overnight and put the lid back on, don't clean the roller – instead, load it fully and slide it into a plastic bag. This will save you time, energy, water and paint.

> **Cleaning rollers:** When you've finished a job using water-based emulsion, squeeze as much paint out of the roller as possible, take it off its handle and put it in the washing machine with your overall and the dust sheets. It's the only way to get them really clean.

TOP TIPS: BE PRACTICAL

Don't open a can or stir your paint with a screwdriver. You can buy a patent can opener and also a brilliant paint stirrer.

Rollers aren't just for emulsion paint – if you aren't good with brushes, you can use them to apply primers, undercoats and top coats on wood as well, even on banisters. You'll find that the long tufted fluffy rollers are best for spindles, as the tufts will get into the carved parts of the wood. Rollers also apply a thinner layer of paint, so three or four layers can be applied without a sign of build-up.

Next time you order a Chinese takeaway, save the chopsticks or ask for extras as they make fabulous paint stirrers, and use the takeaway plastic trays as mini roller trays (or for mixing little bits of filler).

Painting ceilings

> If the main reason for redecorating a room is that you want a fresh new look, the chances are that you won't need to paint the ceiling. But if it does need doing, make sure that you do it before you decorate anything else, so that you don't need to worry about drips – but remember to cover all your furniture with dust sheets. Load your brush or roller and use two or three coats of emulsion, allowing plenty of drying time for each one.

> If you're painting wallpaper, don't worry about getting the ceiling paint on the walls, because you'll paint over it in due course, and it's easier to get a neat line on the walls than the ceiling.

> Daylight doesn't shine directly onto ceilings, so it can be hard to see what you've done and what you haven't. **Try using a wonderful proprietary paint that starts out pink and dries white** – in that way you can see exactly where you've painted.

TOP TIP: PAINTING THE CEILING

Your first coat on a ceiling should go from the far wall to the door, the second coat should be in the opposite direction and then if you need a third coat, go back the original way again. In this way, you won't miss anything and the ceiling won't be patchy.

Painting walls

> When you paint a wall, **start by working from side to side** and **with your second coat, work up and down**. As well as creating an even finish, this also gives your arm a rest! Do one wall at a time to see how well the colour works, and always have your cutting-in brushes handy so that you can **cut in as you go**. That way, your eyes won't get tired and your arms will get a rest.

> Using a roller makes painting a wall an even quicker job. **Push the roller first up and down the wall,** and then from side to side.

Painting woodwork

> Treat all new wood with knotting compound before it's painted – this is an absolute must. Knots are the brown rings on the wood where the branches would have been anchored to the tree with extra-strong fibres. This is why you'll have had trouble if you ever tried to get a screw into a knot without drilling – the wood is just too strong, and it also oozes sticky yellow sap. It's the sap that causes problems if you don't treat the new wood with knotting compound. You'll be able to tell if there's woodwork in your house that hasn't had this treatment from the strange yellow or brown circles on the paint – you will find that they won't clean off with a wash. If this happens with wood in your home, you'll need to sand back down to the bare wood, apply the knotting compound, and then paint on a good wood primer, an undercoat and a topcoat.

> If you want to paint varnished wood, **you'll need to get the wax off first. Use methylated spirits to get back to the wood,** sand down any bumps and fill the dents with wood filler (see page 129). Then apply a coat of aluminium wood primer before you paint on an undercoat and finally the topcoat.

How to paint windows

Tackle these when you've finished decorating the rest of the room, unless you're painting the floor as well, in which case paint the windows and doors before the floor. I hate painting windows, and always get paint on the glass, even when I've covered the edges with masking tape, which is a must. If any windows are sticking or are cracked or faulty, deal with these problems before painting them.

TOOLS REQUIRED

- > **Sugar soap**
- > **Sandpaper**
- > **No-sanding filler**
- > **Tack cloth**
- > **Masking tape**
- > **White spirits**
- > **Three differently sized brushes ranging from 1.2mm (½in) to 5cm (2in)**
- > **Primer and top coat**

ORDER OF PAINTING

First paint the horizontal parts of the frame, starting with the cross-bars. Move onto the vertical pieces and then, finally, the frame, including the sills. You will need to paint sash windows in two stages to allow the frames to be reversed and so get to every part of the woodwork.

1
Remove the curtain rail and any nails and hooks. Wash paintwork with sugar soap and sand. **Fill any holes with no-sanding filler** and sand again.

2
Now sand some more – get it really smooth! Then **wipe the paintwork with a tack cloth** to get rid of all dust and bits.

3
Cover the edges of each pane of glass with masking tape. Then deal with any sticking, cracked or faulty windows (see page 196).

4
Start painting (initally with primer and then, when it's dry, with the top coat) **as close to the glass as possible** using either a 2.5cm (1in) brush or fitch. Paint about 1–2 mm (⅛in) into the glass: if there were any holes in the glazing bars this will fill them.

PAINTING DOORS

Take off all the door furniture or cover it in cling film and masking tape. Wash and sand and fill and sand, just as you did with the windows. Paint in the following order: the mouldings around the edge of the panels, the panels, top and bottom of the door, and then the rest.

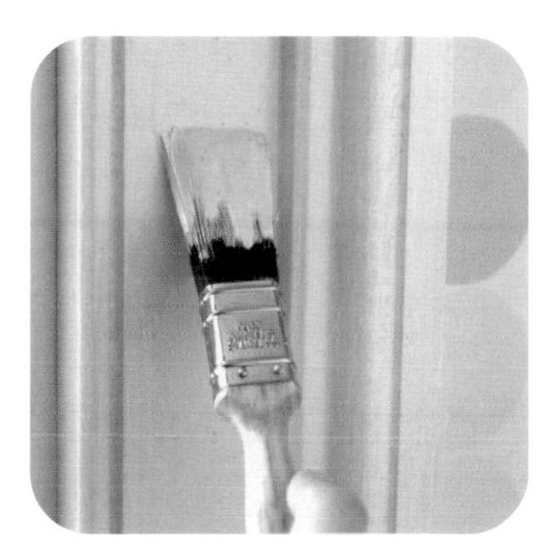

5

Always paint in the direction of the grain, using light strokes and spread it as far as you can. Use as little paint as possible for all parts that will be in contact with each other. With sticking windows, an overdose of paint is the most common culprit. Leave the window open until the paint is dry.

TOP TIP: KEEP YOUR BRUSH CLEAN

If your brush picks up dust and starts to deposit it in the paint, clean the brush by rubbing the bristles on the side of an empty tin, and always have a cloth soaked in white spirit handy in case of accidents. Be a good boy scout or girl guide and BE PREPARED!

Wallpapering

After you've done all the stripping and preparation, wash the walls and rub them down one more time to get rid of all the flaky bits – it's always amazing what's left. If you're papering straight onto new plaster, remember to paint it with PVA first.

How to hang wallpaper

Deciding where to start is important. If you're using patterned paper, it's best to start in the middle of a wall so that the pattern is symmetrical. With lining paper, you can start to the side of a window or door. If you're papering a wall with two windows, hang the first piece of paper between them and work from there, and if you're working around a chimney breast, start with the first sheet right in the middle. Right-handed people usually prefer to work from left to right, and left-handed from right to left.

ESTIMATING QUANTITIES OF WALLPAPER

To work out the quantity of wallpaper you need, draw a diagram of the walls you're going to cover. Label the diagram with the measurements of the height and width of each wall, adding 4–6cm (1½–2¼in) at the top and bottom and 2cm (¾in) at the corners.

Divide the width of the wall by the width of the paper, giving you the number of lengths you'll need.

Multiply this number by the height of the wall. For instance, if you need five lengths at 250cm (98in) each, you'll need 12.5m (13½yd) in total.

Find out how much there is in each roll and buy the appropriate number (see page 207 for more detailed guidelines).

TOOLS REQUIRED

- **Overall with big pockets**
- **2 large buckets**
- **Lots of clean rags**
- **Tape measure**
- **Pencil**
- **Spirit level**
- **Steel rule**
- **Pasting table (or protected big dining room table)**
- **Wallpaper**
- **Scissors**
- **Wallpaper paste**
- **Pasting brush**
- **Plastic sheets or bin bags**
- **Paperhanger's brush**
- **Stepladder**
- **Scalpel**
- **Decorator's caulk**

1

Fill a bucket with clean water and immerse the clean rags. Starting at your chosen point, **mark the wall close to the ceiling** where the first sheet will finish widthways.

2

At this point, use a spirit level and steel rule to **draw a vertical line the height of the wall.** Measure out as many full lengths of wallpaper as you need, allowing 4–6cm (1½–2¼in) excess at the top and bottom, and cut them on your pasting table using scissors.

3
Mix the wallpaper paste in the other bucket following the manufacturer's instructions. Put warm water in the bucket and pour in the paste flakes, **stirring with your hand or a kitchen whisk** until all are dissolved.

4
Using the pasting table and pasting brush, paste up three lengths of wallpaper, removing any excess with the damp rags. **Fold each end into the middle with the paste on the inside.**

5
Paste the area of the wall that will be covered by the first sheet to make it easier to slide the paper around on and to get the air bubbles out.

TOP TIPS: MAKE LIFE AS EASY AS POSSIBLE

Use a stepladder for any area that is above shoulder height. Think of the exercise as you climb up and down those steps. Make sure it's properly set up and see also my advice on pages 18–19.

Do use a proper paste brush – it's designed to pick up as much paste as possible. With the paper brush, I'd recommend one made of manmade fibres for beginners, because it's stronger than the bristle type and easier to use.

The reason for pasting three pieces of wallpaper at one time is that the paper needs time to soak up the paste and expand a little, which then makes it easier to hang. If you think it will take you some time to hang the first sheet and the others might dry out, wrap them in a plastic sheet or bin bag.

Pasted bits of paper stick to everything, and you'll probably end up slipping on one, so get rid of them straight away. I remember doing the splits getting off a ladder onto a bit of wet paper – yes, very funny, that's what everyone else thought as they laughed hysterically instead of helping me to get up. But it could have been very nasty, so don't follow my example.

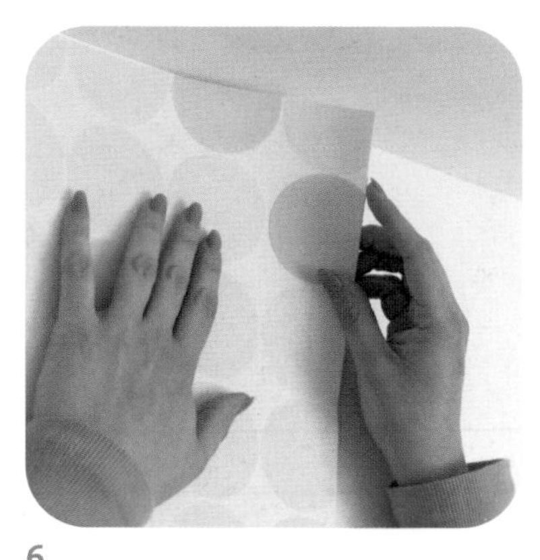

6

Now you'll need the big pockets in your overall. Put the clean wallpaper brush and a clean damp rag in them and put the scissors at the top of the stepladder, and take the first pasted and folded sheet to the top. Unpeel the top edge from the middle **and stick it to the wall close to the ceiling,** allowing the 4–6cm (1½–2¼in) excess for cutting. Allow the weight of the paper to guide itself to the line you've drawn, and work your way down. Unpeel the bottom half of the paper and gently guide that along the line too.

7

Once the paper is vertical, **use the wallpaper brush to brush it out fully onto the wall,** using soft strokes from the centre and top, down and out to the edges and bottom. Be gentle and pretend you've done it a million times before, and it will go on like a treat for you. If you get trapped air bubbles, wait for the adhesive to dry and then use a craft knife to make an incision through the paper. Apply paste and wipe the surface.

8

At the bottom, brush the paper to the wall and **use the back of your scissors to mark the line where the skirting meets the wall**. Peel the wallpaper away from the wall, and cut the paper along the indentation. Brush the paper back onto the wall. Repeat at the top, and then hang the next sheet in the same way. Before hanging the third sheet, paste and fold the next three. Clean off any paste that may be on the surface of the paper with the clean damp rags.

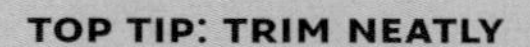

TOP TIP: TRIM NEATLY

Purpose-made wallpaper cutters are available for trimming edges. Roll the sharp wheel along the line to be trimmed and peel away the excess.

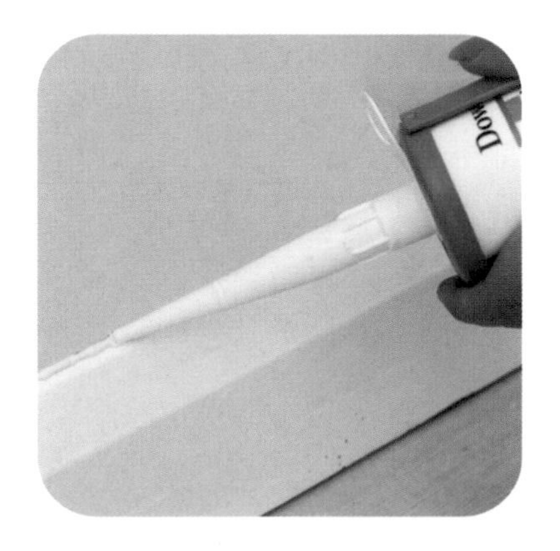

9

Leave the paper to dry for at least eight hours, or overnight. If you are hanging lining paper, **apply a line of decorator's caulk around the edge where the paper meets the skirting**, ceiling and door and window frames, and allow it to dry. This hides the edge – and also seals it from moisture. At the top of the paper, paint over the caulk with the same emulsion used for the ceiling.

TROUBLESHOOTING: WALLPAPERING AROUND TRICKY AREAS

Corner of a frame: Where you need to paper around the corner of a window, door or fireplace, measure the distances involved once you have hung the adjoining sheet, and cut the paper to the right size and shape before pasting, leaving the usual 4–6cm (1½–2¼in) excess at the edges, which you will cut to fit.

Light switches and sockets: When you get to a light switch or socket, turn off the electricity at the mains before hanging the sheet. Once you've hung the top part of the sheet, hold the paper away from the wall and **carefully push your scissors through it** in the middle of where the switch will go – don't try to cut it with a craft knife once it's already against the switch, or you'll ruin the switch as well as the paper. **Clip a cross in the paper** to allow the switch to show, and mark out the corners by denting the paper once the cross has been cut. The switch or socket should slide through very easily.

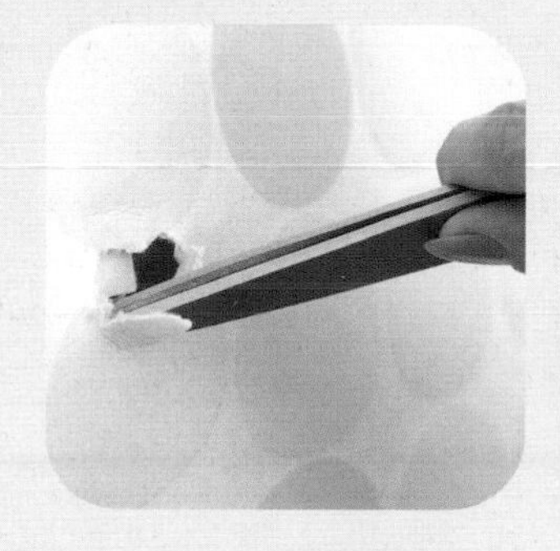

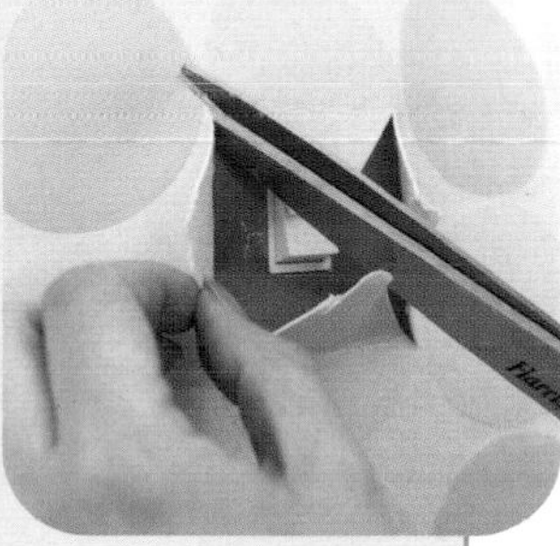

Where two walls meet: Don't ever think you can get to a corner and bend half a sheet round it – even if it looks as if it has worked at the time, a few days later the ripples will appear and it will be a real mess. So, when you reach a corner, hang the paper as usual, **but trim any excess from the width so that only 5cm (2in) of the paper goes around the corner.** Use a seam roller to ensure the paper edge is pressed well against the wall. **Hang the subsequent length of paper so that it is close up to the corner.** For lining paper, trim both pieces of paper right into the corner. If you have a gap when the paper is dry or the paper isn't lying neatly, run a thin line of decorator's caulk into the corner – this will cover a multitude of sins.

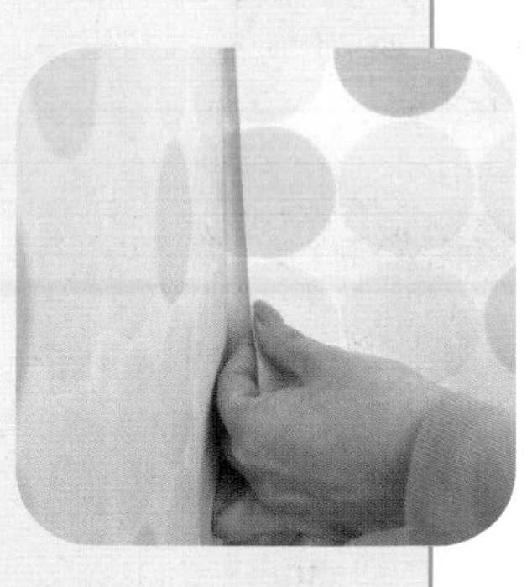

Getting rid of bumps: If, after all your care and attention, you still have a little bump under the paper and it looks as if it's an old wood chip, lift it out with a scalpel like a splinter once the paper is dry. Once it's out, apply a bit of paste to patch the paper down again.

Patching wallpaper

It is possible to replace bits of damaged wallpaper? Of course, you'll always be able to see the join on close inspection, but it's so much cheaper and easier than redoing the whole room that you can probably live with that. There are two simple methods of doing it – tearing and cutting.

How to use the tear method

This method is so simple that you'll wonder why you have never seen it done before.

TOOLS REQUIRED

> **Spare wallpaper**
> **Wallpaper paste**

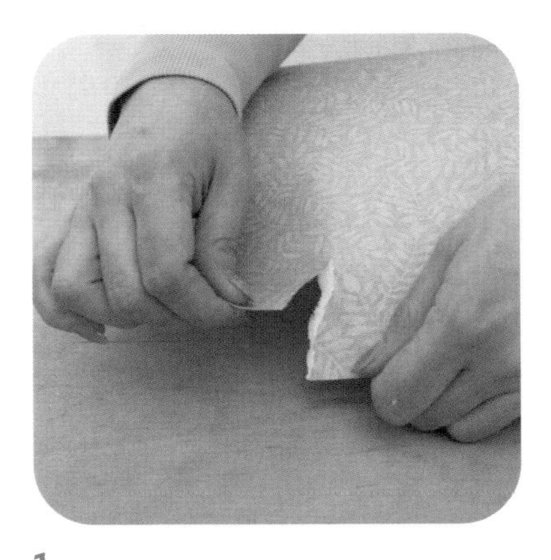

1

Take a small piece of spare wallpaper and tear it – you'll see that it's actually two pieces of paper stuck together: the patterned or coloured paper, which faces the room, and the plain paper, which faces the wall.

2

Tear out a piece that's larger than the area you need to hide. Then, on the reverse side, **carefully peel off the backing paper around the edge** so that you are just left with a lovely thin bit of print.

3

Add paste to the wallpaper patch and leave to soak as usual. Then just **slide and stick it into place to get a perfect match** with the pattern on the wall.

How to use the cut method

This one's a little more complicated than the tear method, but it gives an even better result.

TOOLS REQUIRED

- **Wallpaper paste**
- **Craft knife**
- **Steel rule**
- **Damp cloth**

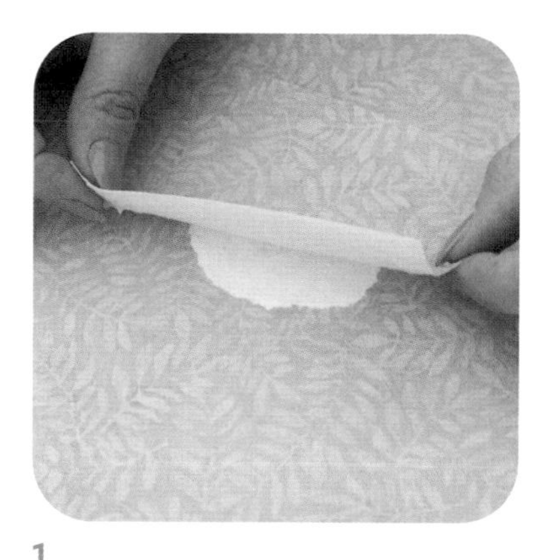

1

Take a piece of wallpaper that's bigger than the area you need to patch, **and paste it over the damaged area, matching up the pattern.** Don't worry about how untidy the edge is - that's to be sorted out later. Leave it for a few days to dry.

2

Use the steel rule and craft knife to **cut a square through the two layers** of wallpaper.

3

Hold a damp cloth to the area, or apply a little steam, until the wallpaper paste has weakened and you can remove the outer layer of wallpaper from around the outside of the square.

4

Release the top square, put it to one side, and **then remove the damaged underlayer**.

5

Replace it with the new square, pasting it properly and pressing firmly before leaving to dry.

CHAPTER TWO

Revive it

Sanding and maintaining floorboards

What do you think your entrance hall looks like when you answer the door to a guest? Find out by going outside with a camera, getting someone to open the door for you and taking a photo of what you see. This is the first impression that visitors get of your home, and the result will probably frighten you. So it's worth making that bit of effort and spending a little money to make sure that all the doorways in your house open onto a welcoming aspect, which is where floorboards, laminate and vinyl come to the fore – read on...

A LESSON ON FLOORBOARDS

Remember that floorboards aren't just for walking on. They also cover a multitude of things, such as water pipes, gas pipes and electricity wires.

Floorboards sit on joists, which are secured by metal plates in the cavities in your walls, preventing them from moving. The joists that hold up the floor are different from the joists that hold up the ceiling, which means that you can't just lay floorboards on the joists in the loft and expect them to hold you – be very careful.

Joists not only support your floor, they also stop the walls from falling in or out, and in the attic they stop the roof from blowing off. So perhaps before you put down that expensive floor, you should check the state of what's underneath. Pull up a few floorboards to see what's going on, and if there is damp or damage or if there is a smell, get in a reputable professional to sort things out. In that way, your beautiful new floor will have firm foundations to rest on.

TOP TIP: MAKE NOTES

Whenever you take up a floor, make a diagram of what's underneath, especially the pipes and the wires. You'll be grateful when you come to make repairs in the future, because it'll mean that you don't have to take up the whole floor again. A friend of mine, who happens to be a director of a well-known timber merchant, forgot to do this, and cost himself two days of hell and a week of the silent treatment from his wife when he shot a nail from a nail gun through the floor into the hot water pipe.

How to sand a floor

Many homes, even those built recently, have solid pine floorboards resting on the joists beneath the carpet or other floor covering, and as long as they're in decent condition and made of solid wood, sanding can transform the dullest, muckiest-looking old floorboards into things of beauty. Sanding is not as difficult as you might think, and will get rid of old stains, varnishes and paint so that you can get back to the bare wood and start afresh.

You'll need to hire a sander from your local hire shop – don't try to do it with a hand sander or a disc attached to your drill. Those can be used for corners and other awkward places where the big sander will not go. Alternatively, you can hire an edge sander as well as a larger one to sand the main part of the room. Talk to the assistant at the hire shop about what kinds of sander you need for your particular room.

TOOLS REQUIRED

> Pipe detector
> Nail punch
> Hammer
> Sanding machine with a good instruction manual
> Sanding discs or belts
> Hand sander
> Edge sander (if necessary)
> Goggles
> Dust mask
> Hard-toed shoes or boots
> Circuit breaker

1
Before you start, **check where your pipes are using a pipe detector and your diagram,** if you have one, and make sure the heads of all screws and nails are beneath the surface of the wood.

2
Screw in the screws and **hammer in any nails that stick out** using the nail punch.

3
If you have any loose boards, screw them down. Nails are not enough to fasten loose boards, because if they're prone to lift, they'll lift a nail out with them, whereas a screw will keep them down.

SAFETY FIRST

As soon as you take up a floorboard, the family moggie will pretend he's escaping from Colditz. The best result is hours of wafting the smell of hot pilchards in front of the hole until he comes out, and the worst is a lot more complicated, such as taking up the whole floor because the idiot has got stuck. Keep all animals away from your work – Auntie Hilda's budgie might faint at the smell of some glues and oil-based paints, and even fish can turn a funny colour if they're not on the other side of a closed door.

SAFETY FIRST

Goggles, hard-toed shoes and a proper dust mask are essential for sanding floors. The dust mask should look like an old-fashioned gas mask – it's designed to stop you inhaling everything from sawdust to paint vapours. Old floorboards tend to be very dirty, and the dust between the boards has been around for many decades, so inhaling it can make you very ill, especially if you have allergies.

4
Check that you have all the equipment and materials that are listed with your machine and read through the instruction manual until you're confident that you understand it. Put on the goggles and hard-toed shoes or boots. Follow the instructions to **attach the sanding disc or belt to the sander.**

5
Put on the dust mask and start sanding the floor. There are various ways of doing it for different machines and yours will tell you how. The basic method is to **travel ACROSS the boards to begin with to level them.**

6
Then travel the length of the boards to go with the grain of the wood. Don't go against the grain on the final sand, as this will lift the soft fibres in the wood, making it fluffy in texture and difficult to seal.

7
Keep checking for nails and screws as you go along – if you catch one it will spark and make a mess of the sanding belt very quickly.

8
Finish off by sanding the corners **with an edge sander or drill attachment.**

AFTER SANDING

After you've finished sanding, the floor must be completely dust-free before you stain or varnish it. Thoroughly vacuum the floor, using a brush attachment if you have one. Clean out the gaps under the skirting boards, and if you feel that there's still dust and dirt you haven't picked up, go over it with a tack cloth, which you can buy from a hardware shop.

This is a large piece of muslin or scrim impregnated with resin or lanoline. One light wipe removes all dust and fluff from a surface and is great for preparation in all painting and decorating – it's such a bonus to have a perfectly dust-free surface. I use mine for some areas of carpentry as well. Don't get carried away, though – if you use it later for dusting, all your furniture will be coated with a fine film of resin.

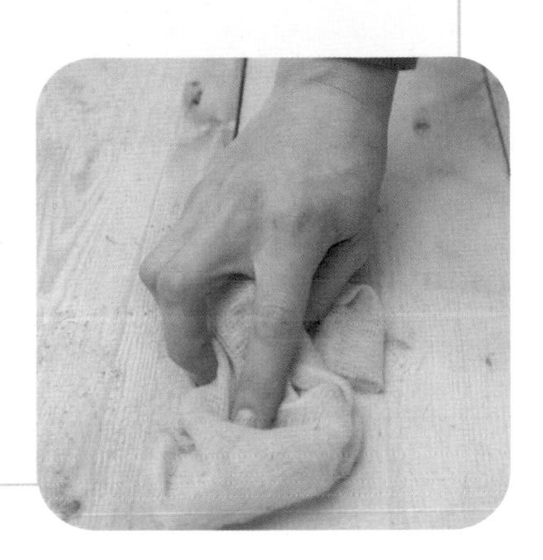

How to fill gaps and cracks

Filling the gaps between floorboards is quite a mucky job. The most common method in the past was to use sawdust and wallpaper paste – what a mess. Another one was to use papier-mâché, but this dries to a very grey colour. It's fine if you're going to paint the floor, but not so good if you're staining and/or varnishing it.

One of the easiest and quickest methods is to use hessian string, or even ordinary string or rope, together with non-waterproof PVA. The thickness of the string or rope should depend on the size of the cracks, but if they vary, you can always double up the string for the wider gaps. Before you start, do a little experiment with the string – put a length of it under the tap and see how much it expands when it's wet. This will help you to judge how much you need. Hessian or sisal will expand and lengthen when wet, and will dry longer and fatter than it was when you started.

TOOLS REQUIRED

> **Non-waterproof PVA**
> **Basin**
> **Ball of string, rope or hessian string**
> **Kneeler pad**
> **Pallet knife**
> **Damp sponge**
> **Sandpaper**

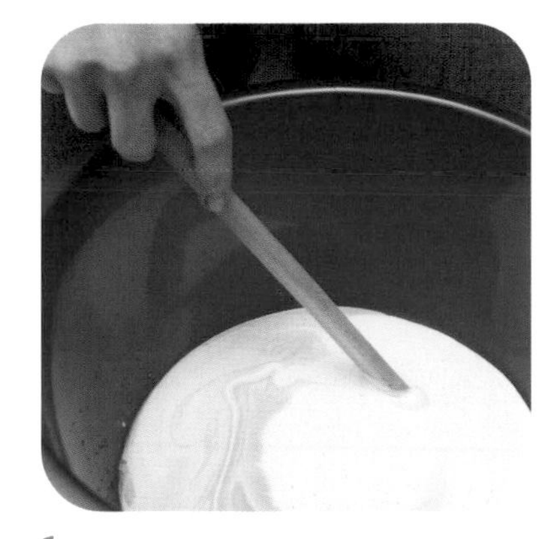

1

Pour the contents of the full can of PVA into the basin. Fill the empty can with warm water, to ensure you get the same quantity, and tip this into the basin too. **Stir to mix.**

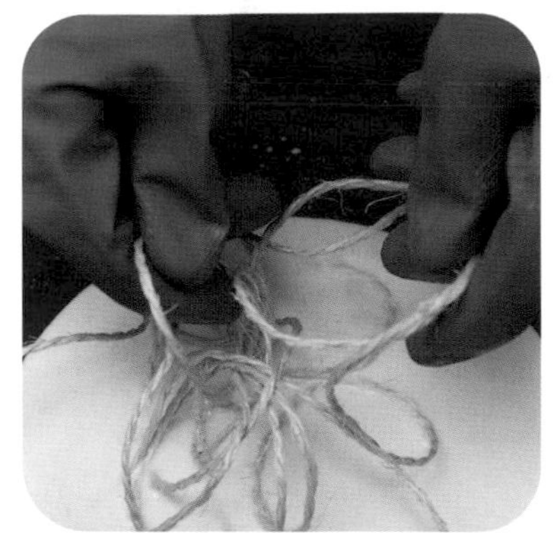

2

Unravel the ball of string and cut into lengths approximately 60cm (2ft) longer than the gaps you're going to fill. For gaps where you're going to double up the string, cut two lengths together. **Cut as many lengths as you need and immerse them in the PVA mixture.** Leave for 20 minutes so the string is soaked.

TOP TIP: QUICK REPAIR

If you've got an aggravating little piece of flooring that's fallen into three pieces, but you can't replace it because you can't get a perfect match, take up the pieces and spread clear or translucent silicone sealant on the joist. Take the first piece of flooring and place it in the hole where it belongs, and spread sealant down the side where it will meet the next piece of flooring. Do the same with the next piece and the next, and then clean off the excess silicone and leave for eight hours. Silicone sealant is usually used in bathrooms but this is a great extra use for it and your damaged floor is fixed.

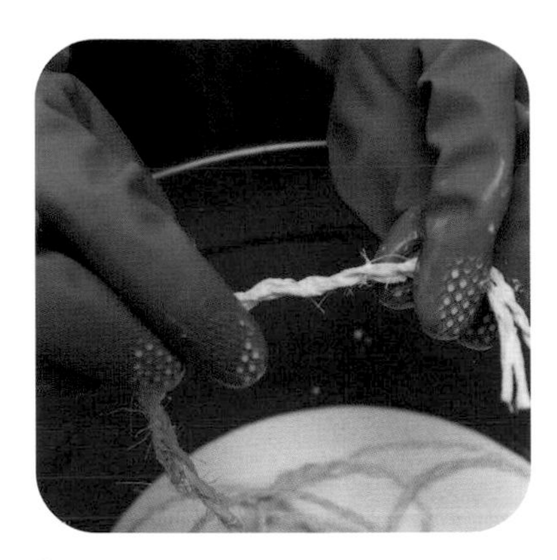

3
If the crack is quite wide and you need two pieces of string, **twist them together and pull them through your fingers** to get rid of any excess PVA. If you are using only one piece, do the same thing, twisting it on its own.

4
Anchor the end of the string at one end of the gap by tying a bulky knot and pushing it into the space between the floorboards with a pallet knife. **Push the string into the gap, twisting it a second time as you work.** Check the string is slightly below the level of the floorboards to keep it safe from trampling feet and the vacuum cleaner.

5
Wipe off the excess PVA from the floor with a damp sponge. If any of it dries on the floorboards, rub it off with sandpaper. Leave the string to dry for a couple of days. If there are any bits of string sticking up, they can be sanded off.

TROUBLESHOOTING: FIXING CREAKS

I've always deliberately kept my bottom stair creaking. It's a very reassuring sound, and when children are little, they may not make much noise, but when you hear the stair creaking it lets you know where the little mites are, bless them. And if there's an intruder, they'll make themselves known as soon as they hit that first squeaky step, so that you can hit the panic button for help.

For the rest of the rooms, however, you'll want to get rid of the noise. Move all the furniture and take up your floor covering. Underneath will be the floorboards, supported by the joists beneath. Joists run in the opposite direction to the floorboards, and the boards should be attached to the joists at every junction with two nails or screws. If these are loose or missing, the floorboard will squeak when you tread on it, and you'll need to tighten or replace them.

First walk around the floor till you get a squeak, then, when you've identified where you think the missing screw is, use a pipe detector to check that there are no wires or pipes in the vicinity. You need to be wary because joists can be cut for pipes to run through them – they're supposed to be at least 5cm (2in) under the floor, but they rarely are. If the coast is clear, screw down the board.

Staining and sealing a floor

You have punched in all the nails and screwed down the loose boards; you have made a diagram of what's going on under the floorboards and you have sanded. Although you say it yourself, it looks pretty good. But how do you keep it looking good? Well, apart from waxing, there are numerous choices – just look below. With a large rug in the middle of the floor, heaven will have been created. The best thing about jobs like this is sitting back once the work is finished and remembering what a mess it was before.

FINISHING FLOORBOARDS

Now you've got back to the original wood, you have a number of options for finishing it:

Varnish: You can seal the boards with a clear varnish to protect them, keeping the existing colour of the wood. Or use a coloured varnish, which stains at the same time as sealing.

Woodstain: You can stain the boards before you seal them – there's a vast range of different colours on the market, and the colour you choose will depend on the style of the building, your décor and your personal taste. It will also vary depending on the exact type of wood – if you have a spare board, test the stain on that to check that you have exactly the right colour, though there's no point in doing this on a different piece of wood.

Paint: If your boards are in good condition, you may be able to paint them without sanding, but they will need to be squeaky clean – keep sweeping and vacuuming, especially around the skirting boards. If you have wax on the floor in places, use the hot iron and brown paper method or, failing this, use a coat of aluminium wood primer to make sure the paint will stick. You can buy specialist floor paints, which are very effective, and they do come in some super colours. You may need two or three coats.

SAFETY FIRST

Always resist the temptation to smoke when you're working on your house! My Dad used to smoke roll-ups, which Mum hated, and as he grew older he got a bit careless and a little forgetful. One day when he was pottering away in his workshop there was a big explosion. We all ran out and he staggered towards us looking very poorly – no eyebrows or eyelashes, just crusty cinders where they'd been, and his lovely green tweed jacket was brown down the front and still green at the back. Poor old Dad – talk about going off with a whoosh! We ran to put out the fire, then I did the daughterly thing of being concerned about him, but broke into convulsions of laughter when we found out he'd dropped his fag into an open can of some mixture he was using to French polish a cabinet. Fortunately, on that occasion no more than his pride was hurt, and it did him a bit of good because he stopped smoking after that. But you might not be so lucky.

How to stain a floor

The instructions on the tin will tell you exactly how to apply the woodstain, but remember that you will get a much better finish if you do the whole floor in one go. Before starting work, open all the doors and windows in the house or flat to give yourself plenty of fresh air and get rid of the fumes.

The colour you choose will depend on the room's style.

TOOLS REQUIRED

- > **Face mask**
- > **Hard-toed boots**
- > **Kneeler pad**
- > **Woodstain**
- > **Paintbrush or small, short-haired roller**

1

When painting, work from the furthest corner with your back to the door, and **work backwards so the last piece of wood you stain is at the threshold.** Work the stain in with the paintbrush or short-haired roller. Don't go over the same area too many times and try to keep a rhythm going.

2

If you have to stop in the middle, feather out the stain on the floor so that it becomes fainter and fainter. This will make a better start when you get going again. If you stop in a line and then start in a line, you'll have a double strength stain there, which looks horrid. And if you just can't do this, **use the ends of the floorboards as your lines.**

SEALING A FLOOR

Once your floor is the colour you want it, you need to seal it to protect it from scratches, stains and water damage. Floor sealant is usually called varnish in DIY superstores. **You can seal the floor directly after sanding it** if you want to preserve the wood's natural colour, though the colour will naturally darken and deepen a little when you apply the sealant. Make sure the floor is completely free of dust before you start – there is no point in sealing all the dirt to the floor, and if you do, the dust will get knocked off, breaking the seal.

Laying wood laminates and floors

What is laminate flooring? It's usually a layer of MDF, or 'medium-density fibreboard', coated with a picture of wood or thin layer of real wood, which is laminated under heat, resulting in an incredibly hard surface. Nowadays, the boards usually have edges that snap together, making the wonderfully satisfying sound 'click clack'.

Check the floor beneath

A badly laid floor can result in water damage, especially in kitchens. Once I had a phone call from a very sweet young lady. She'd decided it was time to get the laminate floor laid in her kitchen that she'd been dreaming of ever since she'd moved in. As I entered the kitchen I got that sinking feeling, quite literally – the floor under the vinyl felt like a sponge beneath my feet. As I peeled back the vinyl, an awful stench hit me. The builders had laid a concrete base, then a 7.5cm (3in) thick layer of polystyrene and finally a layer of cheap chipboard, which had disintegrated.

The bottom of the kitchen cupboards were blown, too. They had soaked up so much water that the wood was swollen and distorted. I asked whether she knew of any leaks and she thought there might be small ones from the draining board and the washing machine. The moral of this story is that a badly laid floor in combination with water is a lethal mix. Before laying any type of flooring, you must check that the floor is sound beneath and, when you are laying it, make sure you DIP – Do It Properly. It is especially important that you use the correct quality of flooring in your kitchen or bathroom.

TOP TIP: INSULATION

We think of insulation being in the loft, but it's a good thing to have in floors to soundproof between your own room or apartment and the one below, and also to protect from the draughts that whistle through the cracks in the floorboards and make black marks around the edge of your carpet. Whenever you're buying new flooring, whether it's solid wood, laminate or carpet, ask in the shop about underlay and make sure you get the kind of underlay that will suit your insulation needs.

How to lay a laminate floor

Many different patterns, grades and thicknesses of laminate flooring are available. If you're laying it in a bathroom or kitchen, make sure you choose the appropriate waterproof board – it usually has a green-coloured MDF base. Professionals can lay a laminate floor in a couple of hours, including sealing it and fixing the borders, but as a novice give yourself a long weekend. It's backbreaking work and is very hard on the knees unless you use knee pads. As well as the boards themselves, you'll also need to lay an underlay – either soundproofing felt pads or, more usually, a plastic underlay. The best kind is grey and comes in a concertina pack – it's a little more expensive, but I've found that it's top stuff.

And, finally, there is the border moulding, which you need to lay to hide the gap running around the edge of the room. You can buy it to match your laminates and you'll sometimes have a choice of shapes – I prefer scotia, which is concave, but you may prefer quadrant, which is convex (*quad* meaning 'quarter' in Latin).

If there's a fireplace in the room, start there and lay the boards parallel to it. If not, it usually looks better if the boards are parallel with the longer walls.

TOOLS REQUIRED

- > **Underlay**
- > **Laminate floorboards**
- > **Spacers**
- > **Knee pads**
- > **Pencil**
- > **Jig saw and special blade with the teeth pointing downwards (ask in the shop for the right one for cutting laminates)**
- > **G-clamps**
- > **Mitre block**
- > **Box saw**
- > **Scotia or quadrant border edging**
- > **Door bar to match your laminates – select the right one for the type of flooring on the other side of the door, and don't be afraid to ask the shop assistant**

TOP TIP: SAW CAREFULLY

The top of a laminated board is very slippery, so take extra care when sawing it – the board must be tightly held on a workbench or a really sturdy table using G-clamps.

1
Put down the underlay, **cutting each piece to fit the length of the room.** You don't need to fix it to the floor – the laminate floorboards will eventually hold it in place.

2
Start laying the boards lengthways, **joining each new board to the next and using the spacers** to ensure there is a 1.2cm (½in) gap between the boards and the skirting board to allow the boards to expand. The 'click-clack' structure of the fitting means that it isn't necessary to glue or nail the boards to the floor or to one another.

3
When you reach the end of the row, you'll usually finish with part of a board. Measure the space you need to fill, remembering to leave a 1.2cm (½in) gap at the end, and then **saw the next board to the correct length** using the jig saw.

4
Use the remaining piece of board **to start off the next row.** This stops the boards from joining in the same place and making a weak section. Always lay the rows either from left to right or from right to left, and don't change once you've started.

6

When laying the boards next to a door, you must be able to slide them under the architrave, which is the ornamental wooden moulding that surrounds the door and stands out slightly from the skirting board. Place a scrap piece of laminate board on the bare floor next to the doorway and draw a line on the architrave 2mm (⅛in) above the top of the board. Then carefully **saw off the bottom of the architrave using a tenon saw,** making sure you don't cut into the doorframe. Don't worry if you've cut it off slightly too high – you can always correct it with filler (see page 129) and paint. It won't show.

7

Keep laying out the boards until you reach the final row. If the space is narrower than the width of your boards, you'll have to cut the board along its length with the jig saw. Measure the width you need twice, making sure you leave that 1.2cm (½in) expansion gap, **and then mark it at either end of the board and draw a line all the way along.**

8

Once you've cut the last boards to the right size, click them into place and the floor will look like one big piece of flooring. If the last strip needs a bit of help to clear the skirting board, **use a little pressure with your foot.**

LAYING A SOLID WOOD FLOOR

Now let's go back to your hallway, the entrance to your domain. Laying laminate in a hallway is not a good idea, no matter how high quality – there's just too much traffic. All you need is a couple of stones embedded in the soles of trainers and the floor is ruined. What you really need is a solid wood floor, which can be repaired with that trusty hired sanding machine.

There are many types of wood flooring, and some have click-clack edges just like laminates and can be laid in just the same way. However, there are lots of others, such as tongue and groove and parquet. It may take some research to find the right one and even more work to install but don't be put off. Also, don't expect instant gratification. The manufacturers will supply fitting instructions, and most suppliers have a free helpline, so use it, as they have plenty of tips about laying their particular type of floor. If your solid wood floor isn't already sealed, seal it as you would floorboards (see page 171).

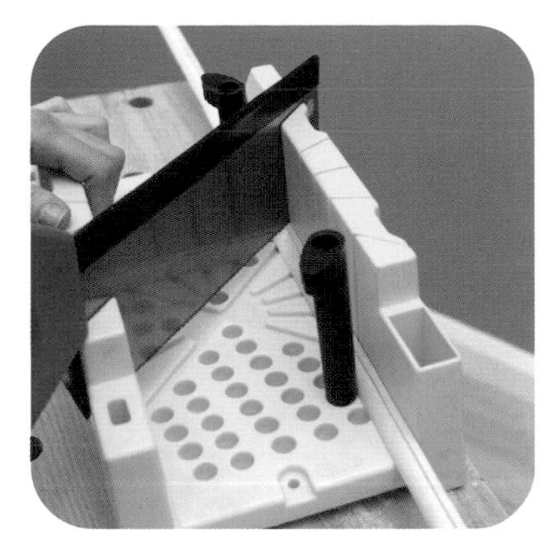

9

To lay the border moulding, cut it to size using a box saw. At the corners, you'll need to saw mitred ends at 45° angles so that the two pieces will fit together – **use a mitre block to guide you.**

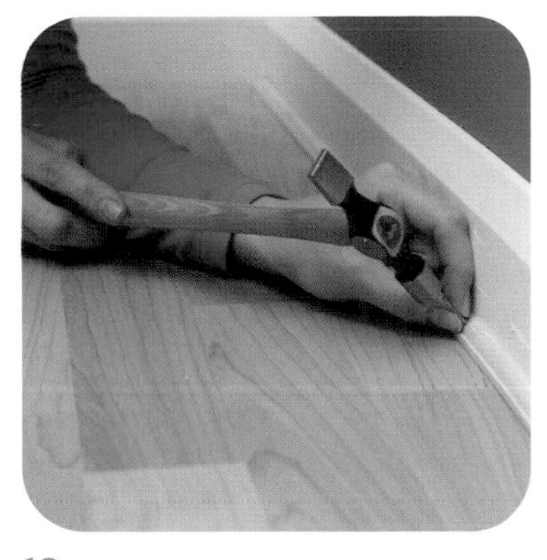

10

Use panel pins or clear silicone (see page 125) **to fix the moulding to the wall or skirting board.** Never fix it to the laminate floorboards, or the boards won't have room to expand into the gap.

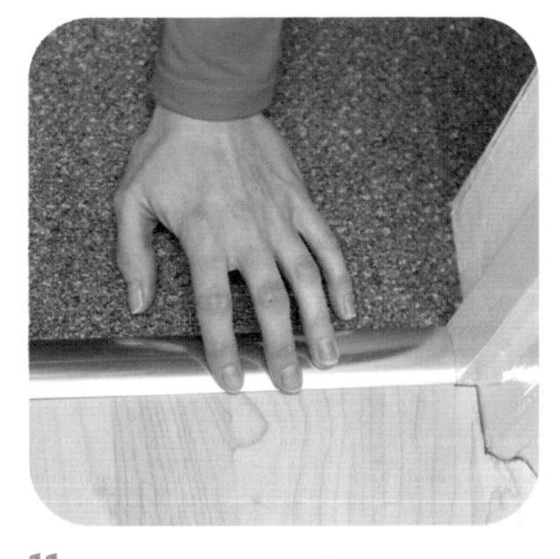

11

Lay the door bar over the entrance and **screw or stick it to it to the floorboard or carpet** beneath. Never fix it to the laminated board for the same reason as before.

Laying vinyl floors

Laying vinyl is not as difficult as it sounds, although you really do need a perfectly level floor. The best material for levelling floorboards is 4mm (⅙in) thick plywood. If it happens to get wet, it won't buckle and roll, and you can just lay it in the same way as a laminate floor, with a space of 1.2cm (½in) around the edges for expansion (see page 172). Don't join the plywood in the middle of the floor, rather place one sheet of ply in the centre and work around it. That way, the part you walk on the most will be solid. For a concrete floor, use a self-levelling compound mixed with liquid latex to make it pliable.

How to lay vinyl

There are so many different types of vinyl on the market, including lots of wood, stone and tile imitations, so take your time choosing the perfect finish for your room. When you've brought your vinyl home, the first thing you need to do is lay it out in another room of the same temperature as the one you're laying it in for an hour or so. This will allow the vinyl to relax and warm up, making sure that you can cut it to the right size. Cutting vinyl to size is quite a hairy job, but it looks so good when it's finished, and if it's the thin stuff, you may get away with doing it in two or three hours.

TOOLS REQUIRED

- **Sheet of vinyl floor covering**
- **Measuring tape**
- **Marker pen**
- **Craft knife with ordinary blade and hook blade**
- **Steel rule**
- **Silicone sealant if the vinyl is being laid in a bathroom (see page 125)**

1

Before you even pick up the knife, **draw the shape of the room on the vinyl.** Do as much as you can by measuring, and then for difficult bits, such as toilet and sink pedestals, the trick is to make paper templates, which you can then draw around on the back of the vinyl (see Troubleshooting, opposite). You might prefer to draw the outline on the reverse of the vinyl, as here, but remember that when you turn it over the shape will be reversed. So if something is not symmetrical, mark the lines on the right side.

2

Use an ordinary blade in a craft knife to cut straight lines by pressing down with a steel rule along the line you've drawn on the vinyl and **running the knife along its edge.** Make sure the vinyl is marginally larger than it needs to be in all directions. You can always cut it down a little more when you come to lay it on the floor, but if you cut it too small there's nothing you can do about it.

TROUBLESHOOTING: CUTTING OUT TRICKY SHAPES

Making a paper template is a matter of trial and error: measuring, drawing and cutting until it's just right. At least when you mess it up it's just paper and not your new floor covering.

With symmetrical shapes such as a toilet pedestal, create a template of half of the toilet and then fold the paper in half before cutting it so that you get the whole thing. **If there was vinyl or carpet already on the floor, you can use this as your template, saving a lot of time and trouble.**

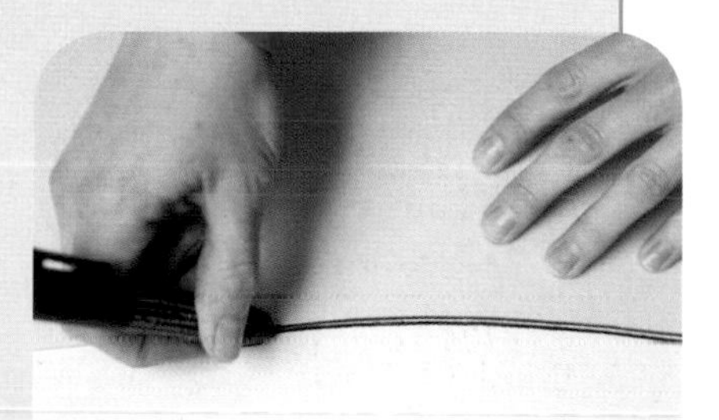

SAFETY FIRST

Dispose of old craft knife blades by wrapping them in newspaper, sealing the paper with sticky tape and then putting them between two pieces of cardboard or wrap in cardboard. The first time you ever cut yourself on one of these blades is hopefully also the last. In my job I use a lot of scalpels and it's essential to be extremely careful about getting rid of them.

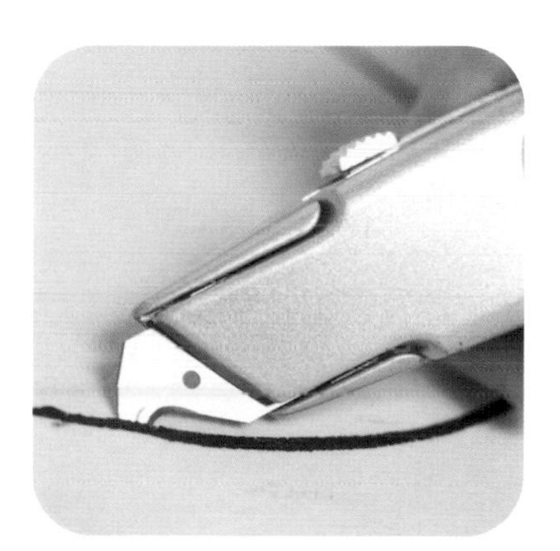

3

Switch to the hook blade for curves, corners and other difficult shapes. This is sharp only at the end and on the inside curve, so that you can insert it through the vinyl and pull it towards you.

4

Lay the vinyl on the floor and slide it under the skirting boards. If it's a bit too big, cut off a little more. When you're sure it's perfect, fasten it down at the doorway with a door bar. If the vinyl is in a bathroom, use silicone to seal around the base of all your bathroom furniture (see page 125).

TOP TIP: CUT CAREFULLY

To make sure you're used to the feel of the craft knife and are confident that it's under control, practise cutting on a spare piece of vinyl before you start on the real thing. If you feel tired while you're doing the cutting, go away and have a cup of tea and then come back when you're feeling better. Don't waste your nice new floor by rushing it, but on the other hand, don't do as my sister did and take a year to cut the vinyl for her own kitchen while doing a smashing job of all the clients' floors!

Chiselling and planing

I was seven when I learnt to use a chisel. It's still one of my favourite tools – a tiny edge of steel that does so much work. The blade should be very sharp and is shaped so the flat side will cut into the wood and the 30-degree angle on the other side will force the wood out of the way when you whack it with a mallet. Read these pages and then you can safely go on to revive doors as outlined on pages 180–3.

Using a chisel

> Try using a chisel on some scraps of wood and see what happens. Ideally, you should use a 2.5cm (1in) chisel for this exercise, but you can do it with a smaller one if you like. First, use a pencil to draw a rectangle 2.5 x 5cm (1 x 2in) on the surface of the wood. **Then place the blade vertically on one of the lines with the flat side facing outwards and give the end of the handle several taps with a mallet, to a depth of around 5mm (¼in).** Continue around the rectangle. The wood is already being forced away, as you'll find out if you turn the chisel around and try it the other way (don't try too hard, though!).

> Repeat this technique to make 5mm (¼in) cuts every 5mm (¼in) across the rectangle, holding the chisel well down the handle to make it easier to move the blade and get an equal distance between the cuts. It looks like lots of little chips in a line.

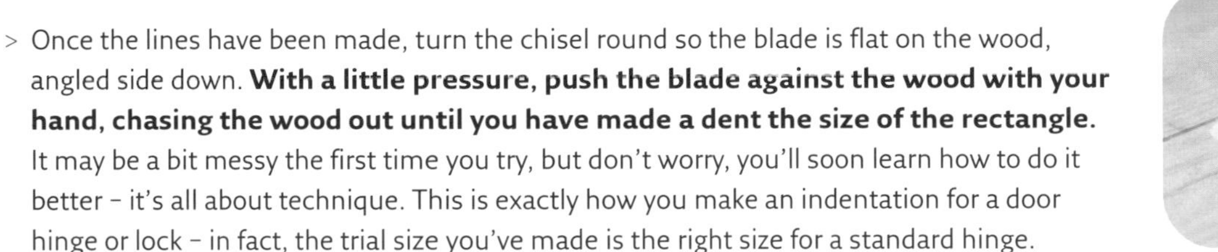

> Once the lines have been made, turn the chisel round so the blade is flat on the wood, angled side down. **With a little pressure, push the blade against the wood with your hand, chasing the wood out until you have made a dent the size of the rectangle.** It may be a bit messy the first time you try, but don't worry, you'll soon learn how to do it better – it's all about technique. This is exactly how you make an indentation for a door hinge or lock – in fact, the trial size you've made is the right size for a standard hinge.

SHARPENING YOUR CHISEL

Sharpening a chisel is an art. In the tools section of this book, it was suggested that you buy a set of three chisels and a sharpening stone. Now is the time to find out how to use that stone.

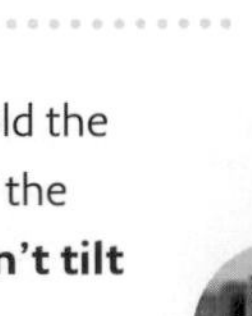

Put some fine oil, such as light white liquid engine oil, on the stone and hold the angled side of the blade against it at 30 degrees. Never sharpen from the flat side of the blade. **Slowly draw a figure of eight on the stone, making sure that you don't tilt the blade as you go** – tilting it will damage the corners.

When you've finished, wipe the blade with an old piece of leather to get rid of any burrs.

TOP TIP: CHISELLING

To keep the depth even, always try to use the same number and pressure of strokes for each cut. If it isn't even, a latch, say (see overleaf), will be tilted or a hinge badly set. Between three and five short but firm taps usually works - rub the chisel into the wood gently. If it's sharp enough, each gentle stroke will release a sliver of wood shaving. This is called paring.

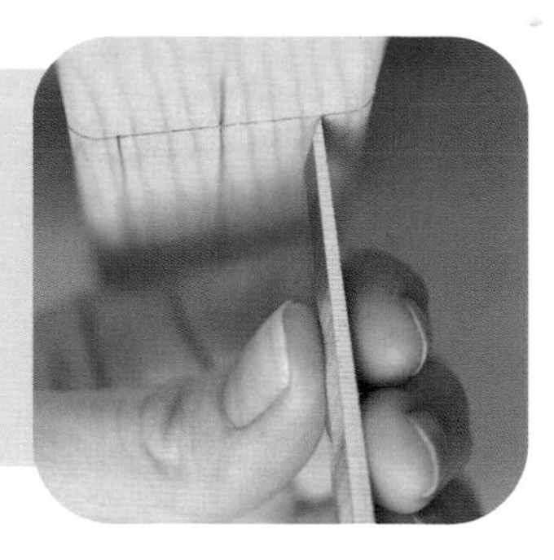

Using a plane

Positioning the blade correctly can be very tricky. If, after reading the instructions, you're still not sure how to do this, let the tool shop help you. It should be positioned just below the plate - any higher off the base and you will crack or break it. To use the plane, guide it gently and quickly over the wood by holding the handle at the front of it. Always mark on the wood where you want to plane to - and don't go any further! You will get the knack very quickly.

TROUBLESHOOTING: EASING DOORS

If a door is sticking on a carpet, open it to the point where it sticks. Take a water-soluble felt-tipped pen (no graffiti, please!) and, pressing your hand down into the carpet, **draw a line on the door to show how much of it needs come off.** It is an art, but when you start drawing you realise what the technique is. Then remove the door by unscrewing the hinges, and rest it somewhere very safe, such as on a kitchen or dining table, making sure that you've padded the locks and handles thoroughly to stop them from scratching and, if possible, pressing the top end against a wall.

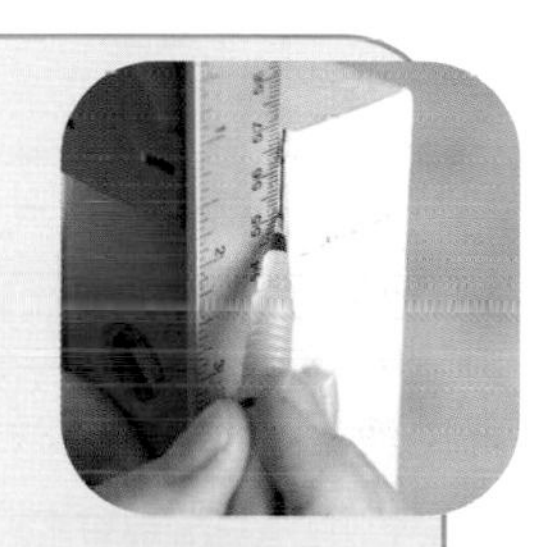

Remove the excess wood with a plane (see above). Protect the carpet and try to keep the dust on the table - an electric plane will make a serious mess, and you can't shut the door to keep it in the room, because the door is on the table! But if you have the right adaptor, you can attach the vacuum cleaner to the plane. It's quite easy and will save so much mess.

Don't plane all the way down to the mark you've made - I know it's a pain, but you should go half way and **then put the door back up with just one screw in each hinge** to see whether it still sticks. Quite often you'll find that you don't need to take off as much as you thought. Once the door no longer sticks, take it down again and give the bottom a good sanding. I also like to put primer or undercoat on the bottom. Wait until the paint is completely dry and put the door back up again with a little help from a friend.

Reviving doors

The door sticks, the latches don't work and the knobs are hanging off. Furthermore, there are great gouges in the paintwork – all in all, the doors look pretty 'orrid. Start by taking off all the handles and door plates and start again. Use all the strategies for filling and painting (see pages 128–9 and 150–5) and then use the following techniques for putting on new latches and handles. The same tools and techniques are used for locks and, of course, there are always the manufacturer's instructions.

How to fit a handle and latch

'Door furniture' is the name for locks, handles, latches, knobs and knockers. Always purchase door furniture from a reputable locksmith or a DIY superstore. Go armed with the size and thickness of the door, and when you've bought what you were looking for, read the fitting instructions thoroughly. It is also important that you investigate your handle and latch, all the different parts and the fitting instructions until you're confident that you know how it fits into the door.

TOOLS REQUIRED

- > **Handle, latch, latch plate and door plate (these should come as a set)**
- > **Pencil**
- > **Steel rule**
- > **Chisel**
- > **Electric drill**
- > **Spade bit of the correct size (see opposite)**
- > **Wood drill bit the size of the handle shaft**

HANDLE AND LATCH

From top right clockwise:
handle
shaft
door plate
screw plate
handle
screws
latch and latch plate

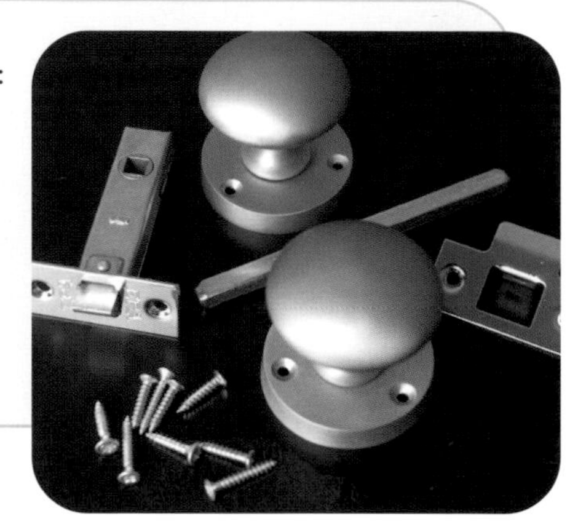

1
Measure the size of the latch plate and **draw a rectangle on the edge of the door** to the same size ensuring it is centred to the space – it might help to draw a line down the centre of the door first.

2
Chisel just inside the latch plate line (see page 178), making a dent that is just deep enough to allow the metal of the latch plate to sit inside the door.

3
With a ruler, draw two diagonal lines from each corner **of the latch plate indent.**

TOP TIPS: GOOD TECHNIQUE

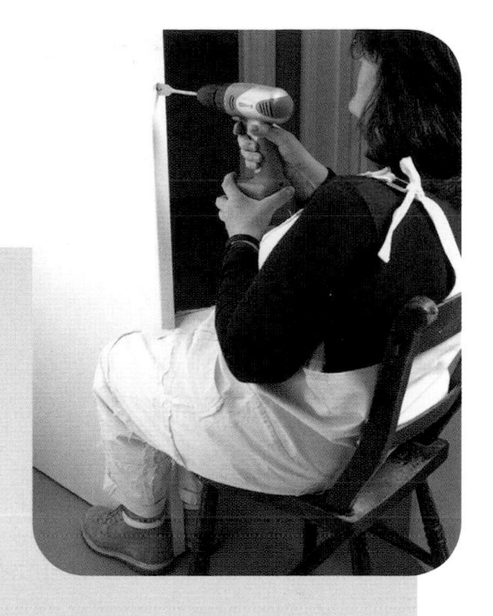

When you're drilling holes through the door, try sitting on a chair and gripping the door between your knees. Have another chair handy for all the bits and pieces – it works a treat for me.

When you're using a chisel to cut the rebate for a latch or lock into the edge of a door, remember that the flat side will cut straight into the wood. So always have the flat side of the chisel facing towards the outside of the door.

4
Fit a spade bit into your drill that matches the width of the end of the latch that sits furthest into the door (usually 23mm or just under 1in – a millimetre over is no problem, but don't make it any larger, or there won't be enough wood for the screws to hold the latch in place). **Use red electrical tape as described on page 49 to mark the length of the latch outline.**

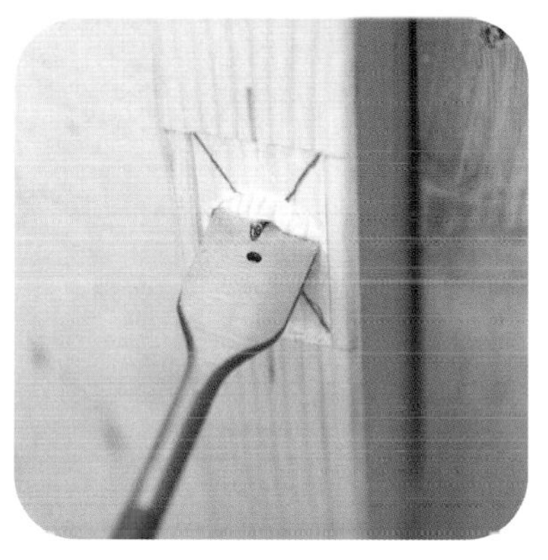

5
Place the spade bit where the lines meet and, keeping the door steady, **drill slowly straight into the door** until the red tape mark is reached. Refer to the hole in the latch for the positioning of the shaft for the handles and mark the position on each side of the door, ensuring they align correctly. Using the wood drill bit, drill half the hole from one side and then complete it on the other side – if you drill straight through, you'll make a mess of the wood on the exit side.

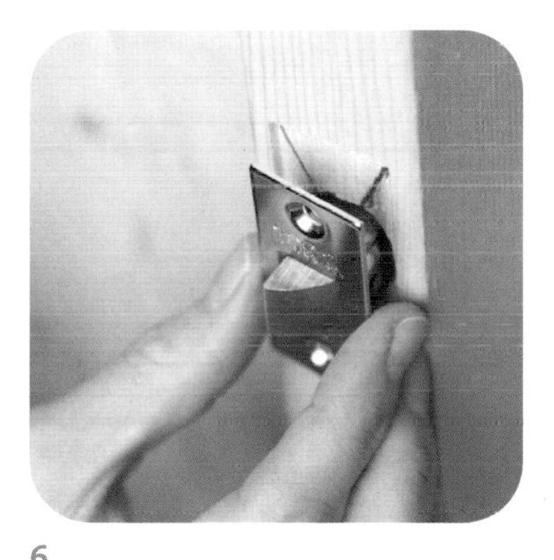

6
Slide the latch into the hole from the edge of the door. It will probably have a little piece of metal that moves from end to end as the latch works – make sure that it's free or the latch will stick. Ensure the latch plate is fitting comfortably in the dent and screw in place. Insert the shaft ready to attach the handles (see Troubleshooting box, overleaf).

7
To make a hole in the door jamb for the latch to fit into, partially close the door so the latch tooth just touches the door jamb. **Draw lines on the door jamb where the top and bottom of the tooth touch it**.

8
Open the door and line up the square hole in the door plate with the marks you have made. Use the opening in the door plate as a template to **draw a rectangle on the door jamb where you'll cut a hole with your small chisel** to make the hole for the latch tooth.

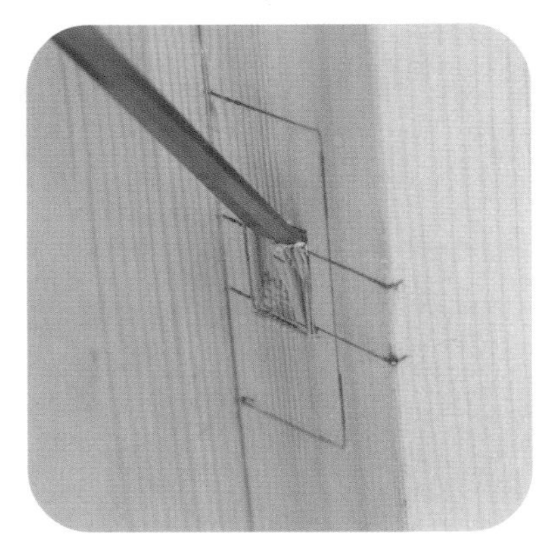

9
Put the door plate to one side and **make the hole with your chisel** – this time, it will be much deeper than the one you made for the latch plate. Check the hole is big enough by closing the door and ensuring the latch goes into the hole.

TROUBLESHOOTING: ENSURING A GOOD FIT

On lever handles, there should be a grub screw and a spring mechanism that operates the latch on the other. Attach the handle with the spring first, and then **use the grub screw to attach the other one.** Tighten with an allen key. Now test the handle. If it doesn't work, you've probably got the pitch of the hole through the door wrong, which means tension is put on the handle shaft – it won't work unless it's completely level. Take it out and adjust the hole with a chisel until the handle works perfectly and you finally have a door that will not shake, rattle and roll.

10
Hold the door plate against the jamb again and this time draw around the outside of the plate, making sure it's properly aligned. Then chisel a shallow indentation the depth of the plate, and **screw the door plate to the door jamb. Job done!**

How to fit a cylinder lock

Good house protection is increasingly important. Once you've mastered the art of fixing a door handle and its associated latch plate, you can move onto fitting a cylinder lock, should you so desire.

TOOLS REQUIRED

- > **Cylinder lock**
- > **Pencil**
- > **Steel rule**
- > **Chisel**
- > **Electric drill**
- > **Spade bit of the correct size (see opposite)**
- > **Wood drill bit the size of the handle shaft**

1
Mark the position of the lock, as in Step 1 on page 180, using either the lock or the template that is sometimes provided, and then **drill an appropriately sized hole for the cylinder** (see Step 5 on page 181).

2
Push the cylinder into the hole from the outside to check the length of the bar. Snip off to the correct length – the bar is marked to help you. Reinsert into the door and then **screw the mounting plate for the lock to the door**.

3
Attach the lock body to the mounting plate and screw in place. Use the lock body as a guideline for marking and making the latch plate recess on the door jamb.

4
Follow Steps 8, 9 and 10 opposite for chiselling a recess for the latch plate. Finally, **screw the plate into position** and now you and Auntie Hilda are as safe as houses.

Rejuvenating kitchen doors

Your kitchen is looking distressed. The cupboard doors are badly scratched and bashed, and the paint is peeling and has been scorched from being too close to the oven. Before you go out and spend a fortune on a new kitchen, it's worth realising that it's probably only the doors that need to be replaced – all main dealers in the UK use the same-sized base boxes, though beware of those made in Sweden, which are completely different.

How to change cupboard doors

Measure the existing doors and take the list to the superstore to choose your new kitchen style. This is also the perfect time to change those sad handles.

TOOLS REQUIRED

- **Tape measure**
- **Screwdriver**
- **Selection of screws**
- **Hacksaw (optional)**

TOP TIP: PLUG THE GAP

If the holes for the screws in the cabinet sides aren't looking good, cut small wall plugs to the correct depth and place them in the holes. Use new screws to match the size and depth of the wall plug.

1

Once you've got your new doors, **undo the screws on each of the hinges of the existing doors** and remove the doors, leaving the hinges attached to the base units. Then simply pop the new doors onto the old hinges and replace the screws.

2

Fix the new handles to the doors before or after you put them onto the cupboards. Hang one of the doors and **experiment with the position of the handle** until it looks absolutely right. Measure the position and check that all the others go in exactly the same place on the door front.

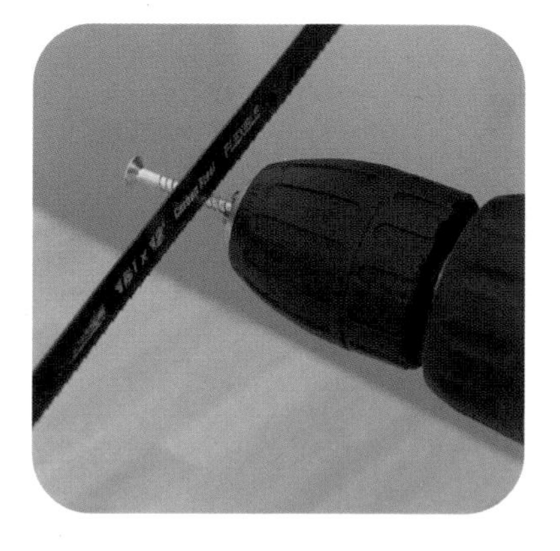

3

If you've bought a pack of handles with multi-length screws, you might find you don't have enough of the right length. Either buy more of the right length or cut the longer ones to size. **Insert a screw into a drill as if it were a drill bit,** tighten and cut with a hacksaw. Alternatively, you can use a vice.

OTHER SIMPLE DOOR CHANGES

How to replace non-standard cupboard doors: If your mum or dad ever said to you, 'Don't slam that door!' the chances were that it wasn't just the noise they were worried about. Every time you slam a door, a little grain of mortar drifts apart from its pals and dies, a little chip of wood squeals and loses the will to live, and screws just lose their grip. It's so sad, but enter Mrs Fixit on her white stallion, armed with drills and bits and bags of goodies to put it right.

Take the measurements of the door, including the thickness, to a superstore that has a wood-cutting service. Ask them to cut a piece of the correct thickness of MDF to the right size for your door, and buy a piano hinge of the same length or slightly shorter. A piano hinge is very long and thin and runs from the top to the bottom of the door and will remain really robust, even if it has a lot of use.

Screw the hinge into the door using the screws provided, and then make marks on the cupboard where each screw will go. To set the door straight, put in only the top screw, and then open and close the door a few times to make sure there are no restrictions – if there are any problems, take the screw out again, make the correct adjustments and start again.

Some cupboard sides may not be wide enough for the hinge to attach securely. If so, screw a piece of wood 2.5 x 5cm (1 x 2in) to the cupboard side with the 5cm (2in) edge butted against the cupboard side and the 2.5cm (1in) edge facing the front, aligned with the front edge of the cupboard. This will give a much wider surface onto which the hinge can be screwed and it can be easily painted to match the interior.

A simple door design: For added design interest to the MDF door you've just made, add a raised lip around the edge. All you need to do is saw a 10cm (4in) strip of 3mm (⅛in) MDF to fit each side and mitre the ends. **Glue them onto the door, prime the MDF and paint over it** (see pages 150–3 for decorating advice).

Reviving kitchen surfaces

We can't all get rid of a complete kitchen just because it's tatty and tired, and luckily we don't have to. Built-in obsolescence is a modern concept, and unless your kitchen is irredeemably broken or the current design doesn't suit your purpose, you should look at the alternatives even if you do have enough money to throw it away and start again. Every time we unthinkingly discard something that could be re-used, we waste the planet's resources. In fact, it's really quite easy to give your old kitchen the kiss of life. A few bright ideas will get you up and running in the competition for the kitchen of the year. Let's have a look at a few different surfaces and how to keep them pristine, and if you've inherited the house of horrors, let's try to make your money stretch as far as possible.

Work surfaces

- **Laminate:** You can fill any chips in laminated worktops with white epoxy resin putty (see page 40). Purchase the correct colour fillers and use the coloured glue that is produced for sticking on the trim on the sides of laminate worktops. Alternatively, **fill a chip with the white putty and then use an appropriate coloured paint to complete the job.**

- **Marble:** Although marble is very occasionally used as a work surface, it is far better to use granite. However, if you feel strongly enough about using marble, **rub it down with marble polish as soon as it is installed as marble is porous**. It will then probably never stain unless you spill something dreadful. If you're removing paint from marble, use a special cleaner from the marble supplier and start on an edge that won't show too much so that you can see how your restoration will work.

- **Granite:** I'm not sure how granite worktops started to be put into our kitchens, but I'm very wary of them. Every time you knock something over it chips or breaks, and although when you look at the surface it seems smooth and shiny, squat down and look at it at eye level and you'll see that it has thousands of little pits. These harbour germs, and because granite isn't organic like wood, it has no antibacterial qualities. So, if you chip a granite worktop, get in touch with a granite supplier to request a repair pack and full instructions.

- **Wood:** If you are buying a new kitchen, ask your installer to use a wood treatment around the hole for the tap. If the tap drips or runs onto the wood, you should get it repaired as soon as possible. Some wooden work surfaces are varnished, which means that one tiny chip allows the water in. If the water gets under the tap and into the body of the wood, it's going to rot. If this happens, you can rub it down and bleach it, but prevention is better than cure.

Floors

> **Limestone :** This is used frequently by builders in new kitchens and bathrooms but it's very porous and should be sealed by the builder as soon as it's laid. Make sure you see that this is done – the stone can look exactly the same before and after, and the only way of finding out is to compare it very closely with a small piece of untreated stone of exactly the same type. As long as it's been sealed, cleaning limestone is just a case of a good wash with a mop or squeegee and a gentle cleaner.

> **Quarry and terracotta tiles (below):** Tiles are a good surface for kitchen floors, but they need polishing with wax, especially if they haven't been sealed. If you are around when the floor is being laid, ensure it is sealed with an appropriate solution (often containing linseed oil). It should be worked well into the surface with a paintbrush. Thereafter a wax polish applied every few months is sufficient to maintain protection against staining. Any chipped edges can be rubbed down with sandpaper.

How to paint tiles

You have moved in to a house with avocado tiles on the splashback behind the work surface, and they're so beautifully done that you just can't bear the idea of scrapping them and spending a lot of money on buying new ones. The answer is to paint them. There are quite a few paints on the market that are specifically designed for this job, but you will have a few things to do before the paint goes on.

TOOLS REQUIRED

- **A pack of protective gloves**
- **Sugar soap**
- **Paint scraper**
- **Methylated spirits**
- **Loads of lint-free cloths – but not your tack cloth**
- **Masking tape**
- **Plastic dust sheets**
- **Very fine small 15cm (6in) rollers**
- **Very fine artist's brush or proprietary grout pen**
- **The right type of paint for the type and location of the tiles, with a separate colour for the grout lines if you want to paint those in (I would choose a colour four shades lighter or darker than the tile)**
- **The correct primer to go with the paint**
- **The appropriate brush or roller cleaner**

1

Wash the original tiles and grout so they are completely clean and free from grease. Use sugar soap and scrape off any sticky patches with a paint scraper. Then wash again, and go over everything with a **cloth dipped in methylated spirits.** Buff up and polish with a clean dry cloth, and don't worry if the grout turns purple – the methylated spirit sometimes leaves this colouring when it evaporates, but it's harmless and you'll paint over it.

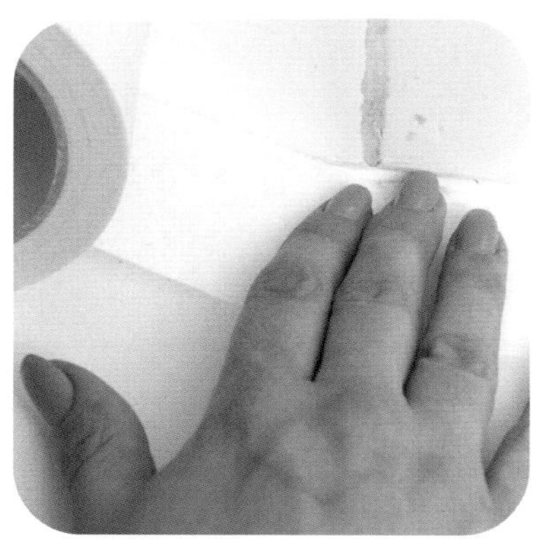

2

Apply masking tape around the edges of the area that you're going to paint, and cover everything else nearby with plastic dust sheets. Cut these so that they fit properly, or you'll be tripping over them all day.

3

Open all nearby windows and doors before you start painting – this paint is quite smelly. **Apply a very thin coat of the primer undercoat with a roller,** trying to keep it even. Paint right over the grout, because you can paint it the same colour as the tiles, or paint the grout lines back in at the end if you prefer.

4
Let the paint dry and apply a second coat of primer undercoat. Once that's dry, **apply two top coats.** Again, keep the coats thin and don't overpaint – if you feel that you need a third top coat, go for it.

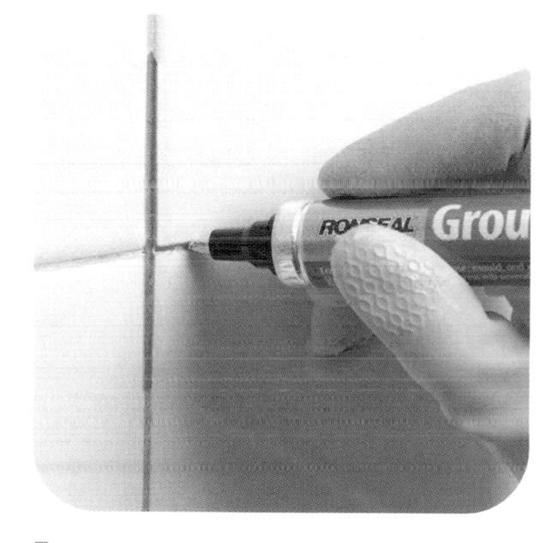

5
If you want the grout lines to show in a different colour, **paint them with a proprietary grout pen.** This is also useful in white if you just want to give your grout lines a pick-up. You can also colour in using a very fine artist's brush. The thing about grout lines is that they don't have to be perfect, and if you decide you don't like them, just wait until they're dry and paint over the top.

Repairing a Belfast sink

> Oh, woe, you have chipped the Belfast sink and can see the yellow interior – it's not looking good. Don't worry, use epoxy resin putty. Clean and dry the chipped area, **then rub together the two parts of the putty** to mix the putty with the hardener. Apply it to the chip and **smooth the surface with a filling knife**, then smooth it again **with a wet finger** until the surface is exactly the right shape and the chip has disappeared. This will dry rock hard and can then be sanded and painted with an oil-based paint to give just the right shiny finish.

> Either bicarbonate of soda or a non-scratch cleaner are best for keeping a Belfast sink clean. Over the years the inside will become pitted from dropping things in the sink, and when this happens, clean it, wait until it's dry and touch up the spots with bath enamel paint.

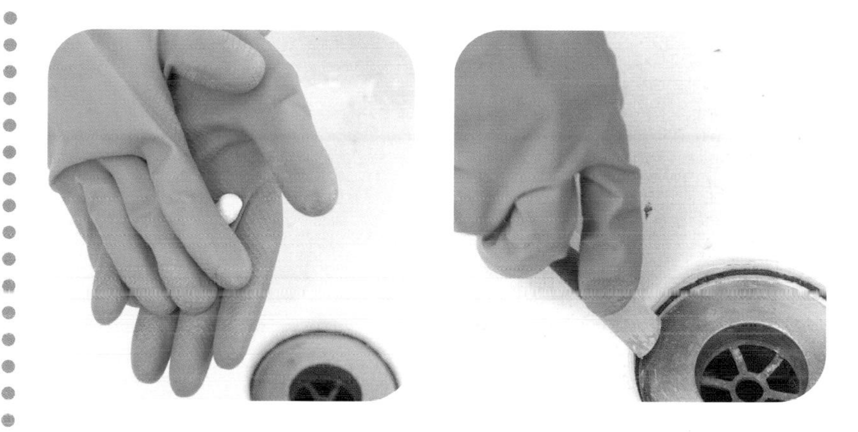

CHAPTER THREE

Maintain it

Cleaning and maintaining

Have you ever thought about what will happen when Auntie Hilda shuffles off this mortal coil and bequeaths you her worldly goods? Some are reproductions and have only sentimental value, but the big bits are fab. If you keep them in good condition, you'll be able to pass them on in your turn, or even sell them, as long as you don't let them fall apart through neglect or ruin them with over-reviving.

Glass

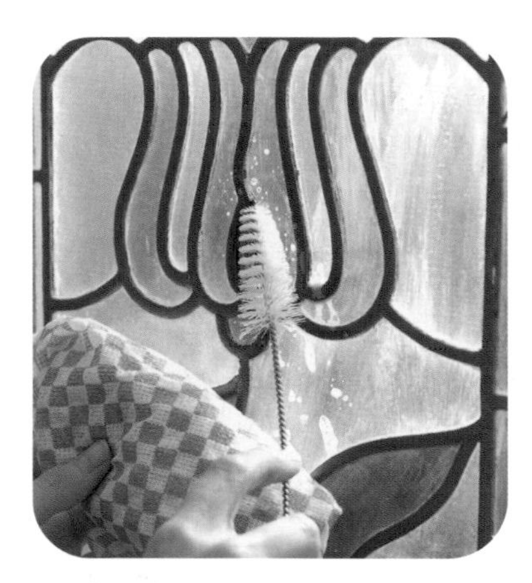

There's nothing quite like sparkling glass. Mum used to clean the inside while Dad went up the ladder on the outside. As he got older it was up to me to do the outside, and with my Mum on the other side of the pane of glass I had to do as I was told. All we ever used was vinegar, newspaper and soft cloths to finish – usually these were dilapidated knickers that had been cut into squares so that the neighbours wouldn't work it out. Now I use a little washing-up liquid and a lot of soft cloths – they are every bit as good, if not better, than a proprietary cleaner.

> **Leaded and stained glass:** This is wonderful stuff, with such a wide range of pretty colours and designs. Even on a seriously dull day it can brighten the lowest spirit. But it can get absolutely filthy if it's damaged. Remove the complete window and take it to a professional restorer, or, for a more straightforward cleaning job, consider doing it yourself.

> Use a baby's bottle brush – the bigger, the better, as the handle is then stronger – a nail brush or toothbrush, and have plenty of soft cloths to hand. **Gently scrub with washing-up liquid and be prepared to get wet**. If the glass has become pitted with acidic dirt, a little bleach helps.

> Once you're content that the glass is clean, **apply a little black boot polish with a tiny brush to the leading and rub it in well, especially into any cracks**. Make sure you don't get it on the glass – it's not a problem in most cases, but if the glass has been acid etched, the stain will stick. If you do smear it on, rub it off with a soft cloth or boot brush straightaway.

Paintwork

I have found that a great many clients that I visit ask to have their 'white work' painted – the skirting boards, the doors and the door and window frames. But actually, a lot of the time all the paintwork needs is a good scrub down. It saves a fortune, and if, when you've finished, you find that it still needs painting, well, you've already done the washing down.

> To revive your paintwork, give the surface a good wash down with sugar soap following the instructions on the bottle or box and using the three bucket method for cleaning (see page 123). It's important to keep paintwork clean and not let the dirt stay there for long, as it starts to eat into the paint. This is especially important outside.

Wood

Resist the temptation to polish your furniture every week. It doesn't need it, and when you do polish you should use the finest, lightest, solid polish. Use it very sparingly and only once a year – one small tin will last for 20 years. Don't use spray polish on antiques as you'll lose the years of wax build-up – that's called the patina. Just make sure that you dust regularly.

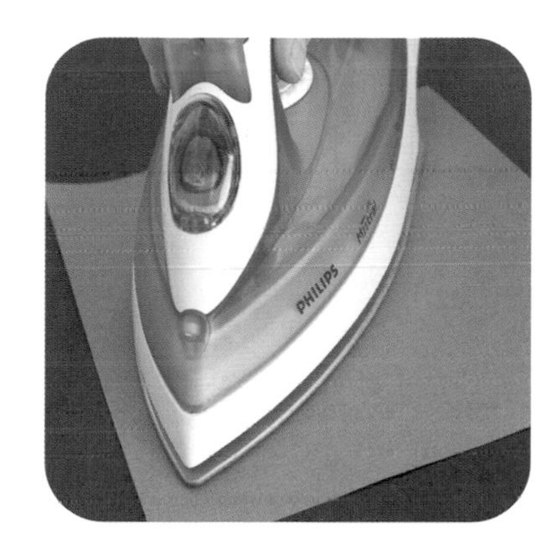

> **Polish it:** For stripped old pine or really rough wood, use solid polish in a tin. Read all the instructions on the tin to check that it's suitable to use on the surface you're treating, and use a damp cloth or duster to apply it.

> **Iron it:** The vicar has called and has put his very hot mug of coffee on Auntie Hilda's bureau, resulting in a round white ring on the surface. You are in shock, but try using **a hot, dry iron on a piece of brown paper,** and iron until the stain disappears.

> **Oil it:** Using kitchen paper, **wipe light white olive oil very sparingly over the suface,** making sure you don't over-oil the sides of the surfaces, and wipe off with kitchen paper until no more oil comes off. To prevent black bacteria from appearing on a wooden sink top, around the taps and in places where water collects, I find the olive oil treatment helps. Also, ask your plumber to seal the wood after he has drilled the hole for the taps.

> **Fill it:** Bashes and holes in your skirting board and door mouldings can look really messy. There are many different wood fillers on the market to help you put them right. They're sold in lots of different colours, most of which bear no relation to the colour of the wood they're supposed to be imitating – it's best to use them as a base that you can paint over.

> **Wax it:** For small areas in wood that you aren't going to paint, such as a scratch on a dining room table, wax is a good filler. It's sold in a block and all you need to do is warm it up in the palm of your hand and apply it to the wood. Wax usually comes in a pack of three colours so mix together two or three of the sticks to get the right shade. **Apply the wax, then level it off and polish the table** – even Auntie Hilda will never know.

How to deal with rusty metal

If your fridge is working perfectly, you can't change it just because it's gone rusty at the bottom. The same applies if the soap box on your dishwasher or your washing machine has got clogged and has leaked, first making the paint peel off and then rusting the metal. One day we'll have machines in which every part is made from recyclable plastic and it will never go rusty and will never go into landfill, but for the time being we need ways of dealing with rust. It's the same method that you'd use for treating the rust on your car, so most of the materials you'll need can be bought from a car accessories shop.

TOOLS REQUIRED

- **Wire wool**
- **Rust cure chemical treatment (paints on white but turns blue)**
- **Aluminium mesh**
- **Car body filler (preferably 'easy sand')**
- **Sandpaper**
- **Metal primer**
- **White enamel paint**

1

Rub off the flaky paint and rust with the wire wool. You may find that the rust has eaten through the metal in which case remove as much as possible – but look out for wires behind the metal you're treating. Remember that you're digging into the guts of your equipment.

2

Treat the rust with the rust cure, making sure you get it as far into the inside of the metal as possible. Rust cure is a white liquid that should turn the remains of the rust back into steel. But the more rust you've got rid of, the better the finish will be.

3

Bridge any big holes with aluminium mesh, **the smaller ones with car body filler.** This is a beige, putty-like substance that comes in a tin with a tube of bright red hardener. Read the instructions to find out the right quantities, and apply the hardener to the putty base. Smear it on and be quick, as it starts to harden quickly but will sand down easily.

4

Once the car body filler is applied, leave it for a few hours, **then sand it down until it's baby smooth.** Paint on the grey metal primer, which comes in a tin or an aerosol – an aerosol is probably easier for the novice. Spray or paint it on, and leave it to dry.

5

Finally, **paint or spray white enamel paint over the area** – or, if you've always secretly wanted a bright red fridge, this is your chance to get carried away and spray the whole lot! Always spray lightly and do several coats, leaving it to dry between each one. If the enamel runs, wipe it off and start again.

TOP TIP: SHAKE THAT CAN

When using an aerosol paint, always shake it vigorously for a long time. Keep shaking and turning the can while you work – you'll find the more you shake the can, the better the spray will be. You'll hear a rattling in the can as you shake it. That's the ball bearings placed in the paint to act as a stirrer, so keep them rolling.

TREATING OTHER SURFACES

Rusty railings: If you're one of the lucky ones whose house has kept its old metal railings, don't give up on them if they're a bit old and rusty. Most of them vanished in the last stages of the Second World War, when they were taken with old pots and pans to make aircraft. The bitter pill was that they were the wrong kind of steel, but if you do have a garden gate or fence, look after it and it'll last a lifetime. You can treat it in just the same way as you did the rust on the old fridge.

Acrylic: The old stereo cover looks like someone's gone over it with sandpaper, and what used to be crystal clear is now very cloudy. Try a little metal polish on a duster, and rub hard for a few seconds before polishing. You'll see the surface start to clear, and your precious piece of equipment will stop being such an eyesore. You can use this on radios, stereos, televisions and the white plastic at the corners of your tiles – and if you get polish on the grout, you can just scrub it off.

Mending a chipped bath: There are plenty of good products on the market for filling and repainting chips in the bath. As contractors, if we chip a bath, we have to replace it, we cannot mend it and I've only ever done it once, which was quite enough. It cost me dear, and although the client was shocked, he was so pleased when we put it right with no fuss or bother. But if it's your bath and you who's done the damage, you might not want to make the same decision. Just follow the instructions on the pack you've bought, and leave yourself plenty of time. If the pack says to leave it for 24 hours, leave it for 48.

Limescale: This will ruin most things in the bathroom and kitchen, so get rid of it as soon as you can. Believe it or not, your blunt chisel will make an impression as long as you wet it first. If you're going to paint the bath afterwards, you can use sandpaper to help you get rid of it as well. Once you've got rid of the limescale, buy an electrical water softener to attach to the main cold water pipe coming into the house. This will prevent new limescale from building up.

Maintaining windows

When it comes to unjamming stuck windows and doors, you'll almost always need a little help from a friend. Lots of jobs around the house can be done on your own, but it may be that you just need an extra pair of hands to shift or lift things. If you think it's going to be too heavy, it probably will be too heavy, so get a friend in to help, even if it's just to read the book out loud. If the window is jammed, first try holding a telephone directory against the frame and hitting it with a hammer. This should at least mean the paint will come unstuck (the usual cause of a jammed window) and allow you to deal with it.

How to replace a pane of glass

I have a real fear of glass and always try to treat it with respect. If you're repairing a window, you may have to sit outside on the sill or use a ladder, so please, please, please make sure you are safe.

TOOLS REQUIRED

- **Packing tape**
- **Sharp chisel**
- **Putty**
- **Glass cut to measure (see Step 3)**
- **Wood preserver**
- **Window putty**
- **Glass tacks**
- **Tack hammer**
- **Putty knife**

TOP TIP: EASY DOES IT

My Dad always said that three or four light coats of paint were better than two heavy ones on a window – take note of the results of over-zealous painting!

1

Stick brown packing tape on each side of the pane **in a criss-cross pattern,** making sure you leave no bare glass. This will prevent shards of glass from flying around.

2

Remove the putty from both sides of the broken pane with a sharp chisel and take out the glass, being careful not to ruin the frame. At this point you could treat the wood with some wood preserver – it's a good discipline to do this every time you expose bare wood on the outside of your house and will save a fortune in the long run.

3

Measure the exact hole that the glass will go into and take the measurement to the glass cutter. He will cut a piece of glass to the right size allowing for the putty, which will act as a buffer and save it from vibration.

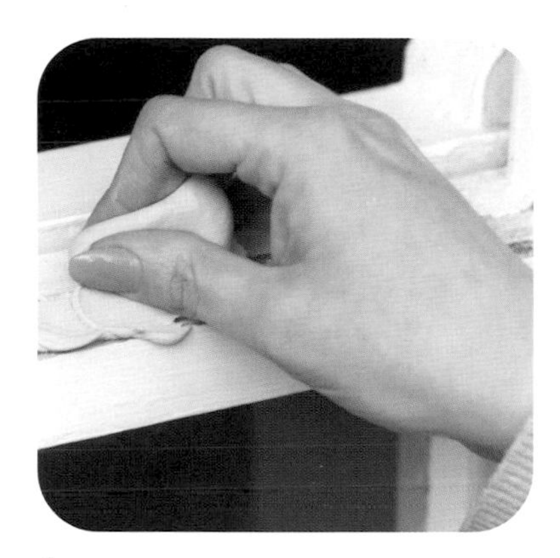

4
Run a tiny amount of putty into the inside part of the frame and insert the glass, pressing it home onto the putty.

5
Hold a piece of paper over the glass and use the tack hammer to tap the tacks into place on each side of the glass. Slide the tack hammer along the paper to tap the tack, rather than just aiming for the tack itself, or you'll risk breaking the glass.

6
Roll out the putty and **use the putty knife to spread it evenly around the glass.** The knife has an angled blade that will give you that perfect shaped edge. If it won't slide, a little water helps. The instructions on the putty tin will tell you how long you need to leave it to dry before painting.

REPAIRING FILLETS AND SILLS

Auntie Hilda's eyes lit up the day I said I was going to do the fillets. She thought I was talking about fillet steak, but no, it's the concrete filling around the outside of exterior windows and doors. If the old fillets have fallen out, replacing them is a good opportunity to look at the part of the window frame that's usually hidden by the concrete fillets, and paint on a little wood preservative. Let this dry and then run a line of silicone right next to the frame. This will help to get rid of draughts. Finally, apply the new cement, making sure you match the other windows in the house to give a consistent style.

If you have broken or rotten interior window sills, first look on the outside for cracks where the water can get through and fill with car body filler – it's weatherproof and paints up a treat. For larger rotten areas, chop out any bad wood with your set of chisels and treat what remains with a wood hardener. Once it's dry, paint also with wood preservative. Then you can set about filling the gaps with car body filler, building it up until you get a rough shape and then sand it down to match the rest of the wood. Once you know the outside of the window is safe to the elements, repeat with the interior sill. Repaint the whole window sill for the ultimate finish.

Draughtproofing

When my sister and I were little we used to wake in the mornings and giggle a lot on those really cold, cold days. We would try to get dressed in bed and then make a dash for the warmth of the kitchen. At night times in the little sitting room we used to huddle round the fire – our fronts were warm but our backs frozen from the draught that came through the windows. It is such an uncomfortable position to be in that I always greet any new method of keeping out draughts with distinctly open arms.

How to draughtproof a window

You've had the loft insulated, the back door draughtproofed and your windows are protected by the heaviest curtains in all creation, but the house is still cold. The problem is that you're losing the heat through the glass and, oh dear, you can't afford double glazing. Well, 20 years ago when we were all freezing, I bought a piece of 4mm (⅙in) acrylic every month to Velcro to one window after another. The acrylic looks like glass but it's not as cold. Use 5cm (2in) wide Velcro, because the draughts around the window can suck the acrylic in and out, and anything too narrow would soon come undone.

TOOLS REQUIRED

> **Acrylic sheets**
> **Scissors**
> **Roll 5cm (2in) wide white Velcro**

1

Have the acrylic cut to the window frame measurements. **Then stick the loopy part of the Velcro to the frame.**

2

Ensure that the acrylic sheet is clean on both sides - but most especially the side facing the window. **Stick the fluffy part of the Velcro** to that side of the acrylic

3

Push the panel onto the window and instantly feel the difference. The beauty is that Velcro breathes, so you do get air, the dust from outside stays out, and the windows don't steam up. Unlike secondary glazing, if you need to get out of the window, you just rip it off and you're free. By the end of the winter it's paid for itself, and during the summer the panels can come down. Wash the paintwork and scrub the loopy Velcro. With curtains up you can't really see it – but if you lean out of the window, mind you don't get stuck to the bottom bit!

TROUBLESHOOTING: MRS FIXIT'S PATENT DRAUGHTPROOFING AND INSULATION METHODS

Gas and electricity bills increase all the time, and to be kind to our purses as well as to the planet, we must try to make an effort not to use so much power.

Dad made a wonderful invention from the old kitchen range. When the range was taken out, he took it to his workshop at the end of the garden and sat on it while he worked. For a laugh one day, he put an electric lamp inside with bits of crinkled cellophane to mock-up a fire and make it feel more homely. He left it on for a couple of hours, forgetting all about it, and then sat on it. To his surprise and our amusement it was very hot – the light bulb had heated the cast iron, which was retaining the heat. There were also bricks in the oven and even they were warm. Without realising, Dad had built his own storage heater! Soon we adapted this invention for other purposes and put a light bulb in a tin can in the rabbit hutch too. Very simple and very successful ... but let's get back to human homes.

A draughty chimney is a big offender when it comes to losing heat. I use the same kind of polyester wadding that duvets are made out of and stick a big wedge up the chimney. It's fab and it breathes, so you get warmth and ventilation – but don't light your fire while it's up the chimney ...

The other usual suspect is the skirting board. You only have to look at the black marks on the carpet to show you where the draughts are coming from. Just pull the carpet away from the gripper rods, pull back and tape it to itself. Go round under the skirting board and between the floorboards with decorator's caulk. This is a thick white filler that comes in a big tube. The beauty of caulk is that it is water soluble, so it will stretch a bit and allow the boards and skirting to expand and contract with the weather. Smooth it in with your fingers, being careful not to hurt them on the gripper rod. After 8–12 hours, put the carpet back and you'll be amazed – not only will it be less draughty, but when you clean the carpet, it will stay clean.

There are many other cheap methods of draughtproofing on the market. You can have a **'V' spring or a plastic brush, which are strips that you attach to various parts of the window** and are fixed in place in accordance with the manufacturer's instructions. But if your draughts are that bad, you may be better off finding out why the window fits so badly. Too many layers of paint is the most common offender, so strip them off and start again.

Recognising condensation and damp

Whenever you see signs of condensation and damp, it's important that you find the cause quickly and then deal with it promptly, because it isn't going away, and the longer you leave it, the more likely it is to cause expensive and extensive damage to your house.

Condensation

Condensation happens when warm, wet air hits a cold surface and cools down, making the water vapour condense into droplets and eventually causing peppery black patches to start to appear on ceilings or walls. This is a form of fungus, and its spores can cause bad headaches and nausea, so it's important to get rid of it for the sake of your health as well as your house.

> If you use a tumble dryer, make sure you have a proper external venting kit, leading the hot air out through the wall behind the dryer. It's not enough just to hang a hose out of a window, because the water vapour will just blow back in or drip down the wall.

> Strip any wallpaper from the affected area and treat the walls with an anti-fungal spray. Windows can be treated with an anti-fungal cleaner or just bleach, but make sure you rinse it off very thoroughly.

> **Install extractor fans** in kitchens and bathrooms. In new-build housing, regulations insist that extractor fans are installed.

> Be sure that the cause of the condensation has been sorted out before you redecorate.

TOP TIP: WHAT, NO VENT?

If you're buying a tumble dryer for a room where it's difficult to fit an external vent, get one with a condenser – I have one, and it's fantastic.

Permeating damp

This is usually caused by a slow leak from a fixing under a bath or sink, and by the time you see staining on the ceiling, it will have been going for a while.

> In the room above the damp patch, inspect all the pipes and fittings in the area. Tighten all the nuts on the piping and replace any broken or worn washers in sink waste units or taps – see page 100. If there are gaps in the sealing around a bath or sink, see page 122 to find out how to remove and replace it.

> Make sure you've found and fixed the source of the water before doing any repairs or redecoration of the stained ceiling or wall.

> Resist the temptation to put oil-based paint over the stain – **you can buy special paint with chemicals that will help not only to seal but also cover the stain.**

> Once the area has dried out, wallpaper can be carefully pasted back on with clean hands and new paste – usually you'll just need a teaspoonful applied with a child's paintbrush.

> If there's damp showing in a wall or ceiling and it doesn't seem to come either from the ground (see below) or from the room above, you've probably got a problem with permeating damp from outside the house. It's very common, and the usual reason is that your guttering is blocked, causing water to cascade down the side of the house (see page 107).

Rising damp

Rising damp is water soaked up in walls from the ground by bricks and plaster.The only way to stop it is with a damp-proof course, and so rising damp is a sign that you either don't have one, or that it has become faulty in some way, allowing the water to get through.

> The first sign of rising damp is often a smell, followed by a stain creeping up the walls.

> The **plaster will start to bubble, and the paint and wallpaper will start to be damaged**. It never moves very fast, but don't ignore it – catch it as soon as possible. If you leave it too long, the plaster may start falling off the wall.

> The solution is usually to have a chemical damp barrier injection into the brickwork all around the house and into any chimney breasts on the ground floor by a professional.

> Once the source of the damp has been blocked off, you can redecorate, which will sometimes mean stripping the plaster right back to the brickwork in the affected area.

TOP TIP: CHECK THE DAMP COURSE

Check the outside of the house to make sure that you haven't laid a path too high or stacked rubbish against the wall, allowing water to enter the brickwork above the damp course.

PART FOUR
REFERENCE

Materials: wood

I have always had a love of wood since my early years watching my Dad transform a pile of scruffy wood into the most beautiful piece of furniture. Wood is warm to the touch, pleasing to the eye and will last as long as you let it. Treat it with respect and it will love you for the rest of your life.

SOFTWOOD

Type	What is it?	Sizes	Uses
Sawn softwood	Unplaned (rough) wood	Many sizes from 5 x 2.5cm (2 x 1in) upwards	General building, timber frames
Treated sawn softwood	Pressure treated to impregnate wood preservatives	Many sizes from 5 x 2.5cm (2 x 1in) upwards	General building outdoors, fences, sheds, areas that get wet
Prepared softwood	Planed planks	Various lengths, widths and thicknesses available to match anything you already have	Floorboards, general
Planed wood for battens	Prepared softwood	5 x 2.5cm (2 x 1in) 5 x 7.5cm (2 x 3in) for studding	Framework, cladding, plasterboarding
Tongue and groove	Planks cut to fit together	Various	Floorboards, cladding
Panel moulding	Thin strips of wood	Various	Decorative finishes on flush doors, panel borders
Architrave	Wide strips with a decorative profile	Various	Trim around doorways
Picture rail and dado	Mouldings with decorative profile	Various	Trim around upper and lower halves of walls
Skirting board	Thin planks, often with a decoratively carved profile	Various	Decorative and protective trim where walls meet

There are three types of wooden materials: hardwood, softwood, and man-made board – the sawdust of the other woods mixed with resins and formed into boards.

> Hardwood comes from deciduous broad-leaved trees like oak and the trees of the rainforest. It is usually harder, more attractive and much more expensive than softwood. Many sources of hardwood are now endangered, so check yours comes from a sustainable source. Make sure it's certificated and has been stamped on the wood. Good wood yards will always be able to show you point of origin certificates as well as clearly stamping the wood.

> Softwood comes from evergreen coniferous trees like pines and firs. It can have a lot of knots, which should be treated before decorating. If it will be visible, buy planed wood for a smooth surface. This means it will be a few millimetres thinner than its original size.

> There are lots of man-made materials around that are used in the home. They are generally very easy to work with, but cutting them creates a lot of dust so wear a mask, especially when cutting MDF, as the sawdust contains some very noxious chemicals. They can also be covered with veneer, a thin layer of fine wood that makes a more attractive surface.

MAN-MADE MATERIALS

Material	What is it?	Sizes	Uses
Plywood	Thin wood veneers glued together under pressure	Thicknesses: 3–18mm (⅛–¾in) • Standard sheet size: 244 x 122cm (8 x 4ft)	General-purpose board
Fibreboard (MDF)	Wood fibres mixed with resin that is compressed and cut into sheets	Thicknesses: 3–35mm (⅛–1⅓in) • Standard sheet size: 244 x 122cm (8 x 4ft) • Grooved board available for curves, 6mm (¼in) thick • Tongue-and-groove effect in a water-resistant panel for baths • Fire-resistant sheets for near fires or for building housing for TV, video or sound equipment in kitchens. It is distinguished by a red colour in the cut ends or sides	General-purpose board, can be bent into curves
Laminate: floor	Chipboard or MDF bonded with laminate or wood veneer	Thickness: 9mm (⅜in)	Floors!
Laminate: worktop	Chipboard or MDF bonded with a selection of colours and finishes	Thickness of 5–6cm (2–2¼in), usually with a curved edge	Kitchen surfaces

Materials: paint and paper

The art of decoration will give you great pleasure. The sense of achievement when you can sit back and say, 'I did that' never fails to kick in. As you do your prep work, remember that through this you will have a good finish, no matter how hard you try to muck it up or how bored you get. When decorating, there is always a point where it feels like you are wading through treacle, but don't fret, it always gets done. Your choice of materials matters, so here is a run-down on your products.

PAINT CHOICES

Paint	Finish	Good for	Coverage
Matt emulsion	Dull, flat	Walls, ceilings	16m^2/litre (87 sq yd/gal)
Vinyl matt emulsion	Dull, flat	Uneven walls	16m^2/litre (87 sq yd/gal)
Vinyl silk emulsion	Medium sheen	Walls in busy or dirty locations	15m^2/litre (82 sq yd/gal)
Eggshell (oil or water based)	Medium sheen	Woodwork	16m^2/litre (87 sq yd/gal)
Gloss (oil based)	Shiny	Wood and metal	17m^2/litre (92 sq yd/gal)
Quick-drying gloss (water based)	Slightly shiny	Wood and metal	15m^2/litre (82 sq yd/gal)
Water-based paints for brickwork	Matt or soft sheen	Internal or external brickwork	15m^2/litre (82 sq yd/gal)
Varnish (water based)	Shiny or matt, hardwearing	Large-scale areas such as in heavy-usage areas like a passageway	10m^2/litre (85 sq yd/gal)
Woodstain (water based)	Natural/coloured	Shows the grain of the wood	22m^2/litre (120 sq yd/gal)

WALLPAPER

CHOICES

Type	Finish	Good for
Embossed	Thick texture, raised finish	Uneven walls that need to be washed
Flock/Relief	Pattern makes a velvety texture	Uneven walls
Lining	Smooth	Base for papering or painting
Printed	Patterned	Smooth walls
Vinyl	Shiny, highly patterned, metallic	High-traffic areas or walls that get dirty
Woodchip	Rough texture	Hiding rough walls

HOW MANY ROLLS DO YOU NEED? – WALLS

	Distance around room, including doors and windows							
Wall height	10m (33ft)	12m (39ft)	14m (46ft)	16m (52ft)	18m (59ft)	20m (66ft)	22m (72ft)	24m (79ft)
2.1–2.3m (7–7ft 6in)	5	5	6	7	8	9	10	11
2.3–2.4m (7ft 6in–8ft)	5	6	7	8	9	10	10	11
2.4–2.6m (8ft–8ft 6in)	5	6	7	9	10	11	12	13
2.6–2.7m (8ft 6in–9ft)	5	6	7	9	10	11	12	13
2.7–2.9m (9ft–9ft 6in)	6	7	8	9	10	12	12	14

HOW MANY ROLLS DO YOU NEED? – CEILINGS

Distance around room	(30–40ft) 9–12m	(42–50ft) 13–15m	(55–60ft) 17–18m	(65–70ft) 20–21m	(75–80ft) 23–24m	(85–90ft) 26–27m	(95–100ft) 29–30m
Rolls needed	2	3	4	6	7	9	10

Materials: tiles

Choosing tiles doesn't have to be a minefield. I always suggest to my clients that they keep every picture they like of a shower or bathroom from magazines and that they research tiles through suppliers and also on the internet. You can't look at too many pictures because it is only through doing this that you start to find out what is available and also discover what style you would choose to have in your own home.

Establishing your style

> Sort through the pictures you've collected and divide them into one pile of those you like and another of those you don't. Then take the pile of pictures you like and do it again and again until a pattern has emerged, showing you what is instinctively attractive to you. This really works because it forces you to spend a bit more time thinking about it than you otherwise might do.

Tiles for different surfaces

> Try to use wall tiles for walls and floor tiles for floors, as they are made from different materials and perform different jobs. Floor tiles are extremely strong and are sometimes slightly thicker than wall tiles. They can resist a lot of wear and tear, but they are also more difficult to cut and drill through.

> If you really want to have the same tiles for both the floor and walls of your bathroom, please remember that although you can use floor tiles on the walls, you should never use wall tiles on the floor. They quite simply aren't strong enough.

> One of my pet hates is tiles on window sills – if you want the sills covered, why not have a piece of glass or acrylic made to fit? Acrylic is great, because if it scratches, you just need to give it a quick rub with metal polish and it's gone. If you can afford it, a beautiful piece of marble on the window sill will make a bathroom come alive, and it's more cost-effective than you may think because even a small piece makes a big difference – just make sure that you protect it with the right sealant.

WALL TILES

Type	Finish
Ceramic (glazed)	Shiny, hardwearing, can be patterned
Ceramic (matt)	Dull, hardwearing – may need sealing, can be patterned
Cork	Soft, good for noticeboards and sound insulation
Marble	Luxurious (and expensive)
Mirror	Create an impression of space
Mosaic (also know as chips) glass or ceramic	Blocks of small squares, or strips to make a border, can create your own picture or pattern
Plastic	Contain pieces of computer rubbish – really wild
Metal	Very 21st century with a choice of patterned or plain
Terracotta	Textured

Sizes and materials

Tiles range in size from large slabs of slate to tiny Victorian path tiles. In general, use small tiles in small places and large tiles in large places. But this is a matter of taste and there are no absolute rules, just as long as you think it through carefully.

> **Ceramic and stone tiles:** Ceramic is the most common wall tile material, but you can have tiles in a huge range of materials, including many types of stone, such as slate, York stone and so on. Be especially careful with tumbled marble tiles and don't apply too much grouting.

> **Mosaic tiles** manage to be both big and small at the same time – small tiles are fixed together on backing sheets to make large ones, with thin gaps for putting grout between the individual pieces. They are really effective and one of the easiest ways to get an almost perfect finish, especially as you don't need spacers.

> **Glass tiles** are my pet hate for novices unless they take up a really small area and you can protect them while you're working. Glass can have a porous surface that accepts the grout, and you just can't get it out, so if you get grout on the glass, they'll never be the same again. Glass mosaic tiles make this even more difficult because there's so much grout involved.

FLOOR TILES

Type	Finish	Good for
Brick	Warm and rustic	Linking exterior and interior
Ceramic	Various, shiny and matt	Decorative effects
Granite	Shades of grey, wearing to a softer sheen	Heavy traffic areas
Limestone	Sandy colour, requires sealing	Adding warmth
Marble	Cool, formal	Creating an elegant effect
Quarry and terracotta	Rustic	Kitchens, utility rooms, creating patterns
Slate	Slip-resistant	Entrances and utility rooms
Metal	Varied, for that wow factor or to look industrial	Hard-wearing areas

Hiring a builder or tradesperson

Now that you've learnt how to Do It Properly in a wide range of situations, you should feel much more in control of your home. But part of being in control is knowing when you need help, and this section is all about the sorts of jobs where you need to hire a professional to do the work for you, such as a major maintenance job or a redevelopment of your home. Just because you're not doing the work yourself doesn't mean you're not involved – in fact, when you're employing someone else you need to be just as much in charge as you are for DIY. It's all a matter of recognising your contractor's greater knowledge and experience, and getting the most out of him or her to achieve the results you want.

Developing your home

You've decided that you want to extend the house at the back, or that the loft will make the perfect place for an extra bedroom, and you need to know how to get from your dream to reality.

Drawing up the plans

The first people you'll need to hire are an architect and a structural engineer. Sometimes your architect will decide whether or not the latter is necessary. In both cases, unless you have a personal recommendation, contact your local council's planning office for information – they often have lists, and for the sake of an easy life are likely only to recommend good ones.

> **Architects** bring an element of creativity, and will help you to come up with a design as well as drawing up plans for the job. They can also oversee the whole job, including keeping an eye on your contractors, but this tends to be expensive. However, the job is more likely to be completed on time due to penalty clauses in an architect's contract with the contractor. It might also help prevent technical problems arising.

> **Structural engineers** usually charge less than architects. They will not have creative input, but they can draw up plans for designs you are already sure of. They also make sure that a building's shape, design and the materials are strong enough to withstand anything that's thrown at them. Structural engineers are a mine of information, so ask them lots of questions when they visit. Your architect will take the engineer's recommendations into the plans.

Applying for planning permission

Planning permission is dealt with by your local council's planning office, and it's a good idea to involve them as early as possible. Even though there are some sorts of development that don't need permission, such as certain types of extension, you'll still need to check with the planning office to make sure your project is exempt, and they can give you a certificate to confirm this.

If you do need to apply for planning permission, the application process varies depending on the local council – some ask you to send in an application form with your plans, while others ask that you visit the planning office personally – so get in touch with yours to find out what to do. I've always found that my local planning office prefers it if plans are quite rough and ready at the outset, because if you go to them with beautifully drawn plans they think you're just expecting them to rubber stamp them. But some local authorities have very precise guidelines for the type and standard of plan they're prepared to consider. Talk this through with your planning office before you make your application.

Once you've submitted the completed application forms with the plans and the correct fee, the council should acknowledge your application and will place it on the planning register so that it can be inspected by the public, as well as consulting other organisations in some cases. They should decide the application within eight weeks or seek your consent to extend the period. If they refuse your application, they must give reasons for the decision, and you can ask them whether changing the plans could make a difference. If this is the case, you can go back to the architect and engineer with the recommendations, and modify your plans for resubmission.

Adjoining properties

Your property may be freehold or leasehold, and it may be detached, semi-detached, terraced or part of an apartment building. This will all affect the way you deal with any changes you make to your property.

> **Freehold and leasehold:** Freehold ownership means that you own a property outright, whereas leasehold ownership means that you have bought the right to live there for a specified number of years. With a leasehold arrangement, the leaseholders will generally pay annual ground rent to the freeholder or landlord. As a leaseholder you are likely to need the permission of the freeholder in order to make any major alterations to your property.

> **Party wall agreements:** Even if you own your house, if it is semi-detached or terraced, you share some walls with your neighbours. These shared walls are called 'party walls', and under the terms of the Party Wall Act of 1996 you must get permission from all adjoining owners if you intend to work on them. Further information about the Act is available from HMSO.

Getting contractors' estimates

Once you've had permission from the council and any relevant neighbours, you're ready to hire a contractor. Make sure you get at least three estimates. The plans will help you in briefing the contractors, and if there's a huge discrepancy in cost or if the numbers just don't make sense to you, one option is to get a quantity survey done – this helps give an idea of the costing of materials.

Working with contractors

When you are working with contractors, remember that you are doing just that, working, even though you may be in your own home. They are your employees, and you should treat them with the same professionalism as you would any other colleague. Always be there to say hello in the morning with a hot cuppa to help start the jumbo jets, and then keep out of their way. At the end of the day ask about the day's progress and what's planned for the next day, and discuss any problems calmly, giving yourself time to think about it if necessary.

MAJOR MAINTENANCE

Major maintenance includes those jobs that maintain your house rather than develop it, but which need to be done properly to avoid costing a fortune in repairs. For instance:

> Anything to do with gas should be done by a registered professional with a Corgi certificate.

> A major plumbing restructure, such as the installation of a new boiler or new radiators, should be done by a professional plumber.

> You are legally required to have all major electrical works certificated, which means they must either be done or checked by a registered electrician (see also page 76).

> Work such as knocking down a wall will need plans drawn up by a structural engineer or architect and building regulations approval.

> Major roofing and sewer work must be done by an expert.

> And any other work that you don't feel comfortable doing yourself!

The best way of getting a contractor is by word of mouth. When you see a builder working on the house opposite, wait until he's gone and knock on the door to ask the owner about the man, his company, the work that was done and how much he's being paid. If he turns out to be the best thing since sliced bread, get in touch for an estimate and ask for more references.

DON'T be suckered into getting work done for cash with no invoices and no VAT – you're asking for trouble, because in the case of any dispute there will be no record of what the contractor was being paid to do. You need to receive estimates, invoices and terms of trading, together with the insurance certificates.

Glossary

Allen key: Spanner designed to turn an Allen screw.

Allen screw: Screw with a hexagonal socket head.

Appliance: Machine or device powered by electricity.

Architrave: Ornamental wooden moulding that surrounds the door.

Awl: A thin, pointed hand tool with a fluted blade used for piercing wood, leather, etc.

Ball cock (ball valve): A device for regulating the flow of liquid into a tank, cistern, etc., consisting of a floating ball attached at one end of an arm and a valve on the other end, which opens and closes as the floating ball falls and rises with the water in the tank.

Bit: The cutting part of a drill.

Bleed key: Small metal key used to release air in the radiator.

Bradawl: A thin, pointed tool used to pierce wood, leather, or other materials for the insertion of brads, screws, etc.

Cap nut: Nut connecting the radiator valve to the central heating pipe.

Chisel: Tool used for shaping and sculpting wood.

Ceiling rose: A special junction box for connecting a suspended light fitting to a lighting circuit.

Circlip (butterfly clip): A flat spring ring split at one point so that it can be sprung open, passed over a shaft or spindle, and allowed to close into a closely fitting recess to form a collar on the shaft.

Circuit: A complete path through which an electric current can flow.

Circuit breaker: A special switch installed in a consumer unit to protect an individual circuit or a device that can be plugged into a mains socket to be used with power tools. Should a fault occur, the circuit breaker will switch off automatically.

Circular locking disc: Looks like two discs joined to resemble a metal plus sign. The side of the plug that goes into the wood has a gap in it, which sits over the locking bolt. When the disc is turned with a screwdriver, the disc catches the bolt and locks it firmly into place.

Conductor: A component, usually a length of wire, along which an electric current will pass.

Consumer unit: A box, situated near the meter, which contains the fuses or miniature circuit breakers (MCBs) protecting all the circuits within the home. It also houses the main isolating switch that cuts the power to your home.

Countersink: To cut a tapered recess that allows the head of a screw to be flush with a surface, or the tapered recess itself.

Damp-proof course: A layer of impervious material that prevents moisture rising from the ground into the walls of a building.

Dimmer switch: A switch that changes the level of light by varying the electric current through a lamp.

Double glazing: Two panes of glass in a window, fitted to reduce the transmission of heat, sound, etc.

Dowel: A fastener – usually wooden – that is inserted into holes in two adjacent pieces, with a resin or glue to hold them together.

Drain cock: Used for emptying all the water from your central heating system. It resembles a tap and will usually be found close to the boiler on the return pipe.

Earth: A connection between an electrical circuit and the earth (ground), or a terminal to which the connection is made.

Emulsion: A paint in which the pigment is suspended in a vehicle, usually a synthetic resin, that is dispersed in water as an emulsion. It usually has a mat finish.

Epoxy resin: Synthetic adhesive coating or filler.

Feed-and-expansion tank: Maintains the correct level of water in the heating system and also allows for the expansion of water in the radiators and pipes when they become hot.

Fixing bolts: Bolts used with an Allen key for fixing together parts. They go directly through two pieces and lock them together.

Flex, flexible cord: Electrical conductors made from numerous wire filaments enclosed in PVC insulation. Usually, two or more insulated conductors are sheathed within an outer layer of PVC. This type of flexible cord is invariably used to carry electricity from wall sockets or similar outlets to electrical appliances.

Fuse: Protective device containing a wire that is designed to melt at a predetermined temperature when the current exceeds a certain value.

Fuse box: Where the in-coming electric current is split to feed the different circuits in your house, with a fuse or MCB (miniature circuit breaker) guarding each one.

Gauge: Thickness, diameter.

Gauge rod: Piece of timber used to measure precisely the distances in a room to work out how many tiles will fit in each part and exactly where they will go.

Grout: A fine white paste that can be used to fill spaces between tiles on the floor or wall.

Grout float: Used for smoothing grout between tiles. It usually has a large handle on it to allow the user to apply plenty of pressure.

Grub screw: A small headless screw having a slot cut for a screwdriver or a socket for a hexagon key and used to secure a sliding component in a determined position.

Gypsum: White or colourless mineral used to make cements and plasters.

Hessian string: Strong, coarse string made from hemp or jute.

Insulating tape: Colour-coded self-adhesive tape, usually made from PVC.

Insulation: Materials used to reduce the transmission of heat or sound. Or a non-conductive material surrounding electrical wires or connections to prevent the passage of electricity.

Jig saw: A mechanical saw with a fine steel blade for cutting either straight or intricate curves in sheets of material.

Joist: A horizontal wooden or metal beam used to support a structure such as a floor or ceiling.

Knotting compound: A sealer applied over knots in new wood before priming to prevent resin from exuding.

Laminate flooring: A layer of MDF coated with a picture of wood or a thin layer of real wood, which is laminated under heat, resulting in a strong, hard surface.

Lath and plaster: A method of finishing a timber-frame wall or ceiling. Narrow strips of wood are nailed to the studs or joists to provide a supporting framework for plaster or tiles.

Light fitting: Whole of the unit that connects the bulb to the wiring in the ceiling or wall, with the connection usually concealed by a plain circular box or an ornamental ceiling rose.

Live: The section of an electrical circuit that carries the flow of current to an appliance. Also known as phase.

Mallet: A tool resembling a hammer but having a large head of wood, copper, lead, leather, etc.

Mastic: Any of several sticky putty-like substances used as a filler, adhesive, or seal in wood, plaster or masonry. They are usually applied with a gun.

MDF: Medium-density fibreboard.

Mitre, mitre joint: A corner joint formed between two pieces of material, especially wood, by cutting bevels of equal angles at the ends of each piece.

Mitre block: A block of wood with slots for cutting mitre joints with a saw.

Moulding: Decorative trim around ceilings and floors, used to prevent draughts and protect floorboards.

Neutral: The section of an electrical circuit that carries the flow of current back to source.

Notched spreader: An essential tool for spreading tile adhesive.

Olive: Copper ring used to make a watertight seal.

Open-vented heating system: Boiler is separate from any hot water tank supplying the taps, and the system usually includes a storage tank and a feed-and-expansion tank.

Pelmet: An ornamental drapery or board fixed above a window to conceal the curtain rail.

Perforator: Hand tool that makes holes in old wallpaper so that water and steam can penetrate.

Piano hinge: Long, thin hinge that runs from the top to the bottom of the door and creates a strong fastening.

Pilot hole: A small-diameter hole drilled prior to the insertion of a woodscrew to act as a guide for its thread.

Pincers: Metal tool with handles and jaws that is used for gripping and pulling things.

Plane: Block with a steel blade to shave wood.

Plasterboard: Wallboard with a gypsum plaster core bonded to layers of paper or fibreboard.

Primer: The first coat of a paint system applied to protect wood or metal. A wood primer reduces the absorption of subsequent undercoats and top coats. A metal primer prevents corrosion.

PTFE tape (polytetrafluoroethylene): Tape used for sealing joints in pipework.

Purlin: A horizontal beam that provides intermediate support for the common rafters of a roof construction.

Putty: A stiff paste made of whiting and linseed oil that is used to fix glass panes into frames and to fill cracks or holes in woodwork, etc.

PVA (polyvinyl acetate): Synthetic resin mainly used in latex paints and adhesives.

PVC (polyvinyl chloride): Synthetic plastic material.

Radiator valve: Located at the bottom of a radiator, these are the valves at either end that control the flow of hot water into and out of the radiator, usually with an adjustable valve at one end and a fixed valve at the other, which can only be adjusted with a spanner.

RCD (residual current device): A device that regulates the flow of electrical current through the live and neutral wires of a circuit. When an RCD detects an imbalance caused by earth leakage, it cuts off the supply of electricity as a safety precaution.

Sander, sanding machine: Power tool used to sand surfaces, particularly wood.

Sanding discs or belts: Converts table or band saws into sanding machines to sand curves or edges.

Score-and-snap pliers: Used for cutting straight lines on tiles that aren't too thick.

Scotia moulding: Deep concave moulding.

Sealed heating systems: Usually found in conjunction with a combination boiler, which supplies hot water both to a sealed central heating system and to the taps.

Sheathing: The outer layer of insulation surrounding an electrical cable or flex.

Short circuit: The accidental re-routing of electricity to earth, which increases the current flow, resulting in a blown fuse.

Spanner: A steel hand tool with a handle carrying jaws or a hole of particular shape designed to grip a nut or bolt head.

Spirit level: Indicator that establishes the horizontal or vertical when a bubble is centred in a tube of liquid.

Stain: Dye that is used to protect and treat materials, usually wood.

Strut: A structural member used mainly in compression, especially as part of a framework.

Studs: The vertical members of a timber-frame wall.

Surge: Large momentary increase in mains voltage. Sometimes referred to as a voltage spike.

Tack cloth: A large piece of muslin infused with resin or lanoline.

Tenon: The projecting end of a piece of wood formed to fit into a corresponding mortise in another piece.

Tenon saw: A small fine-toothed saw with a strong back, used especially for cutting tenons.

Terminal: A connection to which the bared ends of electrical cable or flex are attached.

Toggle bolt: Long thin bolt with two wings attached on the end specifically designed for plasterboard or lath and plaster, which distributes the load over a larger area than an ordinary wall plug.

Top coat: The outer layer of a paint system.

Torque: Any force or system of forces that causes or tends to cause rotation.

Undercoat: A layer or layers of paint used to obliterate the colour of a primer and build a protective body of paint before applying a top coat.

Underlay: Felt, rubber, plastic, etc., laid beneath carpet or floorboards to increase insulation and resilience.

Valve: Device that shuts off, starts, regulates, or controls the flow of a fluid.

Varnish: A preparation consisting of a solvent, a drying oil, and usually resin or rubber for application to a surface to produce a hard, glossy, usually transparent, coating.

Washer: Flat rubber disk that is placed under a nut to prevent leaks.

Useful addresses

CURTAINS

Bradley Collection
Lion Barn, Maitland Road
Needham Market
Suffolk IP6 8NS
Tel: 0845 118 7224
Web: www.bradleycollection.co.uk
(curtain accessories)

Curtains2go
PO Box 7922
Nottingham NG9 6ZG
Tel: 0870 050 7901
Email: sales@curtains-2go.co.uk
Web: www.curtains-2go.co.uk
(curtains, poles, supplies)

Curtain Poles Direct
Freepost No. 6632
Edmonton
London N18 3BR
Tel: 0870 460 1122
Email: customerservice@curtainpolesdirect.co.uk
Web: www.curtainpolesdirect.co.uk
(curtains, poles, supplies)

Luxaflex
Tel: 0161 947 4904 (for stockists)
Email: Info.consumer@luxaflex-sunway.co.uk
Web: www.luxaflex.com
(made-to-measure blinds)

Wilman Interiors
Heasandford Industrial Estate
Widow Hill Road,
Burnley
Lancs BB10 2TJ
Tel: 0128 272 7300
Email: wilman.enteprises@cwvgroup.com
Web: www.wilman.co.uk
(curtains, poles, supplies)

FLOORING

Alternative Flooring Company
3B Stephenson Close
East Portway,
Andover
Hampshire SP10 3RU
Tel: 0126 433 5111
Email: sales@alternativeflooring.com
Web: www.alternative-flooring.com
(natural flooring)

Floors-2-Go
74 Newtown Row
Birmingham B6 4HA
Email: info@floors2go.co.uk
Web: www.floors2go.co.uk
(flooring superstore, laminate flooring)

Floor Depot
130 Aztec
Aztec West
Bristol BS32 4UB
Tel: 0870 200 0998
Web: www.floordepot.co.uk
(flooring superstore, laminate flooring)

Floor Store Direct
13A Heybridge Way
Leyton
London E10 7NQ
Tel: 0800 953 0686
Email: sales@floorstoredirect.com
Web: www.floorstoredirect.com
(wood floor sales and sander hire)

ifloor.co.uk
Tel: 0800 358 0103
Web: www.ifloor.co.uk
(online flooring superstore, laminate flooring)

GENERAL DIY

Abplas (Plastics)
Merton High Street
London SW19 1DG
Tel: 0208 715 1887;
Email: sales@abplas.com
Web: www.abplas.co.uk
(acrylics, polycarbonate, PVC, polystyrene)

Alloway Timber
80-82 Upper Richmond Road
Putney,London SW15 2SU
Web: www.allowaytimber.com
Tel: 0208 870 5291
(Timber, retail and trade)

A Gatto
206-212 Garatt Lane
Wandsworth
London SW 18 4EB
Tel: 0208 874 2671
(Tools, retail and trade)

B&Q
Portswood House
1 Hampshire Corporate Park,
Chandlers Ford
Hampshire SO53 3YX
Tel: 0238 025 6256
Web: www.diy.com
(diy superstore, nationwide locations)

Focus DIY
Gawsworth House
Westmere Drive,
Crewe
Cheshire CW1 6XB
Tel: 0800 436 436
Web: www.focusdiy.co.uk
(diy superstore, nationwide locations)

Homebase
Beddington House
Railway Approach,
Wallington
Surrey SM6 0HB
Tel: 0845 980 1800
Web: www.homebase.co.uk
(diy superstore, nationwide locations)

Wickes
120-138 Station Road
Harrow
Middlesex HA1 2QB
Tel: 0500 300 328
Web: www.wickes.co.uk
(diy superstore, nationwide locations)

LIGHTING

Asco Lights
26 Bury New Road
Manchester M8 8EL
Tel: 0870 120 1552
Email: sales@ascolights.co.uk
Web: www.ascolights.co.uk
(lighting and electrical suppliers)

Christopher Wray Lighting
591-593 King's Road
London SW6 2YW
Tel: 0207 384 2888
Web: www.christopher-wray.com
(electrical suppliers)

Lighting Superstore
Unit G11, Avonside Enterprise Park
Melksham,
Wiltshire SN12 8BS
Tel: 0122 570 4442
Email: sales@thelightingsuperstore.co.uk
Web: www.thelightingsuperstore.co.uk
(electrical suppliers)

MK
The Arnold Centre, Paycocke Road
Basildon, Essex SS14 3EA
Tel: 0870 240 3385
Web: www.mkelectric.co.uk
(electrical suppliers)

PAINT
Brewers Paints
327 Putney Bridge Road
Putney, London Sw15 2PG
Tel: 0208 788 9335;
Web: www.brewers.co.uk

Crown Paint
PO Box 37,Crown House, Hollins Road
Darwen, Lancs BB3 0BG
Tel: 0870 240 1127
Web: www.crownpaint.co.uk
(paint suppliers)

Dulux Paints
ICI Paint, Wexham Road
Slough, Berks SL2 5DS
Tel: 0175 355 0000
Web: www.dulux.co.uk
(paint and painting suppliers)

Harris
L.G. Harris & Co. Ltd
Stoke Prior, Bromsgrove
Worcestershire B60 4AE
Tel: 0800 136 982
Email: sales@lgharris.co.uk
Web: www.lgharris.co.uk
(painting and decorating tools)

Ronseal
PO Box 3658
Sheffield S33 0WY
Tel: 0114 240 9469
Email: enquiry@ronseal.co.uk
Web: www.ronseal.co.uk
(wood products and paints)

Sandtex
PO Box 37, Crown House,
Hollins Road
Darwen, Lancs BB3 0BG
Tel: 0870 240 1127
Web: www.sandtex.co.uk
(paint and painting supplies)

TILES
Fired Earth
3 Twyford Mill, Oxford Road
Adderbury OX17 3SX
Tel: 0129 581 2088
Email: enquiries@firedearth.com
Web: www.firedearth.com

Johnson Tiles
H&R Johnson Tiles Ltd
Harewood Street, Tunstall
Stoke on Trent ST6 5JZ
Tel: 0178 257 5575
Email: sales@johnson-tiles.com
Web: www.johnson-tiles.com
(floor and wall tile suppliers)

Langley London Ltd
Calver Quay, Calver Road
Warrington WA2 8UD
Tel: 0845 230 1515
Email: mail@langleylondon.co.uk
Web: www.langleylondon.co.uk

Reed Harris Tiles
Riverside House
27 Carnwath Road,
Fulham, London W6 3HR

Tel: 020 7736 7511;
Web: www.atreedharris.co.uk
(floor and wall tile suppliers)

Topps Tiles
Rushworth House
Handforth, Wilmslow
Cheshire SK9 3HJ
Tel: 0800 783 6262
Web: www.toppstiles.co.uk
(tile superstore, nationwide locations)

Worlds End Tiles
Silverthorne Road
London SW8 3HE
Tel: 0207 819 2100
Web: www.worldsendtiles.co.uk

TOOL HIRE

Brandon Tool Hire
72–75 Feeder Road
St Philips, Bristol BS2 0TQ
Tel: 0870 514 3391
Email: info@brandonhire.plc.uk
Web: www.brandontoolhire.co.uk
(tool hire, nationwide locations)

HSS Hire
25 Willow Lane
Mitcham CR4 4TS
Tel: 0208 260 3100
Email: hire@hss.com
Web: www.hss.com
(tool hire, nationwide locations)

Speedy Hire
Chase House, 16 The Parks
Newton-le-Willows, Merseyside WA12 0JQ
Tel: 0845 601 5129
Web: www.speedyhire.co.uk
(tool hire, nationwide locations)

TOOLS

Black and Decker
Tel: 0175 351 1234
Email: info@blackanddecker.co.uk
Web: www.blackanddecker.co.uk
(power tool suppliers)

Screwfix Direct
Brunel House, Suite D1
Mead Avenue Houndstone Business Park
Yeovil, Somerset BA22 8RD
Tel: 0500 414 141
Email: online@screwfix.com
Web: www.screwfix.com
(mail order tool suppliers)

Stanley Tools
Sheffield Business Park
Sheffield City Airport
Sheffield S3 9PD
Tel: 0870 165 0650
Web: www.stanleyworks.com
(hand tool suppliers)

WALLPAPER

S&A Supplies
258–260 London Road
Westcliff-on-Sea
Essex SS0 7JG
Tel: 0170 243 3945
Email: sandasupplies@yahoo.co.uk
Web: www.sandasupplies.co.uk
(wallpaper and supplies)

Wallpaper Direct
Tel: 0132 343 0886
Email: info@wallpaperdirect.co.uk
Web: www.wallpaperdirect.co.uk
(wallpaper and supplies)

Index